ULTIMATE Cycling Trips WORLD

ANDREW BAIN

Hardie Grant
TRAVEL

Opposite Cycling past Laguna Cancaraca, Huascarán Circuit, Peru *Overleaf left* Sunny cycling on Nice's Promenade des Anglais, French & Italian Riviera *Overleaf right* Riding on the foreshore at Hamdeok, Jeju in South Korea

INTRODUCTION

In the mid-1990s, on the mountain roads of Norway, I met two touring cyclists. It was a time when I had my backpacking life strewn through a car and they had theirs compartmentalised into panniers. We sat eating lunch together on the slopes of a mountain, pinched between fjords. As rain began to fall, we set off on our separate ways, and I muttered a sentence: 'Why cycle when you can drive?'

Within 12 months I'd bored of my driving existence and was hungry for something more intimate and immersive in my travels. I bought a set of well-worn secondhand panniers (from those two cyclists on the Norwegian mountain roads) and set off to cycle 20,000 kilometres (12,427 miles) around Australia. In the two decades since that encounter, I've pedalled tens of thousands of kilometres across large portions of the world, absorbing the planet and its magic in ways that simply aren't possible cocooned inside a motorised vehicle. As Eric Newby once wrote, 'If there is any way of seeing less of a country than from a motor-car, I have yet to experience it.'

I've now cycled through deserts, over mountain ranges and across notoriously tedious stretches of road, such as Australia's Nullarbor; through all of them the exhilaration of cycling prevails in a way that I've found in no other form of travel. On a bike, you feel every small change in the wind and the weather, and you come to know a place's topography as intimately as if you drafted the landscape yourself. People delight to see you – if you've ever wanted somebody to comment on how powerful you must be, ride through their village on a bike fattened with panniers – and even wildlife seems to recognise you as part of the natural order, rather than as a passing tin can.

But it's also true, as in all facets of life, that some bike rides are simply better than others, carrying you to places where wonder trumps weariness, into the lives of towns and villages, or down roads and tracks that flow as naturally as streams. In this book, you'll find comprehensive descriptions of 20 of the finest places in the world in which to cycle, as well as snapshots of another 16 superb cycling routes in the 'Another turn of the pedals' chapter. I don't claim them as the best rides – there's no such measure – but they're rides that contain singular experiences and an array of beauty best seen from a bike, whether it's a gentle rail trail trundle with kids, a journey along the so-called most beautiful road in the world in Canada, or a challenging crossing of the world's highest mountain range.

Each chapter covers inspiring destinations, with descriptive and detailed information. The story of each cycling journey is designed to bring the experience and the place to life, with a 'Nuts & bolts' of practical details to help set your wheels rolling.

Spend any time on a bike and you'll come to understand the folly of my statement beside a Norwegian road. Whether you're simply exploring the idea of bike travel, or you already know the sweetness of life in the saddle, this book is for you. If nothing else it will make clear that on that day in Norway I simply phrased it wrong: 'Why drive when you can cycle?'

tiful Hamdeok

Map of the World

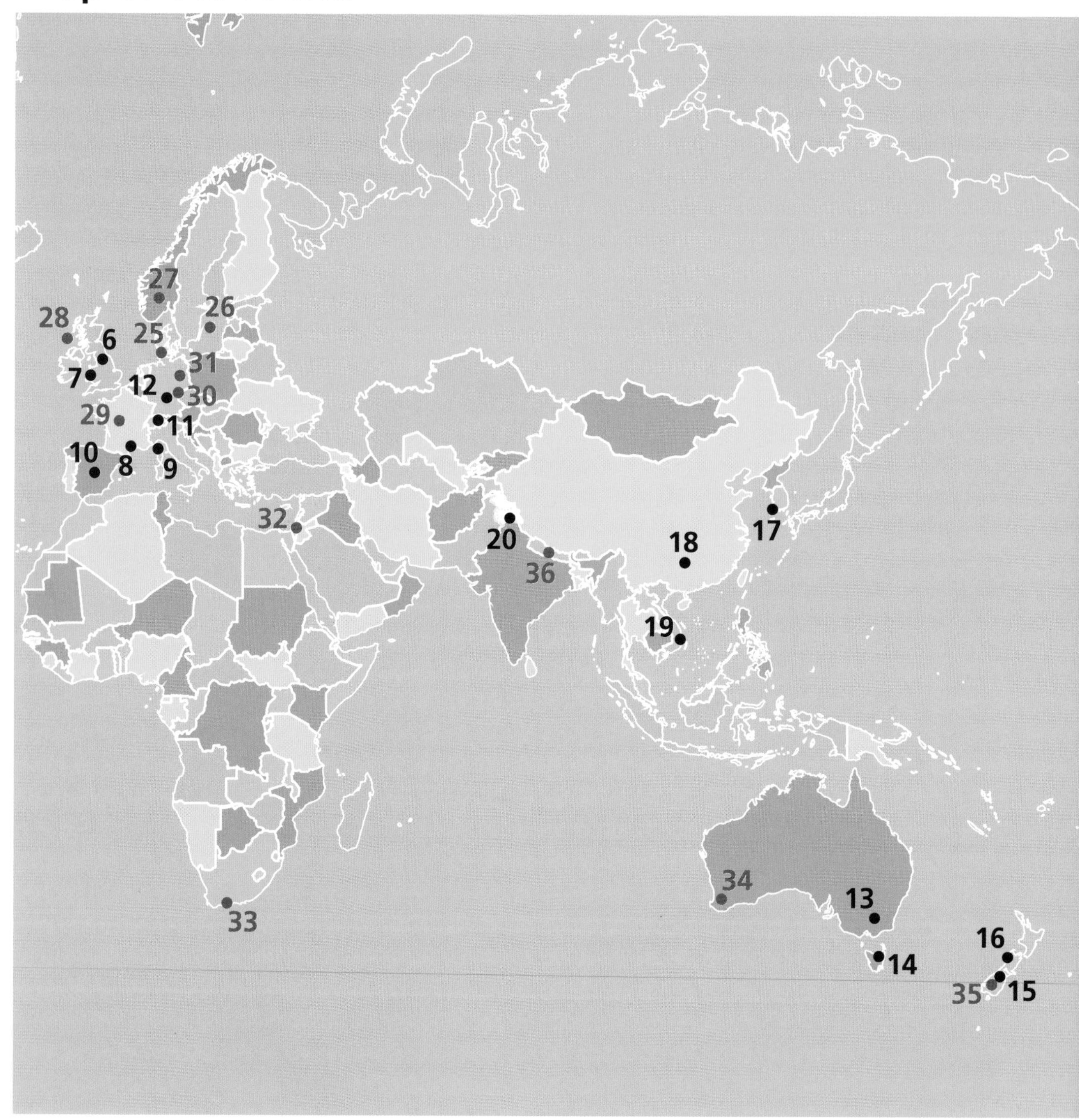

Main routes

1. Icefields Parkway, Canada
2. Prince Edward Island, Canada
3. Maine East Coast Greenway (ECG), USA
4. Cactus Country of Arizona, USA
5. Huascarán Circuit, Peru
6. Coast to Coast, England
7. Lon Las Cymru, Wales
8. Provence, France
9. French & Italian Riviera, France, Monaco & Italy
10. Camino de Santiago, Spain
11. Lakes Route, Switzerland
12. Bavarian Beer Route, Germany
13. Murray to Mountains Rail Trail, Australia
14. East Coast Tasmania, Australia
15. Alps 2 Ocean, New Zealand
16. Old Ghost Road, New Zealand
17. Yeongsan & Jeju, South Korea
18. Guangxi & Guizhou, China
19. Central Vietnam, Vietnam
20. Manali to Leh, India

Another turn of the pedals

21. San Juan Islands, USA
22. Great Divide Mountain Bike Route (GDMBR), USA & Canada
23. Route Verte, Canada
24. Carretera Austral (Ruta 7), Chile
25. Baltic Sea Cycle Route, Denmark
26. Gotland Trail, Sweden
27. Rallarvegen, Norway
28. Hebridean Way, Scotland
29. Loire Valley, France
30. Danube Cycle Path, Germany & Austria
31. Berlin Wall Trail, Germany
32. Jordan Bike Trail, Jordan
33. Garden Route, South Africa
34. Munda Biddi Trail, Australia
35. Otago Central Rail Trail, New Zealand
36. Annapurna Circuit, Nepal

BEST OF THE BEST

BEST MOUNTAIN SCENERY

BEST COAST RIDES

BEST FOR GOURMANDS

BEST FOR TRAFFIC-FREE CYCLING

BEST IN WINTER

BEST AUTUMN COLOURS

BEST MOUNTAIN-BIKING

East Coast Tasmania (Australia), p. 123
Old Ghost Road (New Zealand), p. 145

BEST FOR YOUR SOUL

Camino de Santiago (Spain), p. 87
Lakes Route (Switzerland), p. 95

BEST FOR CROSSING AN ENTIRE COUNTRY

Coast to Coast (England), p. 47
Lon Las Cymru (Wales), p. 59
Lakes Route (Switzerland), p. 95

MOST CHALLENGING RIDES

Huascarán Circuit (Peru), p. 37
Old Ghost Road (New Zealand), p. 145
Manali to Leh (India), p. 183

BEST FOR BEAUTIFUL TOWNS

Provence (France), p. 69
French & Italian Riviera, p. 77
Bavarian Beer Route (Germany), p. 105

Opposite left The Manali-Leh highway near Marhi, India *Opposite right* Vineyard along the Murray to Mountains Rail Trail, Australia *Left* The view from above at Barmouth on Lon Las Cymru, Wales *Right* Prayer flags fly from a ridge above Leh at the end of the Manali to Leh ride, India

It's all about the bike

CHOOSING A BIKE

At its core, bicycle travel is the simplest of activities – hop on a bike and turn the pedals – but there's an astounding number of considerations around even just choosing your bike. The options are manifold - touring bike, mountain bike, hybrid bike, ebike, road bike, recumbent bike and tandem bike - but your decision should be guided by terrain, comfort and whether you need to carry your gear on the bike, which is almost a certainty if you're travelling independently rather than guided. This chapter helps inform your choices.

Touring bikes

As the name on the tin suggests, touring bikes are built with long-distance cycle travel as their prime purpose.

At a glance, touring bikes resemble a road bike, with:

- Drop handlebars (so you can shift your hands around for comfort)
- Wider rims and tyres
- More flexible frames for comfort
- More spokes in the wheels to provide extra strength under loaded weights
- Eyelets in the frames for attaching carrier racks for panniers.

Generally, touring bikes are the best choice for a trip, unless you're heading away from sealed roads, in which case a mountain bike is preferable.

Mountain bikes

On dirt roads and other tracks, mountain bikes provide the most stability and safety. If I think there's even a small chance I'll be able to explore off-road tracks while on a cycle tour, I generally choose a mountain bike to keep all options open.

The 4WDs of the bike world, mountain bikes come with:

- Wide tyres (to create extra grip on loose surfaces)
- Suspension (to absorb the bumps)
- An upright riding position that most cyclists will find more comfortable.

Mountain bikes do increase the workload on sealed roads – all that extra traction – but they're geared well for climbing, so even on a sealed ascent they're welcome companions.

Hybrid bikes

If you want a bike for touring that you can also comfortably pedal around the streets at home, a hybrid is an excellent choice.

Hybrid bikes sit somewhere between a road bike and a mountain bike, with:

- Tyres wider than those on a road bike, but narrower than those on a mountain bike
- Flat handlebars (unlike touring bikes).

Road bikes

Road bikes might be the alpha members of the bike family, but they're the least suitable choice for a cycling trip. They have rigid frames that generally can't carry panniers, making them incompatible with most styles of touring - they're built for speed not sluggish touring, after all. They're really only suited to fully supported guided trips that carry your luggage between stops. Guided road-bike trips over mountain passes through the French Alps, for instance, are very popular.

THE E-SPOT

Electric is unquestionably the new black in cycling. Consider this: in 2018, ebikes outsold normal bikes in the Netherlands; 15 million ebikes are sold in China every year; and the European Cyclists Federation has predicted that 150 million ebikes will have sold in Europe alone by 2030.

Let's be clear on one thing, though - an ebike isn't a motorbike. An ebike is power-assisted. You still have to work but it's casual labour rather than full-time employment - with a push of a button you get battery assistance to reduce the effort of pedalling, while still maintaining power.

The benefits are clear and wide-reaching. In recent years, I've encountered cyclists aged in their seventies who claim they'd have given up touring if ebikes hadn't come along, and other riders who agreed to a cycling trip with a partner or friend only if they could ride an ebike. In some cases, a love of cycling was born.

One potential downside of an ebike is the weight. Ebikes can weigh up to twice as much as a standard bike, and if your battery goes flat during the day, you're suddenly riding a virtual truck. If you're carrying your own bike on flights for cycling trips, an ebike is likely to mean a significant spike in your excess baggage costs (*see* p. xiv). That said, ebikes are almost standard now among the bikes offered by rental companies and guided-trip operators across much of the world, so it's easy to get away without transporting your own.

If you're riding remotely or camping, you'll also want to look into battery-charging opportunities (electricity sources) each night before you set out on an ebike.

CARRYING YOUR GEAR

Panniers

With your choice of bike sorted, the next bit of bike business is deciding how you're going to carry all of your gear. The standard set-up for bike touring is panniers, which are bags that hang from racks over the wheels of your bike – either just two panniers at the rear, or two larger panniers at the rear and two smaller panniers at the front. The back rack and the tops of the rear panniers themselves can also then serve as a kind of shelf for strapping down extra equipment, such as tents or daypacks.

Handlebar bags

It's also worth adding a handlebar bag to your set-up. These hang from, or clip onto, the centre of your handlebars and are good for carrying those small items and valuables that you want access to throughout the course of the riding day. Any time you wander away from your bike, you can simply detach the handlebar bag to keep your valuables with you. It's also a good place in which to carry your camera, so you can quickly capture those candid, impromptu scenes and moments that appear as you ride.

Waterproofing

You can stuff any set of panniers with plastic bags or garbage bags for some primitive form of waterproofing, but I'd recommend investing in fully waterproof panniers, which are produced by the likes of Ortlieb, Altura and Thule, to take away the gamble of keeping gear dry.

Bikepacking

A slicker way of transporting your gear is to have a bikepacking set-up. Bikepacking has grown massively in popularity in recent years, and does away with panniers, using instead a number of smaller bags strapped to the framework of the bike. A typical set-up will include a bag hanging from beneath the bike saddle, a longer roll of gear hanging from the handlebars, a triangular bag snug inside the bike frame, and maybe a small bag sitting on the top tube of the frame just behind the handlebars. It's basically a puzzle of what can fit in where.

You can usually carry less gear when bikepacking – many riders consider this self-imposed limitation an advantage; others will see it as an unnecessary gear diet. It's especially popular for off-road cycle touring and mountain biking, since it makes the bike narrower and lighter. I wouldn't consider riding a trail such as New Zealand's Old Ghost Road (*see* p. 145) in any other way – panniers make the bike too cumbersome and wide on the narrow singletrack.

Bike trailers

The third option for carrying your gear is a bike trailer, which attaches to the rear of your bike and rolls along on a single wheel behind. The trailers hold a single bag, so that it's more like packing a suitcase, rather than packing parcels of gear into individual panniers. Trailers transfer the weight away from your bike, but create an extra weight behind you on a climb, so tend to be a love-them or hate-them item among cyclists.

Stream crossing on the Manali-Leh highway, India

SETTING UP THE BIKE

There are a few small tweaks you might consider making to your bike (or a rental bike) before you set off on a cycling trip. It pays to know at least the basics of bike set-up.

Bar ends

If you're touring on a mountain bike or a hybrid with flat handlebars, the monotony of having your hands locked into a single position all day can become tiring and painful, so a set of bar ends is a good investment. These slot onto the end of the handlebars and angle out like horns, providing an extra range of positions for your hands.

Pedals

Pedal choice is a personal religion among cyclists. Clipless pedals are the choice of many, including myself. With clipless pedals, cleated shoes slot into the pedals, keeping your feet locked in position and improving the efficiency of your pedal stroke, which means more reward for your efforts.

The most suitable form of cleated shoes for touring are mountain-bike shoes, which have the cleat set into a recess in the sole of the shoe, allowing you to also comfortably walk around in them. It's still a good idea to carry at least a second pair of shoes, unless you enjoy sounding like a tap dancer as you walk around towns.

It's best to have done some riding with clipless pedals before setting out on a trip, because when you first ride with cleated shoes, it's a virtual rite of passage to topple over at a few traffic lights because you've forgotten to unclip them as the bike slows to a stop.

The other pedal options are flats (pedals with no attachments) and toe clips, which are a kind of cage into which you slot the front of your shoes. Both allow you to cycle in any shoes, potentially negating the need to carry another pair. Pedal efficiency is lost on flat pedals because your foot tends to move around, especially on bumpy roads. Toe clips provide an excellent compromise – there will still be some movement of your feet but they're generally held in place.

Hydration

You'll often see mountain bikers riding with hydration bladders on their back for drinking water, but on a long cycle tour you'll likely find this unnecessarily stressful on your back, so fit a couple of bottle cages to your bike (there will be points for bolting them onto the bike inside the frame) and carry water bottles, instead.

Hire-bike adjustments

If you're hiring a bike (*see* p. xvii), it's a good idea to bring the saddle from your own bike and fit it to the rental, thus avoiding those first few dreaded days of butt soreness. If you do prefer cycling with clipless pedals, bring your own pedals also to fit to a hire bike.

Preparing to ride

TRAINING & FITNESS

When I set out on my first cycle tour in the late 1990s, I lazily decided that I'd do all my physical preparation on the trip, starting with short daily distances and building towards longer days as I went. In a way it worked, because the trip was so long - 14 months - but only after a whole lot of knee pain, numbness in my hands, fatigue and a butt that felt so raw it might have done a baboon proud. It was a lesson learned the hard way - preparation is key if you're to enjoy rather than endure a cycle trip.

It's worth beginning a dedicated training program a couple of months out from the start of your trip. Start at whatever distance and time is comfortable and build up from there. There are no hard and fast rules about what you have to achieve in training, but I always try to complete at least two or three rides that are longer than my predicted longest day on a trip. It helps physically, but more importantly it helps mentally, creating the confidence and knowledge that the distances you'll be riding are achievable. It really is just about getting hours up on the bike for endurance and comfort.

If you're going to be lugging your own gear on the bike during a trip, it's a good idea to load up the bike to a similar weight on a couple of the training rides - you might be surprised at the extra effort involved, with a loaded bike, especially on climbs. It doesn't matter what you put in the panniers at this stage - just load them up to a weight you think you'll be carrying when touring. You can nut out the puzzle of packing them at home, or even over the first few days of a trip. If you'll be riding through hills and mountains, train where possible in that sort of terrain.

Saddle soreness is common until your body and your bike seat have come to some sort of hard-fought armistice, so wage that war before you begin your bike trip, getting your butt accustomed to a particular saddle (and then take that saddle with you). Knee soreness is another common physical complaint when you first begin to spend time on a bike. If you do experience pain in the knee joints, try adjusting your saddle height and riding in lower gears (so you're spinning faster but with less force).

Opposite Caernarfon Castle on Lon Las Cymru, Wales

PACKING TO RIDE

This is where the conundrums begin. You really want that hardback book you've been meaning to read for months but is it worth the extra ballast as you grind over those mountain passes? That flash new jacket is going look great at dinner each night but it also takes up half a pannier.

If you're riding with panniers (*see* p. xi), packing them is like a cycling version of the Rubik's cube - you know how it should be done but the reality turns out to be far more perplexing than you imagined. One truism of cycle touring is that the particular item of gear that you're trying to find will somehow always be in a different pannier than you thought, so it's good to try to develop a packing system. Keeping particular items in particular panniers - and remembering the system - will save a whole lot of frustration.

I'm not about to tell you what you should take, only that you should be prudent in what you pack. Some items are non-negotiable. This is my tried and tested list:

- Lightweight rain jacket: unless your destination happens to be the desiccated Atacama Desert, pack one. A standard rain jacket will be fine, but cycling-specific rain jackets are longer at the back than front to cover your lower back and butt as you ride leaning over the handlebars. When purchasing a jacket, consider the fact that if it is raining, visibility is likely to be reduced, so make it a brightly coloured one.
- Padded cycling shorts (knicks) are almost a must, unless you have an extremely good relationship with your bike saddle. Ideally, bring two pairs, alternating them each day and washing the pair you've worn each night. If you don't fancy the lycra look, throw another pair of loose shorts over the top when you ride.
- Cycling gloves are another essential. They're typically fingerless, with padding across the fleshy parts of the palm. If you're going to be riding in a cold location, you can also find full-fingered cycling gloves. The padding on the gloves reduces the pressure of your weight as you lean down on the handlebars and if, God forbid, you have an accident, they'll save you some skin.
- Sunglasses will of course dull the bright sunlight but have the added benefit of protecting your eyes against dust and any small stones kicked up by passing vehicles or your own front wheel.

- A first-aid kit is essential and perhaps include a few energy-gel sachets for those moments when your energy levels really flag.
- The items you'll need to carry in the way of bike spares and tools will depend on where you're cycling. A remote ride along, for instance, the Manali–Leh highway in northern India (*see* p. 183) will require far more spare parts than a ride across England's Coast to Coast (*see* p. 47), which is well furnished with bike stores. In general, always carry at least two spare tyre tubes, a set of tyre levers (for removing the tyre), a pump and a puncture repair kit ... and ensure that you know how to change a tyre before you begin riding.
- A bike multi-tool is an excellent friend to carry. It's a compact collection of tools, typically looking a bit like a Swiss Army knife. It'll have the likes of hexagonal wrenches (Allen keys), a tyre lever, a chain tool and a screwdriver. On the one ride for this book in which I forgot to carry a chain tool (for repairing a broken chain), I snapped my chain over the steepest climb on Wales's Lon Las Cymru ride (*see* p. 59), and finished up having to push my bike 8 kilometres (5 miles) through rain into the next town, so I can't stress enough the importance of carrying tools.
- A bike lock is something you certainly need to carry.
- You'll want a camera of some sort, though smartphones have really become the camera of choice. One of my lingering extravagances in bike travel is that I still carry an SLR camera, which is bulky but which I never regret for the quality of the photos. For both security and ease of access, I carry it loose in the handlebar bag, with a tripod strapped to the rear rack for those times I want a low-light dawn or dusk shot, or to capture that waterfall I'm going to cycle past.
- If you're camping, you'll need the standard hiking-style camp equipment, albeit allowing for the greater luxury of not having to carry it all on your back. That means that if I'm cycling alone, I'll usually carry a two-person tent purely for the pleasure of having additional space at night; if I'm travelling with a friend, I'll carry a three-person tent. To this you'll add a sleeping bag and inflatable sleeping mat (mats by the likes of Therm-a-Rest, Exped and Sea to Summit are ideal). You can also purchase lightweight travel pillows in outdoor stores, though I typically use jackets as pillows. If you're going to self-cater, a small camping stove and pans will be necessary, along with camp-style plates, mugs and cutlery.

MAPS

The days of needing to carry a library of paper maps to find your way across a country or region have been consigned to history, though even in the era of electronic mapping I still like to carry one large map covering my entire ride, so I can ponder my progress in a more tactile way each night.

Smartphones are now the map of choice. Google Maps is most often sufficient, but if you want to get more detail, an app such as Avenza Maps allows you to purchase topographic and other maps with GPS positioning to show your location on the map – it's the equivalent of having paper maps, without the need to carry them.

An excellent route planning and tracking app is Ride with GPS – you can search cycling routes created by others in your vicinity, track your rides and create your own routes. Perhaps best of all, the 'route planner' tool will give you elevations and climbs along the way.

FLYING WITH A BIKE

If you're cycling anywhere far from home, and you want to do so with your own bike, you're almost certainly going to need to fly with it. Each airline has its own policy on carrying bikes – some have set charges and others count the weight of the bike as part of your luggage allowance, incurring excess baggage fees (unless you happen to be a master packer). To get a bike onto a plane, you must first do some disassembly and pack it into a bike bag or box.

Bike bags

Bike bags are purpose-built for transporting bikes and can be hard or soft sided. Hard-sided bags provide the greatest protection for your bike, but are weighty (up to about 12kg/26lb), so will add significantly to the cost of each flight you take. They're also only useful if you're able to store the bag somewhere at the start of your ride and you're returning to that place at the end. Some soft-sided bags will roll up so that you can lay them across the back rack of your bike while you ride.

Bike boxes

The most common way to transport bikes for touring is in bike boxes, which are the cardboard boxes in which new bikes are delivered to stores. Bike-store owners are usually happy to give out boxes – they go in the trash otherwise – so ask at your local store for one. Plan ahead also by contacting a store near your ride's end point to see if it'll hold a box for you.

Packing a bike

To pack a bike into a box or bag, remove the pedals, wheels and the seat post and saddle (it's worth marking the height of the seat post before you pull it off the bike to ensure you put it back on at the same height), and turn the handlebars 90 degrees. You can protect the rear derailleur (the gear-changing mechanism by the rear wheel) by unbolting it and taping it to the inside of the chainstay (the section of the frame nearest the chain). Taping a piece of cardboard around the bottom teeth of the front chainwheel should prevent it from puncturing the box or bag. Place the wheels in the box or bag on the opposite side of the frame to the chainwheel. If packing space elsewhere is at a premium, you can always stuff the box or bag with other items.

DIFFICULTY LEVELS

In the Nuts & bolts sections throughout this book, each ride has been assigned a level of difficulty, from easy to hard. These are subjective measures, based on the following.

- Easy – generally flat terrain, with relatively short daily distances. Good rides for novice cyclists.
- Medium – often varying terrain, typically with more sustained climbs and longer cycling days.
- Hard – long cycling days, often in remote areas with few services. Steep climbs and descents likely. Suited to experienced cycle tourers.

Left Bavarian Beer Route, Germany *Right* Stork-ed on the Camino de Santiago, Spain

Lightening the load

There's a time-honoured practice in preparing for a cycle trip that goes a bit like this: you disassemble your bike, pack it into a box or bike bag, lug it to the oversized-baggage counter at an airport, board a plane, collect your bike from another oversized-baggage counter at another airport, and then drag it to a space where you can reassemble your bike, pack your panniers and fit them to the bike. At which point, the cycling to come can feel like the easy bit.

Today, it's not always necessary to go through that pre-ride ritual. The ever-growing popularity of cycling travel has spawned a host of guided trips, pack-carrying services and bike-rental options. If you want to lighten the load a little, here are a few options.

GUIDED TOURS

Logistically, the simplest way to arrange a cycling trip is to take a guided tour, the majority of which are run by dedicated cycle tour operators or adventure travel companies. Typically you'll just need to arrange your flight or other transport to the ride's starting point, and everything else is arranged for you (often including airport transfers), leaving you to concentrate purely on the pedalling.

On guided trips, bikes are normally supplied (sometimes at extra cost), as are helmets, though you can always bring your own helmet and usually your own bike. Accommodation is all booked for you, meals are often included (or at least eaten together as a group), your bags are transferred between overnight stops, and you'll ride with a guide at the front of the group and maybe also at the back. Guides not only point the way, but good ones will provide you with the sort of interpretation and local knowledge that you can rarely acquire when cycling independently. If you're on your own, or quite new to cycling, guided trips also provide peace of mind about support and back-up if something goes wrong – there will usually be someone to fix any punctures, lube your chain each night, dispense any first aid and calmly encourage you on if you're flagging.

It's common to have a minibus as a sag wagon (usually carrying your luggage, plus snacks and spare water), puttering along behind the group. If you're tiring or just don't fancy a particular hill climb, you can hop in the bus and take the easy way across. Depending on the location and trip, the minibus is also often used to shuttle you between sections of riding, so that your trip is a combination of cycling and bus transfers. That means you should end up cycling the best bits of a route, while skipping heavily trafficked or tedious sections of road, but it can also mean that you lose some of the satisfaction and sense of achievement that comes with having pedalled a linear journey from go to whoa.

There are literally hundreds of guided tour operators running cycling trips around the world, and often the most personal experience will come from a locally based company. Some good tour operators that offer a global list of cycling trips include the following:

Backroads (backroads.com)

Butterfield & Robinson (butterfield.com)

Du Vine (duvine.com)

Exodus Travels (exodustravels.com)

Intrepid Travel (intrepidtravel.com)

REI Adventures (rei.com/adventures)

SpiceRoads Cycling (spiceroads.com)

Trek Travel (trektravel.com)

World Expeditions (worldexpeditions.com)

SELF-GUIDED TOURS

An alternative with greater freedom is a supported self-guided cycling tour. There's a lot to like about this form of cycle travel, as you're independent in pretty much every way. The trip operator should supply maps and route notes, making navigation (hopefully) simple, but you're free to move at your own pace, stop anytime and anywhere you like during the day, and you can detour away to whatever catches your attention whenever you wish. There's no guide and you don't pedal with a group, but all the nitty gritty (accommodation, luggage transfers, maps and route notes, and sometimes even train tickets in case you want to skip through a stage) has been pre-arranged, and you don't need to carry all of your gear on the bike.

As with a guided trip, there's invariably a bike supplied (or that you hire through the company) with a helmet and often a small pannier or two for carrying whatever you need through the day.

Luggage transfers might be done by a company employee or a taxi, and you simply leave your bags at your accommodation in the morning and they'll magically turn up at your next stop later in the day.

Meals will almost certainly not be included, meaning you're free to dine as you please rather than being beholden to a company's rusted-on selection of restaurants.

Self-guided tours are most common in Europe, where distances between stops can be short and bike routes are plentiful. Many of the companies that operate guided tours also offer self-guided trips.

BIKE HIRE

In almost all major cities and popular tourist areas, it's possible to hire bikes for extended periods, giving you the freedom to simply select a return date and set out pedalling.

When hiring a bike, there are a few things about which to be mindful. While it's possible to tour on any bicycle, not all hire bikes will be set up suitable to the task. If you're planning on using panniers, you'll need a bike with a rack, so be sure to stipulate that requirement when booking. If you can't find a hire bike with a rack, it's quite feasible to bring a rack with you (a rack can weigh as little as 500g/18oz), but check ahead with the rental company to be sure it's happy with you fitting a rack to its bike. Make certain also that any rental bike comes with a spare tube or two, tyre levers and a lock. Failing that, head to the nearest bike store and buy them – it's a small investment.

True to the laws of supply and demand, bike-hire options tend to become more plentiful around popular cycling routes. Along rides such as the Coast to Coast (England, *see* p. 47), Alps 2 Ocean (New Zealand, *see* p. 135) and the Camino de Santiago (Spain, *see* p. 87), there are often competing bike-hire companies. It's along rides like these that you're most likely to have a choice of bikes, including touring bikes and ebikes.

If you're having trouble finding a suitable hire bike near the start of your ride, try broadening your search. When I cycled Lon Las Cymru (Wales, *see* p. 59), for instance, I found a good touring bike for hire in London, from where it was just a two-hour train trip to the ride's start in Cardiff.

PUBLIC TRANSPORT

So you're setting out to ride from city A to city B but that doesn't mean you necessarily have to pedal every metre of it. Check the public transport networks of the country in which you're riding (a quick online search is often sufficient) and see whether trains and buses will also transport bikes, which they commonly do. If you're flagging, or you just want to hop to a whole other area, you can use a train or bus to cut out the bits you don't want to ride.

Trains are usually the most reliable option for transporting bikes, but do your research because rules and options differ per country and per service, such as city or regional. In Switzerland you can pretty much pop a bike on anything that moves; in South Korea, buses are the most bike-friendly option.

For trains in the likes of the United Kingdom (National Rail), the United States (Amtrak) and France (SNCF), the official online booking page will tell you at the time of booking as to whether a particular service can carry bikes.

Rest stop on the Mori Plains, along the Manali to Leh ride, India

NORTH AMERICA

Icefields Parkway

CANADA

Thread through the Rocky Mountains on one of the world's most beautiful roads.

Icefields Parkway

WHY IT'S SPECIAL

In the bear-filled Canadian Rockies, they have a name for people like me: 'You're meals on wheels,' I'm told with a laugh as I breakfast in a Banff cafe, ready to begin cycling to Jasper, 290 kilometres (180 miles) and five days away. I will be riding along a road that's regularly called the most beautiful in the world, pressed between the pencil-sharp peaks of the Rocky Mountains and below the range's largest icefield, passing meadows of wildflowers, glaciers and alpine lakes so blue it's as though the sky is inverted. Wildlife of all varieties - elk, bighorn sheep, eagles, deer - stroll the meadows and even across the road itself, especially if you incorporate the Bow Valley Parkway into the ride, as I did and would recommend. And yet for all that magnificence, it's still the bears that everybody wants to talk about.

BEST TIME TO RIDE

The Icefields Parkway comes into its own through July and August, when the summer days are long, daytime temperatures hover around 21–23°C (70–73°F) and roadsides are coloured with wildflowers. Traffic is at its heaviest but the wide road shoulder negates it. By October and before May, maximum temperatures are falling to uncomfortable lows (10°C/50°F) in October and April, so other feasible times to ride are May, June and September, though note that June is the area's wettest month, with average rainfall of around 70 millimetres (2.7 inches) in Banff.

RIDE IT

Befitting the complex environment, the Icefields Parkway is a road that took 10 years to construct and is today travelled by more than one million people every year. Among them is a regular stream of cyclists, drawn here by the unquestionable truth of the Parkway's claim to be among the world's most spectacular roads.

That weight of visitor numbers might suggest masses of traffic to contend with, but the Parkway brings unexpected kindnesses to cyclists. This fully sealed road through the Rockies has a wide shoulder along its entire length - at times almost as wide as the traffic lanes - and in a move to preserve its pleasures as a scenic road, large trucks are banned from driving on it.

It's also dotted with accommodation options and more than a dozen campgrounds, providing sleeping options aplenty. None of the campgrounds (except at Lake Louise and at Wapiti, just outside of Jasper) require bookings. Eating possibilities are more scant, with few restaurants and a single general store at Saskatchewan River Crossing, almost midway between Banff and Jasper. If you're self-catering, you'll likely need to carry at least a couple of days of food on your bike.

Nuts & bolts
Distance: 290 kilometres (180 miles)
Days: 5
Ascent: 2500 metres (8200 feet)
Difficulty: Medium
Bike: The ride is entirely on sealed roads, making a tourer or hybrid bike ideal.

Previous Mountain magic on the Icefields Parkway *Opposite top left* Cycling past wildflowers in bloom on the Icefields Parkway *Top right* Pines and peaks near Banff *Bottom left* Black bear in Jasper National Park *Bottom right* The Icefields Parkway curling through the Rocky Mountains

Opposite The wide shoulder of the Icefields Parkway
Left Cycling along the Bow Valley Parkway, Banff
Overleaf The blue water of Peyto Lake as seen from Bow Summit

LOCAL SNAPSHOT

In 1887, in a move to preserve the Cave and Basin Springs in Banff, Canada created its very first national park and only the third national park in the world. Twenty years later it was joined by Jasper National Park. Banff National Park has grown tenfold in size since its establishment and together with the contiguous Jasper (the two intersect atop Sunwapta Pass on the Icefields Parkway) covers an area almost the size of Kuwait or Fiji around the Rocky Mountains. Between them the parks have more than 2500 kilometres (1550 miles) of hiking trails, providing plenty of distraction if you want to leave the bike and set out on foot.

DAY 1

BANFF TO LAKE LOUISE VILLAGE (60KM/37 MILES)

The Icefields Parkway stretches for 230 kilometres (143 miles) between Jasper and Lake Louise, but like most cyclists, I set out from Banff, 60 kilometres (37 miles) south of Lake Louise, adding the Bow Valley Parkway to the journey. This road, which parallels the Trans-Canada Highway, is regarded as one of the best in Canada for wildlife spotting. Which, of course, brings to mind the little subject of bears. 'We saw a grizzly and cub on the Bow Valley Parkway yesterday,' a pair of cyclists tell me before I've even stepped out of the Banff breakfast cafe.

When I leave the cafe and begin my ride, it's with a mixture of the excitement that always hangs over the start of a cycling trip and vague trepidation about this echoing tale of bears. But if there are bears out here, they'll need to stand in the wildlife queue because as I begin along the Bow Valley Parkway, 7 kilometres (4.3 miles) outside of Banff, I'm pedalling into a living Canadian field guide. A bald eagle sits barrel-chested and regal atop a tree, a pair of bighorn sheep clatter across the road and an elk draws a crowd of cars and cameras. Clearly, if a bear ever does appear, I'll be able to spot it by the cars gathered around it like a herd. I ride on, worry-free, with the milky-blue Bow River winding along below me and more bald eagles perched like gargoyles in the trees.

Though the overall trend from Banff to Jasper is downhill (Jasper is more than 300 metres, or 985 feet, lower than Banff), this first day climbs around 400 metres (1300 feet) to Lake Louise. It also brings treats, such as Johnston Canyon, midway through

the day, where you'll almost certainly want to park up and wander for a couple of hours. One of Banff National Park's most popular walks – sometimes even claimed as the most popular in Canada – the narrow canyon is entered on boardwalks bolted to the cliffs. It's a 1-kilometre (1100-yard) walk to the canyon's Lower Falls, which seem almost to pour from inside the cliffs, or you can continue beyond to the Upper Falls and the more distant, brilliantly coloured Ink Pots pools. The latter is a 12-kilometre (7.5-mile return walk, so set out early, and with supplies, if that's your plan.

The Bow Valley Parkway rolls directly into Lake Louise Village, 33 kilometres (20.5 miles) from Johnston Canyon, where I set up camp for the night in the Lake Louise Campground, a sprawling forest site with room for 206 tents. It's wise to book ahead through the Parks Canada website for the popular campground, where the most welcome feature is arguably the fact that it's ringed by an electric fence to dissuade curious bears. If you're not camping, the village has hotels and a hostel, and there's always the option of the ultimate treat – the lavish Fairmont Chateau Lake Louise, high above the village on the shores of the eponymous lake.

For me though, the lake itself will wait until tomorrow.

DAY 2

LAKE LOUISE VILLAGE TO WATERFOWL LAKES CAMPGROUND (59KM/36.5 MILES)

Even if I've reached Canada's most famous body of water in name, I haven't in reality. Though Lake Louise Village is Canada's highest town, the namesake lake is still 200 metres (650 feet) above it, which is fine in any language except a cyclist's. To see this unquestionable highlight of the Canadian Rockies, you must ride uphill for 5 kilometres (3 miles) before you've even advanced your ride towards Jasper. But it's worth it.

I begin at dawn, which comes early in summer this far north on the planet, and shunning the road I rise up the slopes on the shared-use (cyclists and hikers) Tramline Trail, ascending through pine forest on what really was once a tramway, resulting in a manageable gradient of around 4 per cent. In half an hour I'm on the lake's shores, peering across its turquoise waters to the peaks racked behind it. On a breathless dawn, the lake is motionless, reflecting the mountains like a painting hung upside down. If the Icefields Parkway really is the most beautiful road in the world, this is its appropriate beginning.

I return down the slopes on the Tramline Trail and back in Lake Louise Village, my day proper begins. The Icefields Parkway crosses two passes on its course to Jasper, and the climb to the first of them – 2069-metre (6788-foot) Bow Summit – begins immediately.

As mountain climbs go, this one is kind. Though it ascends 500 metres (1640 feet), it's spread across 40 kilometres (25 miles), rising past a string of lakes – Herbert, Hector, Bow – each one bluer and more impressive than the last. It's almost as though I'm swimming uphill.

Seeming to spill across the plunging gap of Bow Summit is another lake, Peyto Lake, bluer than Matisse's nudes and arguably the most spectacular of the Icefields Parkway's lakes. The catch for cyclists is that it's another 70-metre (230-foot) vertical climb on a side road to reach the lookout, with its instantly recognisable view over the lake, but as per the finest laws of physics, what goes up must come down. I've reached the Parkway's highest point, and from here the 40-kilometre (25-mile) climb is matched by a near-40-kilometre descent – quid pro quo – to the Saskatchewan River Crossing, the point where the Mistaya, Saskatchewan and Howse rivers converge. It can be over quickly – little more than an hour of freewheeling joy to spend the night at

Saskatchewan River Crossing - but it can also be broken into two halves and savoured. Midway through the descent, I stop and set up camp at Waterfowl Lakes, beneath the towering tip of Mt Chephren. Like almost all campgrounds along the Parkway, it offers basic national park camping, but with treated drinking water, picnic shelters and food lockers so cyclists (and hikers) can store food away from snack-intent bears. In the campground this night, the scene is like a mini cycling festival. Camped around me are various groups of riders. The trees around my tent sport scratch marks from a bear, and the Mistaya River that flows past camp translates as Grizzly Bear River in the Cree language. But if we are meals on wheels, we're at least a buffet tonight.

DAY 3

WATERFOWL LAKES CAMPGROUND TO COLUMBIA ICEFIELD CAMPGROUND (66KM/41 MILES)

In the morning, the 20 kilometres (12.5 miles) to the Saskatchewan River Crossing passes in a happy downhill blur. I'm escorted across the bridge by swallows and enter what passes as civilisation on the Icefields Parkway. 'The Crossing' contains the road's only petrol station and its sole general store (you'll need to stock up here if you need any supplies to get you through to Jasper - there is nowhere else to do so), as well as a motel, restaurants, a cafe and more unsolicited advice.

'Watch out for bears, won't you,' one of the cafe staff cautions me. 'Between here and Jasper you'll see lots of them.' Terrific. Thanks. My long-gone nerves have suddenly cycled up the Parkway to rejoin me.

Beyond the Saskatchewan River Crossing, the scenery somehow gets only more spectacular as the road undulates along the North Saskatchewan Valley, passing meadows and crossing large gravel flats, with cliffs rising hundreds of metres overhead. Approaching the head of the valley, the cliffs almost clamp shut over the road, with the well-named Weeping Wall streaked with water. From here, I can see the Icefields Parkway ploughing high into the mountains. I have arrived at the base of the second of the road's pass climbs.

Bow Summit may have been the Parkway's highest point, but the shorter, steeper climb to 2035-metre (6676-foot) Sunwapta Pass is its most challenging section. It's a similar gain in altitude - around 500 metres (1640 feet) - but abbreviated into 15 kilometres (9.3 miles), rather than 40 (25). It sweeps through long Big Bend and rises, rises, rises. For the first time I'm out of the saddle, standing on the pedals, trying to extract extra leverage from them, finally rising onto the wide pass, where I cross the unseen line between Banff National Park and Jasper National Park.

Even on this warm day, the wind atop the pass is frigid, betraying the fact that I'm entering the true 'icefields' section of the Icefields Parkway. Frosting the mountains beside the road is the largest icefield in the Rocky Mountains – the Columbia Icefield – busting out of the mountains at various points as glaciers. The most prominent of them is the Athabasca Glacier, just 4 kilometres (2.5 miles) beyond Sunwapta Pass. Two campgrounds – Wilcox Creek Campground and the tent-only Columbia Icefield Campground – lie between the two, providing the chance to take the next morning off the bike and explore the Athabasca Glacier, which is the Icefield Parkway's prize feature.

DAY 4

COLUMBIA ICEFIELD CAMPGROUND TO HONEYMOON LAKE CAMPGROUND (54KM/33.5 MILES)

From the unmissable Columbia Icefield Discovery Centre, 2 kilometres (1.2 miles) from the Columbia Icefield Campground, buses with tractor-sized tyres drive up and onto Athabasca Glacier, said to be the most visited glacier in North America, bringing the world of high mountains into easy reach – rug up for high mountain conditions on a very large ice block. Visits here also include a trip 5 kilometres (3 miles) up the Parkway to the Columbia Icefield Skywalk (buy a package ticket for the two activities to save some cash), a glass-floored walkway (in the mould of the Grand Canyon Skywalk) that overhangs the Sunwapta Valley, nearly 300 metres (985 feet) below.

It's past midday by the time I'm finally cycling this day but I'm in no rush for this journey to end, and having crossed Sunwapta Pass it feels as though Jasper is almost within reach. I'll take any reason to linger on this gorgeous road as it continues to run beside North America's most enchanting mountain range.

I rise over Tangle Ridge, where three bighorn sheep have created a traffic jam as they slurp at a salt lick beside the road. Cars are banked up and cameras are pointed out of windows, at least until the sight of my bike scatters the animals into the hills.

The descent from the ridge passes waterfalls and the outstretched fingers of Stutfield Glacier, before flattening across the braided plains of the Athabasca Valley, with its river that will now lead me all the way into Jasper.

A roaring tailwind blows, and I could easily reach Jasper in an afternoon, but I want to draw out this most lovely of bike rides. I camp the night instead at Honeymoon Lake.

DAY 5

HONEYMOON LAKE CAMPGROUND TO JASPER (51KM/32 MILES)

In the early morning, having been woken at dawn by the alarm call of a distant wolf, I finally ride on for Jasper. Most of the signs of life this early in the day come from the open meadows, rather than the road. Stopped at the edge of the Parkway, I watch as white-tailed deer drink from a lake and bound through the grasses with balletic grace. Behind me, cars whirr blindly past, oblivious to this magical moment no more than a few metres from their windows.

It's the kind of snapshot of life you often only see from a bike - the reward of slow and silent movement. Despite all the warnings, I haven't seen a bear but I've seen so much more since leaving Banff. Is this really the most beautiful road in the world? After five days on a bike, it doesn't seem like hyperbole.

Jasper is Banff's twin and equal, a mountain tourist town par excellence, filled with accommodation, fine eating options and easy access to the likes of Maligne Canyon, one of the deepest canyons in the Canadian Rockies, and the perfectly photogenic Maligne Lake. Aim to spend a few days in the town enjoying life off the bike, or if the pedalling is just getting into your system, it's a 100-kilometre (62-mile) return ride from town to Maligne Lake. It's your call ...

Riding resources

For an overview of the Icefields Parkway, visit: icefieldsparkway.com.
Bikes are available for hire in Banff at:
Ultimate Sports (ultimatebanff.com)
Banff Adventures (banffcycle.com)
Bikes can be returned from Jasper to Banff on the Brewster Express bus (banffjaspercollection.com/brewster-express), if luggage space permits, but book ahead.

Opposite Athabasca Glacier tours at the Columbia Icefield Discovery Centre *Right* Divine detours through pine in Jasper National Park

NORTH AMERICA

Prince Edward Island

CANADA

Cross Canada's smallest province in the company of great food, fine beaches and Anne of Green Gables.

Gulf of
Saint Lawrence/
Golfe du Saint-Laurent
CANADA
N
Green Gables
Heritage
Place
Avonlea
Village
Cavendish
Rustico
Bay
North
Rustico
Beach
PRINCE EDWARD ISLAND
NATIONAL PARK
Brackley
Beach
Tracadie
Bay
Greenwich
Interpretation
Centre
Greenwich
Dunes
St Peters
Bay
Bear
River
BASIN HEAD
PROVINCIAL
PARK
Elmira
Morell
Stanhope
Tracadie
Hunter
River
PRINCE EDWARD ISLAND
Morell
River
Hillsborough River
Souris
Singing Sands
Beach
Northumberland Strait/
Detroit de
Northumberland
Charlottetown
Georgetown
0
10 km
1
2
3
4

Prince Edward Island

WHY IT'S SPECIAL

Cycling a province that rises to no more than 142 metres (465 feet) above sea level and is traversed end-to-end by a rail trail is pure delight, and feels like an entirely fitting and appropriate way to travel on Prince Edward Island (PEI). In 1908, Canada's smallest province became the only North American region to ever ban motor vehicles. Curiously, it was in that same year that Lucy Maud Montgomery's island-defining novel *Anne of Green Gables* was published. More than a century on, both those events still seem to resonate across PEI.

Though cars are long back on the roads, bicycles and the famous redhead remain key features of PEI's tourism landscape. In Cavendish, where Montgomery's novel was set, you can visit the Green Gables house (Green Gables Heritage Place) that inspired the book's location, while *Anne of Green Gables the Musical* has been playing in PEI's capital city, Charlottetown, since 1965, making it Canada's longest-running theatre production. Out in the countryside, the Confederation Trail forms the foundation of great cycle touring around the island.

BEST TIME TO RIDE

Summer temperatures on PEI are gloriously warm, so ride from around June to September to enjoy comfortable conditions and the enticement of the island's beaches and swimming - PEI likes to claim it has the warmest water north of Florida.

From December through March, the Confederation Trail is open only to snowmobiles.

RIDE IT

For cyclists, the compelling features of the island are twofold: PEI is split by the Confederation Trail, a 273-kilometre (170-mile) bike path (with another 160 kilometres, or 100 miles, of branch trails) that follows an abandoned railway line between its eastern and western tips; and the island's highest point is just 142 metres (465 feet) above sea level, meaning there's no such thing as a big hill climb here.

The Confederation Trail was created in the 1990s when PEI's entire rail network was ripped up and converted into bike paths. It stretches from Tignish (west) to Elmira (east), arcing across the island. It's also part of the Great Trail, the trans-Canadian pathway billed as the world's longest recreational trail (24,000 kilometres, or 15,000 miles - and counting), if too much cycling isn't enough.

If the Confederation Trail has one flaw, it's the fact that it's more single-minded than scenic, following a green corridor through the rural heart

Nuts & bolts
Distance: 225 kilometres (140 miles)
Days: 4
Ascent: 1200 metres (3940 feet)
Difficulty: Easy
Bike: The Confederation Trail sections of the ride are unsealed, but a mountain bike would be overkill since they're smooth and hard-packed and the riding is so flat.

Previous The red cliffs of Prince Edward Island National Park

of the island and all but ignoring PEI's beautiful coasts – the trail began life as a practical railway line, after all. For this reason, you'll want to branch off the trail at times, as the ride described here does, a task made even easier by the gentle nature of the island's topography.

LOCAL SNAPSHOT

Prince Edward Island's food is revered, so reward more than equals effort on a cycle trip here. PEI has earned foodie fame for its oysters, lobsters and potatoes (PEI might easily stand for Potatoes Everywhere Island). You won't want to leave without having tried some of the more than 100 varieties of potato grown here, with crops covering more than 5 per cent of the island. The potato industry alone is said to be worth more than $1 billion a year to the island. As you ride, keep an eye out for lobster suppers – there are good ones in Charlottetown and at Fisherman's Wharf in North Rustico. The island is also home to Canada's top cooking school, the Culinary Institute of Canada, meaning the island is awash in great chefs. Even the ice-cream once named by *Reader's Digest* as the best in Canada – COWS Creamery – is made on PEI.

Below Covehead Harbour Lighthouse near Stanhope
Opposite Gazebo on the shores of St Peters Bay

ITINERARY

DAY 1

CHARLOTTETOWN TO CAVENDISH (51KM/32 MILES)

I've come to Prince Edward Island (PEI) not to ride the entire linear route of the Confederation Trail, but to use it as a guiding line of sorts to the island's highlights. I begin in Charlottetown, at the end of one of the trail's branch lines. With a population of just 36,000 people, PEI's capital is a likeable, sophisticated city squeezed into the shape of a country town. Grand architecture furnishes its streets, yet no building stands taller than 10 storeys. It further belies its small size with a dining scene and food to rival far larger cities, and this only sets the scene for a distinctly culinary island.

From Charlottetown, the branch trail runs north for 8 kilometres (5 miles) to meet the main arm of the Confederation Trail, which I follow west to Hunter River, even though ultimately I'm cycling to Elmira at PEI's eastern tip. I leave the trail at Hunter River, taking quiet roads towards the north coast.

On the north coast are the likes of Cavendish and PEI's only national park: Prince Edward Island National Park. I'm riding to Cavendish this first day and have been warned that it's a hilly crossing to the north coast, sometimes in tones that suggest I'll be climbing the equivalent of an Alpine pass. I'm highly sceptical, even though I am passing near to the island's highest point, and yet the warnings are surprisingly prescient – by the time I hit Cavendish, I've totted up climbs totalling nearly 500 metres (1640 feet) on day-one legs. I'm ready for a nap.

Cavendish is PEI's tourist epicentre, and not purely because of its period pieces related to *Anne of Green Gables*. It's a seaside-silly town, a Canadian-style Blackpool filled with amusement parks, water parks and the likes of the Ripley's Believe It or Not Odditorium and Jurassic Bart's Dinosaur Museum.

For fans of LMM, as author Montgomery is affectionately known around the island, there are more compelling reasons to linger in Cavendish. It's home to the Avonlea Village re-creation, Montgomery's childhood home and the Green Gables Heritage Place, which was the farmhouse belonging to Montgomery's cousins that formed the inspiration for the setting of the novel. Today it's a national historic site. It sits at the very heart of Cavendish, among a bevy of hotels and eateries, so it's an easy stop when I arrive. I park my bike and wander into the old farmhouse, which is filled with period furnishings and restored so as to resemble descriptions in

the book. 'Aunt Dorothy had wallpaper like this,' I hear one visitor whisper in the dining room.

DAY 2

CAVENDISH TO STANHOPE (40KM/25 MILES)

More interesting than Cavendish is the national park that stretches east from the town along the coast. It's a park in three parts – a natural trilogy – covering 40 kilometres (25 miles) of PEI's north shore. Running directly along the park's coastline is the Gulf Shore Way bike path, which I follow out of Cavendish, riding atop low red cliffs that occasionally break open into beaches.

The path and the Cavendish section of the national park both end at North Rustico Beach, where I take to roads, looping around protected, oyster-rich Rustico Bay. After 20 kilometres (12.5 miles), I'm returned to the north coast, the national park and the continuation of the Gulf Shore Way bike path, which here runs along the foot of treeless sand dunes behind Brackley Beach. It's like cycling through a golf links, which feels kind of appropriate on an island that bills itself as 'Canada's No 1 golf destination'.

PEI's reputation for fine island produce is founded in its soil, which is so red and perfect that it almost looks edible itself, and by the time I arrive at my hotel in Stanhope this night, my legs are all but painted red in dust – I'm fast becoming one with the island. I've been pedalling for two days and covered 90 kilometres (56 miles), and yet by road I'm just 20 kilometres (12.5 miles) from Charlottetown.

DAY 3

STANHOPE TO ST PETERS BAY (54KM/33.5 MILES)

I pause in the small town of Stanhope for a day as a hurricane rattles and rolls over the island, then continue pedalling my way east. The early pattern of this day is familiar – the Gulf Shore Way bike path and then skirting the shores of Tracadie Bay, nibbled into PEI's north coast.

In the village of Tracadie, at the southern tip of the bay, I rejoin the Confederation Trail, which will be my near-constant companion all the way to the eastern end of the island. Ahead of me, beyond the marshy headwaters of the Hillsborough River – PEI's longest river, where blue herons fly in slow motion and bald eagles sit like Christmas angels atop spruce trees – is the Confederation Trail's most spectacular section. For 11 kilometres (7 miles) the trail hugs the shores of St Peters Bay, crossing the mouths of three rivers on trestle bridges, including the Morell River, one of PEI's few salmon-spawning streams.

At the head of the bay is the town of St Peters Bay, where every cottage seems to have a bay view, looking over mussel beds, and where I stay this final night, in easy reach of arguably PEI's most beautiful natural feature: the Greenwich dunes.

DAY 4

ST PETERS BAY TO ELMIRA VIA GREENWICH DUNES (80KM/50 MILES)

The third piece of the national park, the Greenwich dunes stretch in a line across the mouth of St Peters Bay, 10 kilometres (6 miles) from town. I have just 60 fairly flat kilometres (37 miles) to ride to Elmira, much of it along the Confederation Trail, so I begin my day by pedalling out to the dunes. There's barely a rise in the road along the shores of the bay to the carpark for the dunes, which were added into the national park in 1998 - more than 60 years after its establishment. At the road's end, walking trails begin, heading across a long floating boardwalk, rimmed by bulrushes and through a line of coastal dunes to the beach.

Back at St Peters Bay, the Confederation Trail continues along kilometres of ruler-straight track, passing a series of beaver ponds. For a couple of hours I ride without seeing another soul, other than the chipmunks that bounce across the track. Out here, deep in woods, it's hard to believe that PEI is Canada's most densely populated province.

Past the fancifully named town of Bear River (on an island that has no critter larger than a beaver), I depart the main trail again, turning south onto an 8-kilometre (5-mile) branch trail to the south-coast town of Souris. Though my end goal, Elmira, is most easily reached along the main trail, I have one more detour to make. Around an hour's ride east of Souris, along the coast, is Basin Head Provincial Park. The beach at the park is considered by many to be the island's best - a Canadian travel website once went so far as to name it the best beach in the country - with its fine white sands backed by wine-red cliffs. It has become known as Singing Sands Beach because of the squeak in its sand when you walk on it, or even when the wind shifts it.

At Basin Head, I park my bike for one final time and head onto the sands among a crowd of bodies baking in the sun like sausages on a barbecue. I'm in no hurry since I now have just 12 kilometres (7.5 miles) to ride to Elmira and the finish of the Confederation Trail. In an indication of the narrowness of the island's eastern tip, Elmira sits midway between the north and south coasts, and yet it'll be just a 4-kilometre (2.5-mile) ride from the town to the seaside motel in which I'll spend my final night before returning to Charlottetown.

As I settle into this scene of blue sea, white sand and cliffs as red as PEI's famous lobsters, I am again - as I have been for days - almost overwhelmed by colour. All that's missing is a redhead called Anne and a beautiful house called Green Gables.

Riding resources

Prince Edward Island Tourism has a comprehensive webpage on the Confederation Trail (tourismpei.com/pei-confederation-trail). Charlottetown bike store MacQueen's (macqueens.com) hires out bikes and also offers self-guided tour itineraries, booking your accommodation on the island and transporting your luggage between stops.

Above Crossing the Naufrage River
Opposite Greenwich dunes

NORTH AMERICA

Maine East Coast Greenway (ECG)

USA

Ride border to border in Maine through a seductive mix of towns and hilly country.

CITY OF BELFAST
HARBOR WALK
PUBLIC WELCOME
PLEASE RESPECT
SHIPYARD PROPERTY

Maine East Coast Greenway (ECG)

Nuts & bolts
Distance: 570 kilometres (354 miles)
Days: 7
Ascent: 4900 metres (16,075 feet)
Difficulty: Medium
Bike: A standard touring bike is fine. Only the Down East Sunrise Trail (days 6 and 7) is better suited to fat tyres, but hardly impassable on skinnier ones. Cyclists uneasy on gravel also have an entirely on-road alternative for that stretch.

CONTRIBUTION BY ETHAN GELBER

WHY IT'S SPECIAL

Imagine a long-distance trail that swings within 8 kilometres (5 miles) of 25 million people and yet remains traffic-free – an avenue of rail trails and other paths set aside for hikers, runners, skaters, skiers, dog-walkers, equestrians, wheelchair-users and, of course, cyclists.

That's the East Coast Greenway (ECG), a 4830-kilometre (3000-mile) multi-use trail system stretching from Key West, Florida, to the US–Canada border town of Calais, Maine. Its uplifting goal is to string together a continuous car-less corridor across 450 communities in 15 states (plus Washington, DC), while passing directly through 25 major east coast cities, such as Miami, Savannah, Charleston, Raleigh, Richmond, Baltimore, Philadelphia, New York, Boston and Portland. In Maine, it includes some of the best off-road wilderness trails on the Eastern Seaboard.

The plenitude of communities along the way are brimming with accommodation, farm-to-table restaurants, locally brewed beer, other supplies and services, and lots of attractions. This allows for daily distances to be adjusted according to one's desires and strengths.

Maine's animal community can also be appreciated from the ECG, especially at its wildest moments: crossing Scarborough Marsh (day 1), along the Down East Sunrise Trail (DEST, days 6 and 7) and in the Moosehorn National Wildlife Refuge (day 7). Look for songbirds, waterbirds, wild turkeys, grouse, beavers, eagles, deer and moose, and keep a special eye out for the nesting ospreys on Charlotte Road.

BEST TIME TO RIDE

May through October is ideal. The warmer and drier summer season (June to Aug), is followed by an autumn (Sept and Oct) notorious for its crisp nights and colourful leaves.

RIDE IT

Since discovering the ECG, I've cycled several long segments in New England, but the route from the point at which it enters the state of Maine, at Kittery, to its northern terminus in Calais is, I believe, the most outstanding, delivering a mix of towns and changing landscapes, including one of the best off-road wilderness trails on the Eastern Seaboard.

I divide Maine's ECG into four sections, each showcasing a special quality of the state. The Eastern Trail from Kittery to Portland begins in rolling

Previous A leafy passage through Maine
Opposite top left Kennebec River Trail near Hallowell *Top right* Belfast Harbor Walk
Bottom left Waterfront Walkway Trail, Calais
Bottom right Kids on the trail - Brewer Riverwalk

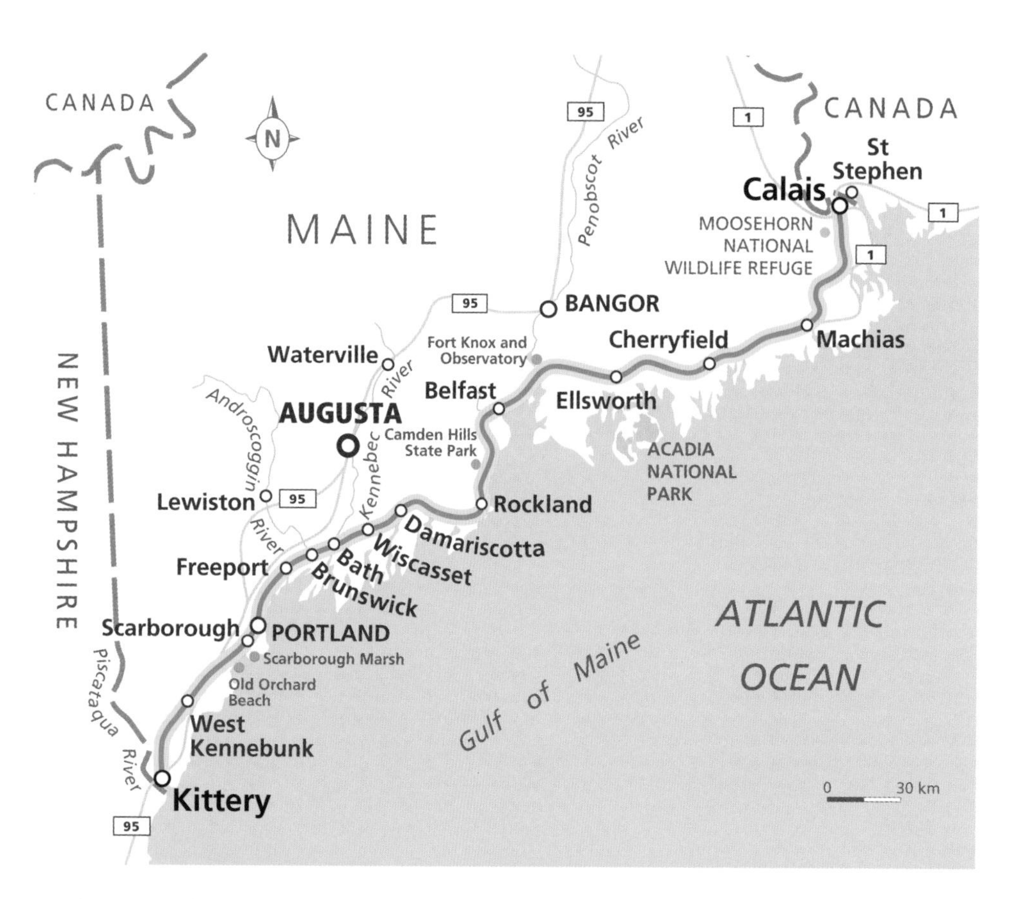

terrain, weaves through clapboard-housed farms and towns, and samples a couple of pleasantly graded and shaded rail trails before finishing in Maine's largest and most populous city. The inland 'spine' route continues on riverside and runs through some of Maine's other lively southern cities: Lewiston, Augusta, Waterville and Bangor. The coastal 'complementary' alternative to the inland spine embraces the best of Midcoast Maine's challenging hills and sea-centric villages. Finally, 140 kilometres (87 miles) of the Down East Sunrise Trail – the longest, unbroken off-road segment of the whole ECG – traverses Downeast Maine's scenic rivers and forests, stopping just short of the international border at Calais, where the ECG calls it quits.

I rode from south to north, though the ECG could just as easily be tackled in the opposite direction. In no real hurry, but with significant previous experience of Maine's unrelenting hills, I allotted a week for the journey, aiming to complete 60 to 100 kilometres (37 to 62 miles) a day.

Helpfully, wherever the Maine ECG follows the course of another established path, like the Eastern Trail or the Down East Sunrise Trail, ECG signposts are clear and common, usually paired with the other trail way-markers. Maps are only necessary along parts of the sometimes-unsigned coastal 'complementary' route (*see* p. 24).

Worthy of note when sharing the road with other vehicles: Maine law requires drivers to leave a distance 'of not less than three feet' when passing cyclists. On roads known to be busy with bikes, conspicuous reminders ensure the awareness of drivers, the vast majority of whom who I found to be patient and respectful.

Opposite Lobster and lemon; fuel for the trail

DAY 1

KITTERY TO PORTLAND (104KM/64.5 MILES)

It takes about 22 kilometres (13.5 miles) to get beyond Kittery and the extended suburbia of gently trafficked roads and green villages along the Piscataqua River, separating Maine from New Hampshire. A first but mild taste of hills ensues – they get much harder later in the week, as well as early rural stretches of forests, fields and working farms. I'm tempted to stop and photograph the big red barns lording over green fields of black-and-white cows, but it soon becomes clear that these will be familiar sights and colours throughout the Maine landscape.

Progress is easy, despite numerous turns to keep to back-country roads. The East Coast Greenway (ECG) is identified by abundant and reassuring route markers, all of them in tandem with those of the 105-kilometre (65-mile) Eastern Trail, which the ECG adopts from Kittery to Portland, and sometimes those of US Bike Route 1, a separate Florida-to-Maine bikeway that only uses regular roads.

Just east of West Kennebunk, 59 kilometres (36.5 miles) into the day, the first off-road section of the Eastern Trail begins. On well-maintained and easily rideable hard-packed earth, the gently graded, 10-kilometre (6.1-mile) path keeps to the old Eastern Railroad Corridor, unused since 1945 and largely an abandoned right-of-way owned by a natural gas pipeline utility company. After navigating so many roads shared with vehicles, the straightforward plunge into placid woodlands is an instant reminder of how idyllic the end-to-end ECG will one day be.

Too soon, the trail is interrupted by the twin towns of Biddeford and Saco. The Eastern Trail Alliance is actively working on an off-road traverse to replace the 7-kilometre (4.4-mile) detour through the towns. Saco is where anyone bent on visiting the 11-kilometre (7-mile) seafront of Old Orchard Beach can take US Bike Route 1 to the coast.

I choose to cruise the second, 13-kilometre (8.2-mile), off-road section of the Eastern Trail. The final third of this corridor is especially pastoral where it crosses Scarborough Marsh, Maine's largest saltwater estuary. I stop to chat with birdwatchers ogling a great blue heron and rattling off other wildlife sightings – a bald eagle, wild turkeys, a deer turtle. They are making their way to the Audubon Center, visible a short walk to the west.

After Scarborough, 90 kilometres (55.8 miles) from Kittery, the South Portland Greenbelt leads to the Casco Bay Bridge for the passage into Portland, Maine's biggest, busiest and most touristed metropolis, replete with everything needed for a recharge, like a dinner of lobster and chowder (known locally as 'lobstah' and 'chowdah').

LOCAL SNAPSHOT

The East Coast Greenway (ECG) is no small undertaking, of course. It was originally launched in 1991 by eight bike enthusiasts and urban planners who shared a dream of this linear park. There was a common belief that it could boost public health, environmental sustainability, economic development and civic engagement.

Since then, identifying existing municipal, county and state-owned trails and then constructing new, connecting segments at an average cost of about $1 million per mile has made the ECG arguably the most ambitious infrastructure project in the US. Three decades after the ECG Alliance began its work, approximately 35 per cent of the ECG is successfully off-limits to motorised vehicles. Detours on tranquil regular roads, streets, footpaths and bridges account for the ever-diminishing remainder.

As the trail's stature grows, projections are that certain segments could see as many as 50 million visitors a year. This would make it the most visited park in the United States. That's a far cry from the seven cyclists who, in only 2004, were the first to ride the ECG from end to end.

DAYS 2–3

PORTLAND TO WISCASSET (84KM/52 MILES); WISCASSET TO ROCKLAND (91KM/56.5 MILES)

There are two paths from Portland to Ellsworth. The ECG 'spine' heads inland along the Androscoggin and Kennebec rivers, before cutting overland back to the coast. It visits Central Maine's most culture-rich cities, including the second- and third-largest – Lewiston and Bangor, respectively – and the state capital of Augusta.

I'm more drawn, however, to the coastal 'complementary' itinerary through Midcoast Maine. The riding over these two days, plus the two that follow, is mostly on quiet roads and alternates between hard hills and easy leisure – the former an energy-sapping rollercoaster of hillocks and hummocks, and the latter through spirit-buoying seaside towns, the combination of which has made Maine's reputation. Common to both are gently curious locals, quizzically asking about my trip, remarking on Maine's unforgiving geography and always ready with directions, insights, kind words and a yarn.

These two days from Portland to Rockland see repeated ascents, rarely exceeding 45 metres (150 feet) at a time, but with a relentless frequency that demands sweaty, whoopie-pie-fuelled determination. Accordingly, I fill up on food and drink supplies whenever I can in the classical New England towns and villages full of distraction: retail-minded Freeport, worldwide headquarters of L.L.Bean; Brunswick, home of Bowdoin College and an active arts and entertainment culture; Bath and its storied maritime past; Wiscasset and Damariscotta, full of antiques and architecture; and art-rich Rockland, site of the famous Farnsworth Art Museum and numerous galleries.

DAYS 4–5

ROCKLAND TO BELFAST (62KM/38.5 MILES); BELFAST TO ELLSWORTH (59KM/36.5 MILES)

The pattern of pasture- and forest-topped rises giving way to inlet-cradled communities continues during the two days between Rockland and Ellsworth, albeit with two important exceptions: the hills get longer and push higher (up to 120 metres, or 400 feet, of elevation gain per climb, sometimes over several kilometres); and the road choices after Belfast become more limited. Luckily, when the ECG has no recourse but primary and busier byways, there's a welcomingly wide shoulder.

For this reason, I plan shorter days, which also leaves time to admire Camden's windjammer-filled harbour and take in the beauty of Camden Hills State Park and Megunticook Lake just past it. It even allows for full exploration of the seafaring history and working wharf on the tongue-twisting Passagassawakeag River city of Belfast, the day 4 overnight stay and site of an intact 19th-century downtown complete with the US's oldest shoe store and a century-old cinema.

On day 5, it's definitely worth pausing on the dramatic Penobscot Narrows Bridge to take in the views over the river, and out to Fort Knox and Bucksport. A climb up the observation tower ends in an even more dramatic vista of the surrounding area.

After this, it's 24 kilometres (15 miles) of Acadia Highway, including a couple of the longest and highest hills on Maine's ECG, with equally excellent views of the road ahead. The final descent finishes outside Ellsworth, friendly gateway to Bar Harbor and Acadia National Park.

DAYS 6–7

ELLSWORTH TO MACHIAS (95KM/59 MILES); MACHIAS TO CALAIS (75KM/46.5 MILES)

The last leg of the ECG is a two-day pull from Ellsworth to Calais, and can be summarised in four words: Down East Sunrise Trail (DEST). Once the Calais Branch Railroad Corridor, it saw its last trains in 1984 and is now a 140-kilometre (87-mile), graded (though not without its ups and downs!) forest passage, with a 3.65-metre (12-foot) wide, compact gravel base that's perfect for multi-season riding. It's also the longest unbroken off-road section of the ECG – a deep dive into the gorgeous natural landscape of Downeast Maine, a habitat for moose, white-tail deer, beavers, eagles, wild turkeys and more.

Although I'm on a standard touring bike, I rarely dismount to walk through a rough patch. Anyone unfazed by the gravel trail surface could stay on it all the way; the DEST veers close enough to most towns to allow for short detours. That said, there's an entirely on-road alternative for cyclists uneasy on the gravel. It's quite a bit longer and, as it stays mostly on Route 1, busier.

To mix things up a bit, I ride the DEST for 44 kilometres (27 miles) and then take a 25-kilometre (15.5-mile) surfaced-road respite on the ECG-mapped parallel route from Cherryfield to Columbia Falls. Returning to the DEST for the 26 kilometres (16 miles) to Machias, the best midway break on the DEST, I get the best of both worlds. After Columbia Falls, I take a moment on a short, wood-plank bridge in the middle of a long backwoods DEST segment to absorb the sounds of nature: frogs and ducks on the river below, birds unseen in pine boughs on both banks. I even hear a distant splash and imagine a beaver or surfacing salmon. This really is the way every ride should be.

From Machias, the ECG sticks to the DEST for 43 kilometres (26.5 miles), pivoting off onto sealed roads for the final zip into Calais. There are just a couple more hills (easy now for practiced Maine legs) on Smith Ridge and Charlotte roads, and a deep-in-the-wilderness ride through Moosehorn National Wildlife Refuge, one-third of which is set aside as hands-off federal wilderness. Along the way, I see eagles, deer, grouse, songbirds and the ospreys nesting on platforms along Charlotte Road.

Just 7 kilometres (4.5 miles) from the end of the ECG, I turn onto Route 1, dropping into downtown Calais, where a small border crossing funnels directly into downtown St Stephen (New Brunswick, Canada).

Eyeing Calais, back across the river, I reflect on long, protected greenways, especially those through the forests and marshes along the DEST, which some people claim is the most spectacular wilderness on the ECG. In the near future, I look forward to riding more similar ECG trails in other states, all while keeping an eye on the progress in Maine. I hope one day to roll without any cars from state line to international border.

Riding resources

Everything you need to know about the East Coast Greenway (ECG), including maps, cue sheets, detailed state-specific information and the ECG Alliance, is available online (greenway.org).
The ECG Alliance's superb mapping tools include web-based and GPS- or mobile-ready versions, as well as detailed cue sheets formatted for print.
For a close-up of the Eastern Trail (the Maine ECG from Kittery to Portland), see: easterntrail.org; for the Down East Sunrise Trail (most of the ECG in eastern Maine), see: sunrisetrail.org.

Opposite The Down East Sunrise Trail near Calais

PEDALLER

Dan Buettner

Minneapolis-based Dan Buettner is a National Geographic fellow and the *New York Times* bestselling author of *The Blue Zones*. He was once issued a speeding ticket while riding his bike near his home.

Find him at bluezones.com.

Where was your first cycle tour?

The first one was from Prudhoe Bay in Alaska to Tierra del Fuego, Argentina from August 1986 until June 1987 – basically, the top of North America to the bottom of South America. It was a world record at the time.

What drew you to cycle travel in the first place?

I had a young friend named Joel Kachael, and we grew up poor, and even though we were making $1.20 an hour as dishwashers, he bought a $750 bicycle. We all kind of caught the bug from him, and then when I was 14 I used to bicycle 120 kilometres (74 miles) from my parents' house to my grandparents' house on a farm. That fostered that early zeal for cycling, that consummate feeling of freedom when you wake and have the road unfold in front of you.

What did you learn on that first trip that has carried through all of your subsequent cycle trips?

Empathy, I think. Travelling in a motorised vehicle strips the experience away from the travel. You're in an air-conditioned bubble; you don't feel the geography, the land, the incline, the decline, the heat, the dust. You're less apt to stop at a random place at the end of a day and meet a random person and end up living in a real-life situation, as opposed to a campground or a hotel. I learned that travelling on bicycles gives you a chance to feel what it's like to live in the places you're visiting and not just skim the surface.

You've been in Guinness World Records for cycling. What records did you set?

I set the record for biking from Alaska to Argentina, for bicycling from the top of Africa to the bottom of Africa, and for bicycling across the Soviet Union. Nobody will ever beat that one because the Soviet Union collapsed the year after we finished – I like to say it wasn't my fault.

What tips would you give someone who's preparing for a cycle tour?

Don't over-plan. Just do it. You don't need much. Get a simple bike – it's often better to have a steel bike than a fancy aluminium bike, because steel bikes can be welded if you break the frame. They're easy to fix.

What does cycle travel give you that other forms of travel don't?

It's the difference between transportation and travel. The word 'travel' has the same root as 'travail', which means work. A true traveller exposes themself to hardships, and through those hardships you not only have real experiences and gain wisdom, but you also gain insight and you develop yourself. Bicycling gives you that in a way that you'll never get on a motorbike or in a car.

Are the rewards of a cycle tour all physical, or are they also mental and emotional?

I've always considered bicycling a rolling sort of meditation. You learn things spasmodically through cycling because it forces you to go slow enough to make small observations that you miss if you're going 60km/h (37mp/h). Most transportation is from point A to point B and in bicycling you notice all the minutiae between the points, and therein lies the richness of it.

Where have been your favourite places to cycle?

I've biked across every continent, but believe it or not my favourite place is Maiden Rock in western Wisconsin and a whole network of trails there that are really Amish roads. More exotically, biking around Lake Atitlan in Guatemala and seeing the lake change different hues of blue as you ride. I loved cycling across the Sahara for its austerity and the attention to detail you develop over time. I loved the southern coast of Africa, from Jeffreys Bay to Cape Town (*see* p. 202).

Where's the one place you'd really like to cycle?

Vietnam, I'm heading there next. I've wanted to ride there for over half a century, and I'm finally going to do it.

Below Cycling through China in 2000 *Opposite* Dan Buettner in his family's ancestral land of Sicily

NORTH AMERICA

Cactus Country of Arizona

USA

A desert adventure with vineyard and mountain detours.

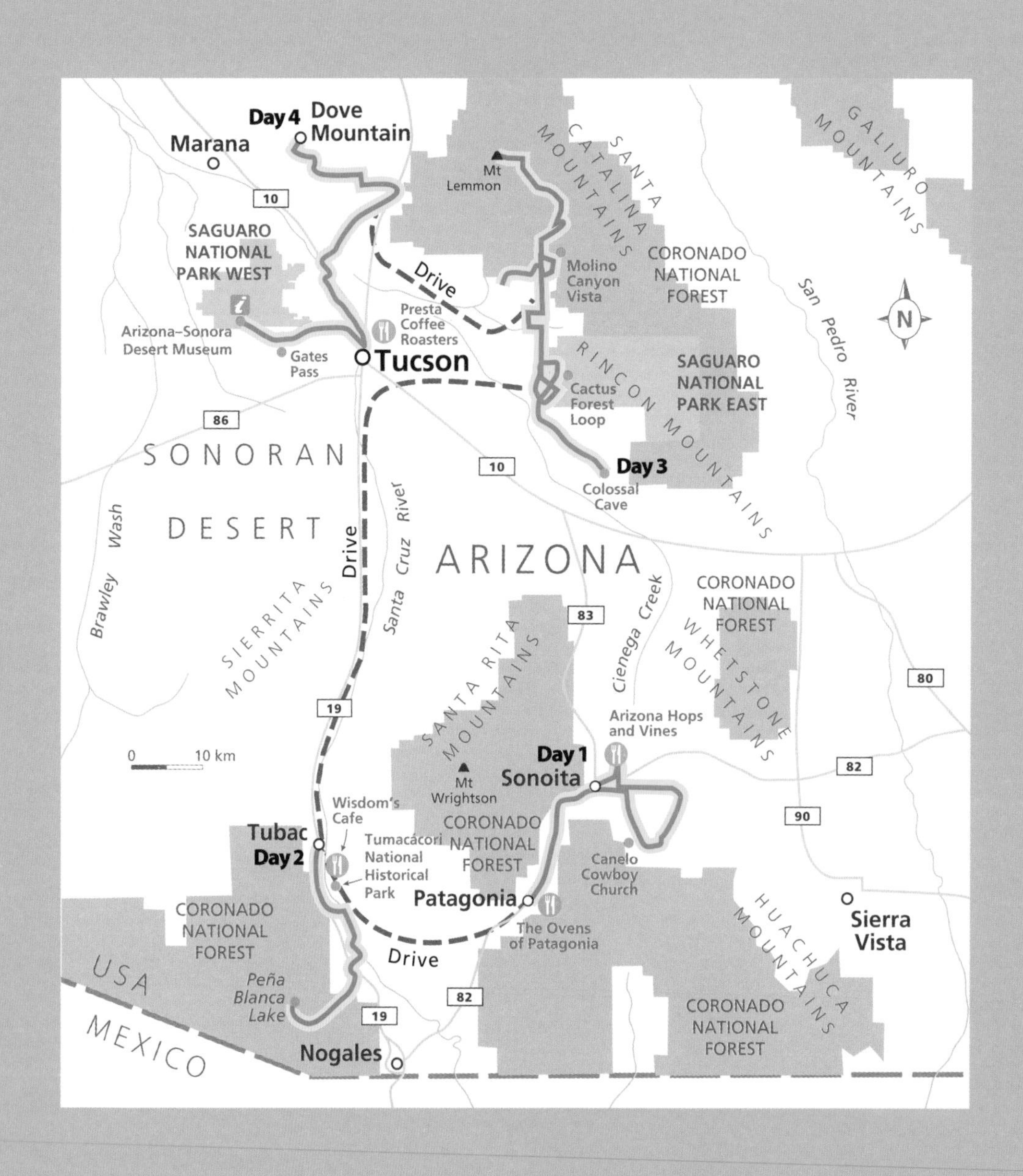
Day 4
Dove Mountain
Marana
10
SAGUARO NATIONAL PARK WEST
Arizona–Sonora Desert Museum
Gates Pass
Mt Lemmon
SANTA CATALINA MOUNTAINS
GALIURO MOUNTAINS
Drive
Molino Canyon Vista
CORONADO NATIONAL FOREST
San Pedro River
N
Presta Coffee Roasters
Tucson
RINCON MOUNTAINS
Cactus Forest Loop
SAGUARO NATIONAL PARK EAST
86
SONORAN
DESERT
10
Day 3
Colossal Cave
Brawley Wash
Drive
Santa Cruz River
ARIZONA
SIERRITA MOUNTAINS
CORONADO NATIONAL FOREST
83
Cienega Creek
WHETSTONE MOUNTAINS
SANTA RITA MOUNTAINS
80
19
Arizona Hops and Vines
0
10 km
Day 1
Sonoita
Mt Wrightson
82
Wisdom's Cafe
90
Tubac
Day 2
CORONADO NATIONAL FOREST
Tumacácori National Historical Park
Canelo Cowboy Church
Patagonia
The Ovens of Patagonia
HUACHUCA MOUNTAINS
Sierra Vista
CORONADO NATIONAL FOREST
USA
Drive
Peña Blanca Lake
82
19
CORONADO NATIONAL FOREST
MEXICO
Nogales

Cactus Country of Arizona

CONTRIBUTION BY JEN MURPHY

WHY IT'S SPECIAL

Wanting to log a few more outdoor kilometres before becoming a slave to my trainer during Colorado's long, snowy winter, I took a friend's advice and booked a trip to Tucson in late November. I'd imagined four days pedalling past Georgia O'Keeffe-worthy landscapes, but the diversity of the ever-changing scenery surprised me. In addition to pale red rocks and seas of cacti, there were mountains and even vineyards nestled in the high desert.

I've found that most wine regions throughout the world double as fantastic cycling destinations and Arizona's wine-producing areas are no different. A self-admitted wine snob, I've always believed that just because all 50 states in the USA can produce wine doesn't mean they should. And while – let's be honest – Arizona is no Napa, it does have some unicorn wines (such as Sand-Reckoner Roussane and Dose Cabezas WineWorks El Nort) and the paradoxical experience of wine tastings in a desert environment.

A 210-kilometre (130-mile) network of bike paths also makes it easy to ride from downtown Tucson into cactus-studded Saguaro National Park. In addition to scenic rolling roads, you can challenge yourself with a revered climb up Mt Lemmon.

BEST TIME TO RIDE

Mild temperatures and blue skies from November through February make this a winter cycling heaven.

RIDE IT

Arizona may not seem like the most hospitable cycling destination. Towering cacti carpet the desert landscape, threatening tyres and cyclists with their thorns. In summer, temperatures boil above 40°C (104°F), causing the motorways to buckle with giant stress fractures. But come late autumn and winter – November through February – southern Arizona transforms into a cycling paradise that rivals off-season pro-training grounds such as Mallorca. While the rest of the country is buried under snow, the Sonoran Desert is blessed with blue skies and mild temperatures hovering around 15°C (59°F).

The region offers exceptionally diverse riding for both expert and recreational mountain bikers and road cyclists. And the city of Tucson, flanked on each side by trail-laced Saguaro National Park, wins the award for having the friendliest bike culture in the south-west, boasting the Loop (a 210-kilometre, or 130-mile, network of paved bicycle paths), events

Nuts & bolts

Distance: 320 kilometres (199 miles)
Days: 4
Ascent: 2500 metres (8200 feet)
Difficulty: Easy-medium
Bike: A road bike with a slightly wider tyre diameter (700×28mm), which can handle the rough roads, is what locals ride. Continental Gator Skins can stand up to the cactus thorns. Be advised to pack tweezers for goathead thorns, too.

Previous The namesake saguaro cacti of cycle-friendly Saguaro National Park

North America

such as the annual El Tour de Tucson (a 160-kilometre, or 100-mile, ride with up to 10,000 participants) and coffee shops where it seems like half the customers are dressed in lycra.

Much of Saguaro National Park can be accessed by the Loop but it's best to rent a car if you want to follow this whole ride and explore wine country and tackle Mt Lemmon. If you don't have a car, you could use a cycling company that has a van.

LOCAL SNAPSHOT

Southern Arizona is one of the oldest continually inhabited places in North America. First occupied by the Hohokam tribes, today it has emerged as a rich melting-pot of cultures. Tucson was officially founded by the Spanish in 1775 and has plenty of historic cycling detours, such as Mission San Xavier del Bac and Tumacácori National Historical Park. Today, the city boasts America's first and only UNESCO City of Gastronomy designation. After riding the trails of the Loop there are plenty of options to refuel, from Downtown Kitchen, run by James Beard-award-winning chef Janos Wilde, to low-key Kukai, a seriously good Japanese spot in a shipping container at MSA Annex.

Opposite Windmill at Sonoita
Right Dwarfed in cactus country

DAY 1

SONOITA TO PATAGONIA (66KM/41 MILES), DRIVE TO TUBAC

I start my trip in Sonoita, a wine-growing region just over an hour's drive south-east of Tucson. Surrounded by the Santa Rita, Huachuca and Whetstone mountain ranges, the bucolic vineyards and country roads provide a lovely backdrop for cycling. The area is situated at an elevation of around 1500 metres (4920 feet), and my lungs immediately feel the altitude as I set out from the town of Sonoita on a 42-kilometre (26-mile) loop ride around an area known as vineyard alley. The generous shoulder on Highway 82 slopes deceptively uphill, taking me past native oak glades and yucca patches, old steel windmills, and the Canelo Cowboy Church, a house of worship with grounds that double as a rodeo arena.

Wineries beckon visitors with 'Tasters Wanted' signs, and at mile marker 23 along Highway 82, I detour up the gravel driveway of Arizona Hops and Vines, a women-run winery with a shaded deck, perfect for a lunch break. I tack on a mellow 24 kilometres (15 miles) to reach Patagonia, a sleepy town straight out of a classic Western movie. I half expect to see giant tumbleweeds rolling down the dusty main street. Having had my fill of wine at tasting rooms in Sonoita, I'm ready to splurge on a slice of made-from-scratch blueberry pie from Ovens of Patagonia, a homely bakery and shop known for its exceptional baked goods. I order a second slice to go, then load my bike on my car and drive 40 minutes north-west on the 1-19N to the gallery-filled town of Tubac for a solid night's sleep.

DAY 2

TUBAC TO PEÑA BLANCA LAKE RETURN (86KM/53 MILES)

The second day I ride an out-and-back route from the town of Tubac, through quiet residential areas, then deep into remote, ranch-studded cowboy country, where I learn quickly that cattle have the right of way on the road. This day there's nearly 500 metres (1640 feet) of elevation gain, but the gruelling inclines are followed by speedy descents that allow me to coast and catch my breath, which is a mixed blessing because between the cattle and the occasional roadkill, the air on certain stretches of the two-lane road is far from fresh. Riding here, I'm less than 20 kilometres (12.5 miles) from the Mexican border, and I'd been advised to keep my passport handy in case I was stopped by border-patrol officers, who police the area. But as I cycle by one roadblock, the only procedure is a friendly wave-through and a kind warning to watch out for the cattle grates ahead on the road.

Once I enter Coronado National Forest, I test my mettle on a final climb to Peña Blanca Lake. I pause at this desert oasis, tucked into the foothills of the Pajarito Mountains, 1219 metres (4000 feet) above sea level, and take in the towering rocky outcroppings and stony hoodoos – the tall, thin spires of weathered rock so emblematic of south-west USA. I'm more prepared for those rollers on my way back and luckily, I'm also prepared for a flat tyre. Goathead thorns – tiny balls covered in barbs – are a cyclist's nemesis out here and are nearly impossible to spot before they inflict damage. I'd been tipped off to pack tweezers in my repair kit in case I needed to extract pricklies, and they came in handy twice today.

A detour to Tumacácori National Historical Park, just 20 minutes ride outside of Tubac, is a must for history nerds or anyone curious about the region's Spanish colonial past. The expansive grounds include a museum, the ruins of three Spanish mission communities and the state's second-oldest church.

Arizona's wine may have a ways to go, but the state has some of the best restaurants in the south-west, and the proximity to Mexico means there's no shortage of authentic Mexican cuisine. Just 3 kilometres (2 miles) south of Tubac, I pull up at Wisdom's Cafe, which has been family run since 1944 and is an institution known for its potent margaritas and fruit burros, a fruit-filled crispy tortilla rolled in cinnamon and sugar. Come dinnertime, live music by a father-and-son duo, who take requests, means that things can get happily rowdy

as tables erupt in sing-alongs of 'Despacito' and 'La Bamba'. Belly full, I settle in for the night at Tubac Golf Resort and Spa, an 8-minute drive (or 20-minute ride) away, and catch my first glimpse of the area's pig-like javalinas roaming the grounds en route to my room.

DAY 3

DRIVE FROM TUBAC TO CACTUS FOREST LOOP IN SAGUARO NATIONAL PARK (1HR); RIDE CACTUS FOREST LOOP (30.5KM/19 MILES) & MT LEMMON (32KM/ 20 MILES); DRIVE MT LEMMON TO MARANA (1.5HR)

My final two days bring me to quintessential cactus country in Saguaro National Park, so named for its columnar cacti that can grow up to 12 metres (39 feet) tall, and it may be America's most cycling-friendly national park. It's a one-hour drive from Tubac to start the Cactus Forest Loop on Saguaro National Park's eastern side. The 30.5-kilometre (19-mile) Loop is a rollercoaster ride so enjoyable that I end up riding it twice, taking care not to lean too hard into the cacti-lined corners. The road is one-way only for cars, which allows me to focus on the sharp, winding descents rather than oncoming traffic.

Some cyclists use this scenic loop as a warm-up before grinding up the Sky Island Scenic Byway to the top of Mt Lemmon. Located at Tucson's north-east corner, the twisting 32-kilometre (20-mile) road is a bucket-list climb for hardcore cyclists. Rising almost 1700 metres (5580 feet) at a steady 4 to 6 per cent grade, it's one of the top-10 sustained distance climbs in the country – you might want to drop the panniers in Tucson to ride this. The reward for conquering Lemmon is a killer view of Tucson and a thrilling 30-minute descent.

While it may be hot and dry at the base, the arid, Saguaro-studded desert eventually transitions as you climb to a landscape and climate more typical of the Pacific Northwest – cool and crisp, and blanketed in ponderosa pines. In winter, it's not unusual to experience snow at the top, so layers of clothing are a must. After seeing quite a few frozen-looking cyclists fly by me on their way down, I opt for just a taste of Lemmon. It's way more steep than I anticipated, and I quickly realise I'd need the better part of a day to summit. My legs burned just from the 8-kilometre (4.9-mile) slog to the Molino Canyon Vista. On the lightning-fast descent, I promise myself I'll come back another year to attempt the top with fresh legs. For now, I recharge my quads with a deep-tissue massage at my luxe home for the evening – the

Ritz-Carlton Dove Mountain resort in the small town of Marana, a 1.5-hour drive from Mt Lemmon.

DAY 4

DOVE MOUNTAIN TO SAGUARO NATIONAL PARK'S TUCSON MOUNTAIN DISTRICT (98KM/61 MILES)

For my final day of riding, I map out a route that doubles as the ultimate sightseeing tour of Tucson. From the foothills of the Santa Catalina Mountains, I veer south-west into the Oro Valley, along the blissfully car-free Cañada del Oro River Park Trail, part of Tucson's Loop network. The bike path is so smooth and well maintained it makes me start thinking I should move to Tucson.

A stretch of 55 kilometres (34 miles) takes me right into the city's vibrant Mercado District, where I refuel with a latte at local cyclist hangout, Presta Coffee Roasters, located within Mercado San Agustín, then continue up and over the iconic Gates Pass. This spectacular, 330-metre (1080-foot) climb over the rainbow-hued Tucson Mountains in Saguaro National Park West leads to the Arizona–Sonora Desert Museum, the state's second-most-visited attraction, behind only a rather impressive ditch known as the Grand Canyon. Part natural history museum, part desert botanical garden and part zoo, this indoor-outdoor attraction is a great place to stretch your legs and observe desert creatures such as coyotes, raptors and furry javalinas.

It's getting late by the time I leave the museum, but I'm feeling ambitious and strong after a few days on the bike, and decide to add on the West Loop Route, another cruisy 43 kilometres (27 miles) around the park, with about 585 metres (1920 feet) of climb. I've learned by now to dodge the fallen chollas, a super-spiny species of cacti that locals call 'jumping cholla' for their strange ability to seemingly attack passing hikers and cyclists. But I haven't been able to evade those pesky goathead thorns, and the task of fixing another flat tyre is a blessing in disguise as it delays my final few kilometres, so that I end up riding towards a magical desert sunset. As the deep-orange sun sinks into the blush-coloured horizon, the mountains take on a celestial glow, and I realise that I've found my version of cycling heaven.

Riding Resources

The books *Cycling Arizona: The Statewide Road Biking Guide* by Christine Maxa and *Biking the Arizona Trail: The Complete Guide to Day-Riding and Thru-Biking* by Andrea Lankford are excellent resources, as is The Arizona Bicycle Association website (bikeaz.org).
Bicycle Ranch (bicycleranch.com) and Transit Cycles (transitcycles.com) are Tucson's go-to bike shops.

Opposite top Expect to see the pig-like javalina *Bottom* Shadowed on Mt Lemmon *Below* Sunset in the foothills of the Santa Catalina Mountains

SOUTH AMERICA

Huascarán Circuit

PERU

Explore the best of the Andes with a challenging circuit through Peru's Cordillera Blanca, a singular place of soaring icy peaks, steep granite walls and tumbling glaciers.

PATRIMONIO MUNDIAL
WORLD HERITAGE • PATRIMOINE MONDIAL
PARQUE
NACIONAL
HUASCARAN

SALOMON
ALCALDE

Huascarán Circuit

CONTRIBUTION BY MARK WATSON

WHY IT'S SPECIAL

The Huascarán Circuit is a crossing of two of the highest passes along Peru's Cordillera Blanca mountain range. The cordillera contains Peru's highest mountain, 6768-metre (22,205-foot) Huascarán, and this ride circumnavigates its extensively glaciated massif, passing many of Peru's other most beautiful mountains.

Few places in the world allow you to cycle in such close proximity to Himalayan-scale mountains, while enjoying the unique and ever-present Indigenous culture of the people who call the biggest tropical mountain range on earth home. Its beauty lies not just in the singular alpine scenery but also in the unique Andean culture of the Quechua people that can be witnessed along the way. These hardy people - descendants of the Inca - farm traditionally in an alpine environment, in much the same way they've done for hundreds of years.

BEST TIME TO RIDE

The route is best ridden from June to August, when the dry season in this region is at its peak. Expect stable weather with clear skies and light wind, but these are the winter months, so night-time temperatures can be as cold as -10°C (14°F) on the highest passes. Days will be warm up high but hot in the valleys.

The shoulder months of May and September are also a reasonable time to go, but the weather will be less settled and afternoon thunderstorms more likely.

RIDE IT

This ride is *the* classic multiday route of the Peruvian Andes, encompassing a challenging double crossing of the main divide of the biggest ice-covered tropical mountain range in the world.

Due to the high altitude reached on this ride and the sheer amount of climbing, it's no trivial undertaking. To avoid acute mountain sickness (AMS) it's crucial to be at least partly acclimatised before you begin the ride. If you have come from sea level, spend two to three days in Carhuaz or Huaraz before your ride and make at least one walk or ride to higher elevation. If you are not already acclimatised, consider sleeping lower than the described route on the first night. It's worth also travelling light, with a minimalist bikepacking set-up, but with sleeping bags and clothing warm enough for camping in sub-zero conditions.

Nuts & bolts
Distance: 230 kilometres (143 miles)
Days: 5
Ascent: 6000 metres (19,700 feet)
Difficulty: Medium-hard
Bike: The ride can be done on any good-quality touring bike but a bikepacking rig with disc brakes and generous climbing gears is best suited to the rigours and long climbs and descents. We rode mountain bikes with 2.4-inch tyres.

Previous View to 6354-metre (21,000-foot) Chopicalqui, near the top of the Portachuelo de Llanganuco pass *Opposite top left* The heights of the Cordillera Blanca from the Portachuelo de Llanganuco pass *Top right* Huascarán National Park entrance *Bottom left* Wild donkeys in Huascarán National Park *Bottom right* Typical mountain village of mud brick homes in the eastern Cordillera Blanca

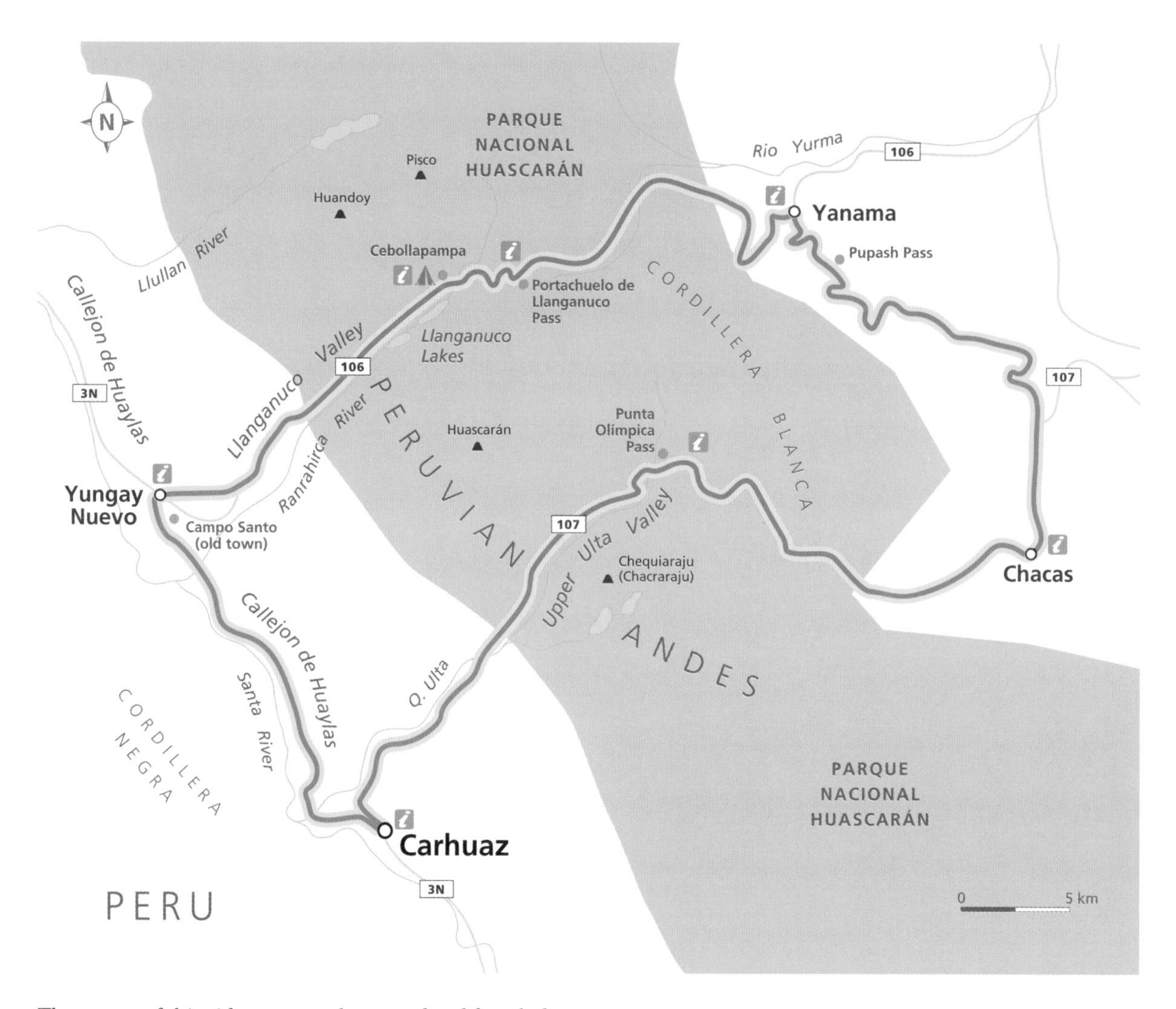

The cruxes of this ride come on the second and fourth days, when you cross the Punta Olímpica and Portachuelo de Llanganuco passes – the route's twin apogees at 4900 metres (16,075 feet) and 4767 metres (15,640 feet), respectively – which even for well-acclimatised bodies will be a challenge.

Basic supplies are available in Chacas and Yanama, so you can avoid having to carry food for the whole circuit from Carhuaz. If you have specific food requirements, including milk powder and granola bars, the best place to shop is Huaraz.

LOCAL SNAPSHOT

As you ride this circuit, it's worth contemplating the tragic fate that befell the Indigenous people of this land and the story of the colonisation of the nation now known as Peru.

Invested with the authority of the Spanish crown, Francisco Pizzaro and 168 ambitious conquistadors arrived in the northern Peruvian city of Cajamarca in 1532 to find an empire in disarray. Well ahead of their arrival, First World disease, introduced by earlier, smaller expeditions, had already begun to decimate the local population. While his subjects may have considered him a god-king, bestowed with absolute power, the previous Inca emperor Huayna Capac was not immune to the ravages of smallpox. He died, along with his immediate heir, four years before Pizzaro's arrival.

A struggle for succession took place between two of Huayna Capac's sons, Atahualpa and Huáscar, leading to civil war that destroyed the unity of the empire. Atahualpa had the backing of the military and ultimately had Huáscar assassinated. Huascarán is a noble namesake of Huáscar.

Atahualpa and a force of thousands faced Pizzaro's small band of well-armed conquistadors in Cajamarca's plaza in November 1532. The conquistadors used the element of surprise, horses and vastly superior weapons to overpower Atahualpa's forces and capture the emperor. A period of negotiation followed, but ultimately Atahualpa was executed by garrotte, a move that was also a sharp knife to the heart of the Inca empire.

Over the following years, the core of the Inca empire was pushed further from its traditional highland seat in Cusco and forced to the edge of the Amazon basin. The Spanish were relentless in their pursuit but the Inca held out. In 1572 the last bastion of Inca resistance – based in the jungle retreat of Espiritu Pampa – was quashed.

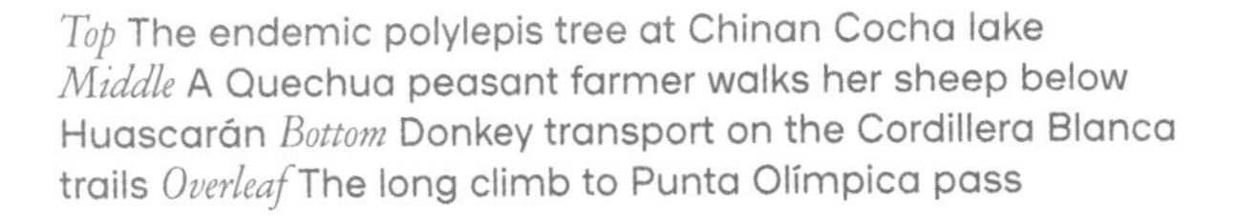

Top The endemic polylepis tree at Chinan Cocha lake *Middle* A Quechua peasant farmer walks her sheep below Huascarán *Bottom* Donkey transport on the Cordillera Blanca trails *Overleaf* The long climb to Punta Olímpica pass

ITINERARY

DAY 1

CARHUAZ TO CAMP IN UPPER ULTA VALLEY (43.5KM/27 MILES)

The starting point is the small Andean town of Carhuaz, busy with the bustle of a weekly early morning market as my partner Hana and I fill our water bottles and pinch our tyres to check the pressure. In preparation for the long climb that awaits, a few drops of lubricant go on the chain, too.

Stalls are set up with a typical sprawl of goods - from the freshest bread to cheap electronics and fertiliser, on market day you can find it all. Strong-looking ladies with bowler hats and colourful layered skirts squat next to piles of fruit, vegetables and the distinctive round white quesos (cheeses) often seen in such markets. I buy a half-round for a few sol - we'll appreciate the extra protein and salt during the long cycling climbs over the coming days.

Amid the sound of Carhuaz's car horns, the melodic calls of the market hawkers and the clatter of sheep hooves on the street, we clip into our pedals and spin up the hill away from the sunny plaza.

As we gain height on the quiet paved road out of Carhuaz, the scale of our surroundings soon becomes apparent. Carhuaz lies in the Callejon de Huaylas, a deep inter-Andean valley. Pinched dramatically between the Cordillera Blanca and its 'sister' range, the arid Cordillera Negra, the callejon (alley) is the artery through which commerce flows in this region. With a hot climate and abundant water fed from glaciers by an intricate network of aqueducts, this valley is rich with agriculture. Llamas and alpacas are a common sight on the hillsides above the road.

After a couple of hours of climbing on the quiet, well-graded road we stop for lunch at a small roadside restaurant. The building is rudimentary: just a cheaply constructed shack with a tin roof and a dirt floor. Inside is a table covered with a gaudy plastic tablecloth, atop which is the standard bowl of aji (spicy tomato chilli) that accompanies most meals in Peru. At the end of the small smoky room, two women are hovering over pots of rice, potatoes and steaming tasty pollo guisado (chicken stew). In typical style, the stew is preceded with a delicious quinoa soup that's sparingly laced with vegetables. The guisado is served with a heap of rice and some waxy textured black potatoes. Chuño, I've come to find out, are potatoes that have been harvested and then naturally freeze-dried during the sub-zero, high-altitude nights of the winter dry season. They're just one type of more than 4000 varieties of potato, an Andean food staple that was

first domesticated on the shores of Lake Titicaca more than 7000 years ago.

After lunch, we climb further until the road enters a broad U-shaped glacial valley and rises gently along the edge of the pampa, the valley's boulder-dotted grassy floor. Ahead I can see where the road kicks up out of the cirque in a series of apparently endless switchbacks, climbing towards the craggy outcrops and heavily crevassed glaciers that shape the upper valley.

We gain height more quickly now, breathing harder but finally stop to camp for the night near a small lookout in the Upper Ulta Valley. It's easy to find a spot away from the road and once the tent is up and a cup of tea brewing, we pause to take in our surroundings. On the opposite side of the valley, Huascarán, a complex mountain of snowfields, steep glaciers and golden granite cliffs, steals the show.

DAY 2

UPPER ULTA VALLEY TO CHACAS (38KM/23.5 MILES)

Spinning the pedals once again, it strikes me that I'm riding though a landscape that has barely changed in the five centuries since Atahualpa defeated his brother Huáscar in civil war to become emperor (*see* p. 41). The Inca would have known glaciers that were longer in their reach towards the valley floors but up here, high above the grazing range of llamas, the land either side of the tarmac strip knows a story much deeper than the rise and fall of an empire.

A gaggle of tourists stands on a pullout near the entrance to a modern tunnel, absorbing the stunning view of crisp white seracs, tumbling water and the raw mountainscape. We pass by, turning onto a dirt road that weaves its way precariously up the side of the peaks, towards the narrow rocky notch of the Punta Olímpica pass. The pass, nudging 5000 metres (16,400 feet), is choked with a patch of snow and we trudge over it, pushing the bikes and anticipating the fresh view we'll have on the other side.

The road's rough across this other side too, but fun, zig-zagging down towards the main road and a series of impossibly blue lakes, coloured by minerals contained in the glacier-pulverised rock. We pick up the main road and a blissfully fast and smooth descent leads us down through the cirque. Glaciers and curvaceous moraines run to near the road edge and soon we're back in the vegetation zone. The red, papery-barked polylepis with their gnarled limbs are distinctive – a native tree that is an icon of the Andean sub-alpine zone.

The long descent delivers us into welcome thicker air and warmth as we roll into the picture-perfect plaza of Chacas. On one side sits a beautiful stone church, crafted from local rock. We're in time for a late lunch and after a filling soup and plate of rice, maize and tasty asado de alpaca (grilled alpaca), we take a rest.

Like most Peruvian alpine villages, many of the buildings of the town are made from mud brick and some are even roofed with traditional thatch, rather than corrugated iron. On most porches, strings of maize – another food staple – hang drying in the harsh sunlight.

DAYS 3–4

CHACAS TO YANAMA (49.5KM/30.5 MILES); YANAMA TO CAMP AT CEBOLLAPAMPA/LLANGANUCO VALLEY (49KM/30 MILES)

The following day we climb on from Chacas, along dirt roads that cross the 4000-metre (13,120-foot) Pupash Pass into a neighbouring valley and the small town of Yanama. It's another scenic day of climbing as we pedal over 1500 vertical metres (4920 vertical feet). Yanama is a pleasant mountain village, and though it lacks the charm of Chacas, it's a good resupply stop and a chance to sleep in richer air before we climb high again.

Rarely steep, though ever-continuous, the dirt-road climb to the second major pass of the route – Portachuelo de Llanganuco – will take us over the crown of the Cordillera Blanca a second time. As we gain height, we transition from the maize fields and grazing animals of Yanama into the alpine zone. It's in the final 300 vertical metres (985 vertical feet) of the long climb that the scenery starts to get spectacular, with our view towards the sky rimmed by precipitous 6000-metre (19,700-foot) peaks – some of the highest in Peru.

It's the pass itself, as we stand in awe (and slightly out of breath), that yields arguably the finest view of the entire circuit. Looking north-west from Portachuelo de Llanganuco, the glaciated skyline of Chacraraju, Pisco and the multiple peaks of Huandoy are impressively photogenic. It has to be one of the world's great mountain views.

What goes up must come down, and we're glad of our 2.4-inch mountain bike tyres as we drop into the switchbacked Himalayan-scale descent to the Llanganuco Valley. Riding one way, the massive east face of Huascarán fills our view; going the other way, it's the granite turrets of Huandoy – it's hard to concentrate fully on the road.

After the relative isolation of the last three days, the valley is busy with tourists coming and going from the famous

Laguna 69 trek. If you have a day to spare, it's a highly recommended hike, offering proximity to glaciated peaks and spectacular views. We stop at Cebollapampa for the night, where there is informal camping and toilets. Just down the valley we can see the turquoise waters of the Llanganuco Lakes sparking in the afternoon light.

DAY 5

CEBOLLAPAMPA/LLANGANUCO VALLEY TO CARHUAZ (50KM/31 MILES)

The greener surroundings are a treat and in the morning we ride down past the lakes, which are walled in by immense cliffs. It's another postcard scene, especially with the lakes framed between the red-barked polylepis trees. The road leads us past the lake outlet and the granite walls, once filled with a kilometres-deep glacier, seem to close in. Huge boulders, arching rock slabs and a tumbling stream accompany the dusty ride down towards Yungay, back in the Callejon de Huaylas.

It's a hot afternoon in the callejon but we're back in the land of plenty and a good lunch is completed with ice-cream before we leave the large town of Yungay Nuevo and continue to the site of the old town.

On 31 May 1970, a powerful earthquake dislodged thousands of tonnes of ice from ice cliffs high on Huascarán. The earthquake was serious, destroying a widespread area of towns and infrastructure between the mountains and the coast, but the avalanche caused an even greater calamity. As the ice collapsed off the mountain's north face, it collected rocks, snow and dirt and propagated into the deadliest avalanche in history. The morass, reaching speeds up to 1000km/h (620mp/h), travelled 15 kilometres (9.3 miles) down the valley, almost completely burying the ancient town of Yungay and killing 20,000 people.

Very little remains of the old town, which is mostly locked metres-deep in debris, but visible parts of a destroyed church and a mangled bus are testament to the force and scale of the disaster. The site has never been excavated and remains as a giant cemetery and memorial park. It's a sobering last stop on this tour of the Cordillera Blanca but it also provides us a chance to reflect on the uncompromising power of nature that has created this dramatic region. We finish the day with a quick 22-kilometre (13.5-mile) paved-road ride to Carhuaz, looking forward to a shower and a celebratory meal after this most memorable of rides.

Riding resources

Julio Olaza, owner of Chakinani Peru (chakinaniperu.com/peru), is a mine of information on cycling in the Cordillera Blanca. He runs supported cycle trips throughout the region, as well as bespoke tours and can provide logistics.

Opposite Savouring the day's last rays as the sun sinks behind Huascarán *Above* The Llanganuco Lakes

EUROPE

Coast to Coast

ENGLAND

Cross the United Kingdom from sea to sea on the country's most popular cycling route.

Coast to Coast

WHY IT'S SPECIAL

Stretching across northern England, from the Irish Sea to the North Sea, the Coast to Coast is the most famous and popular multi-day cycling route in the United Kingdom. And with good reason. It offers the chance to cross an entire country among a fraternity of like-minded cyclists, while taking in a couple of England's most spectacular regions: the Lake District and the Pennines.

Though northern England is renowned as industrial, this is mostly a ride through rural and natural scenes - farms, fells and moors. The ride crosses the poetic Lake District and the high, haunting moors of the Pennines, a mountain range that forms the spine of northern England. It's long enough to be a challenge but not an ordeal, and hilly enough to test legs but not destroy them.

BEST TIME TO RIDE

June to September brings the warmest and best conditions in northern England. In August and September you might get the added bonus of purple-flowering heather across the moors of the Pennines.

RIDE IT

Though officially titled the Sea to Sea ride, the route is almost universally known as the Coast to Coast (borrowing its name from the parallel walking route), and is a combination of shared-use trails at either end, and mostly quiet roads in between. It has two possible start and finish points on each coast - Whitehaven and Workington in the west, Tynemouth and Sunderland in the east. I'm riding from Whitehaven to Tynemouth.

It's a ride that is able to be all things to all cyclists. Some ride it in one massive day, while most, like me, stretch it over three to four days. As one local cyclist described it to me, 'Three days is normal, four is leisurely, five is a pub crawl'. I'm riding it in four days - I'm planning leisurely, with a bit of a pub crawl thrown in.

Nuts & bolts

Distance: 219 kilometres (136 miles)
Days: 4
Ascent: 3200 metres (10,500 feet)
Difficulty: Easy-medium
Bike: The Coast to Coast is well suited to a hybrid or tourer, with most of the ride along sealed roads or hard-packed trails. There's one short mountain bike option into Keswick, but there's an alternative road section.

Previous A green entry to the Lake District in Ennerdale *Opposite top left* The rugged Lake District *Top right* The former Grove Rake lead mine *Bottom left* Moor magic in the Pennines *Bottom right* The Coast to Coast's start in Whitehaven

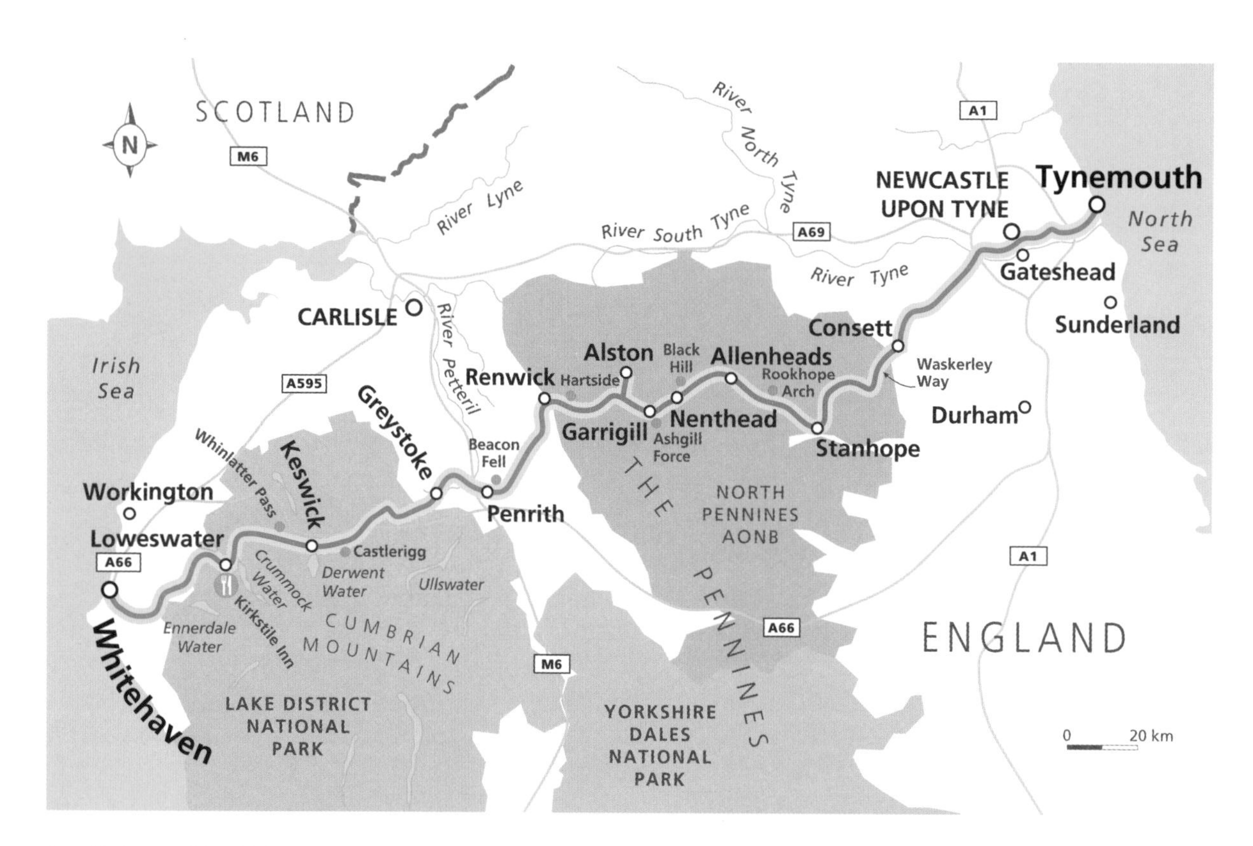

LOCAL SNAPSHOT

Across the top of the Pennines, you'll reach tiny Nenthead, one of the UK's first purpose-designed villages, constructed in the 18th century by the London Lead Mining Company. Though it was inhabited by miners – the town once extracted around 60 per cent of the country's zinc – it was known for a time as the 'town without sin' for the piety of its residents. With its citizens preferring Bibles to beer, the town even had a reading room for the miners, which is now the village store.

Opposite The still surface of Loweswater *Right* The popular tourist town of Keswick

DAY 1

WHITEHAVEN TO KESWICK (48KM/30 MILES)

At the end of a slipway in the seaside town of Whitehaven, a ritual is under way. A young couple stands at the water's edge, dipping the back wheels of their pannier-laden bikes into the sea. As they pedal away across the foreshore pathway, I do the same, wetting the back tyre of my own bike beside a tall metal sculpture etched with the figures 'C2C'. Tradition dictates that Coast to Coast cyclists dip the rear wheel of their bike into the Irish Sea before setting out, and then do the same with their front wheel in the North Sea at the ride's end. Having done my ceremonial christening, I begin riding across the island.

The Coast to Coast is a sea-to-sea route, but its early journey is through lakes. Though it takes a while to leave Whitehaven, winding through its long tail of suburbs, it's less than an hour to the edge of the Lake District, where the westernmost of its lakes, Ennerdale Water, seems to leak out of a deep valley beside the route. Mountains (or fells, as they like to call them around here) stand stacked along the edges of lakes, which seem to float past like clouds at the end of various long descents before I reach Loweswater.

One of the most civilising features of any outdoor activity in the UK is the presence of an abundance of country pubs – places preserved in time, where roasts still rule lunch menus, dogs slumber beneath tables, and wood-fires warm low-ceiling rooms. Near the shores of Loweswater, where the lake this day is as flat as a window pane, I find my first pub solace in the Kirkstile Inn, almost exactly midway through the day. The inn is a classic 16th-century pub, but more importantly, it's near the start of the day's biggest climb, over Whinlatter Pass, making it the perfect lunch stop.

It's a gorgeous few kilometres of riding beyond the Kirkstile Inn, passing manor houses crouched beside oak trees, with views across Crummock Water to the moor-covered peaks that cluster around it.

As passes go, Whinlatter Pass is a gentle place – just a broad break in the hills, with crumbling rock walls that arch down the slopes like the ribs of an upturned boat. From the pass, the ride makes a circuitous entry into Keswick, the ever-popular tourist town on the shores of Derwentwater and my home for the night. As I whip pass tourist traffic jams at the edge of town, I'm feeling smug about my suddenly superior mode of transport, though the rain that will be falling by the next morning will quickly wash away most of my conceit.

DAY 2

KESWICK TO ALSTON (75KM/46.5 MILES)

Pedalling out from Keswick, I briefly divert from the main Coast to Coast route, ascending a steep road to Castlerigg, one of Britain's oldest stone circles, predating Stonehenge, and older even than the Giza Pyramids. The rain is forecast to continue all day, but in that optimistic English way an ice-cream van is already set up on the road outside the circle.

As I ride on, I feel as though I've arrived at the heart of the Lake District. Fells rise around me, dry-stone walls snake across the landscape, and oak trees bloom like giant green mushrooms.

This day will be the longest and hilliest of my four days on the Coast to Coast. A broad valley runs through the mountains between Keswick and Penrith, and while the main road pretty much clings to its base, the trail finds quiet roads that arch up and over the toes of the mountains. From the saddle of my bike, I look down like a drone onto timeless farmhouses, verdant fields covered in constellations of sheep, and the far-removed traffic of the busy A66 road.

Past Greystoke, a town that brings Tarzan swinging to mind (Tarzan was Viscount Greystoke), I see wheat rather than sheep in the fields for the first time, and it

feels like a sign that I'm leaving the Lake District. Villages come quickly now – Blencoe, Laithes, Newton Reigny – as the land briefly flattens out. From a climbing perspective, this short section is a bit like the eye in the storm, pinched between the Lake District fells and the more challenging Pennines, a mountain range often called the 'backbone of England'.

Penrith is near enough to the day's midpoint, creating an ideal lunch stop. The ride out of Penrith isn't the hilliest bit of the day; it just feels like it, as the ride climbs across the slopes of Beacon Fell, where I get my first views of the humpback hills of the Pennines ahead. The long climb into these mountains begins in Renwick, 20 kilometres (12.5 miles) past Penrith.

From Renwick, 200 metres (650 feet) above sea level, the ride ascends almost another 400 metres (1300 feet) to the top of Hartside in less than 8 kilometres (5 miles). I settle into a rhythm and a low gear and crawl my way up into these mountains.

Opposite The market town of Alston
Above Quiet road near Garrigill

Britain's Automobile Association once rated this road over Hartside as one of the world's 10 best drives, and I'm confident that it's even better on a bike, with the route ascending at a comfortable gradient into the barren moors that carpet the Pennines.

There's something inexplicably beautiful about moors. At a glance they're as bleak as a cold front, gathering colour only when the heather blooms in late summer, but they have an innate sense of natural power, as if they'll never really be conquered. Weather conditions can be harsh and changeable, so pack your wet-weather gear in easy reach.

Over the top of Hartside (reflecting the weather conditions, the original cafe built atop Hartside was named Helm Wind Cafe, after the gusts that often rake the area), the road unfurls so gently through Alston Moor that even without pedalling, my bike settles into a natural pace of about 35km/h (22mp/h) – nothing too fast, nothing too slow. Down in the hollows around Leadgate and Alston, the moors merge seamlessly with rural lands straight from a postcard: stone manors, green fields, billowing oak trees and dry-stone walls as neat and intricate as Jenga puzzles.

Alston claims itself as England's highest market town, and has plentiful sleeping and eating options. For Coast to Coast cyclists the town is also noteworthy as the first point at which the ride intersects with the Tyne River. In the truest way, the journey to Tynemouth, where the Tyne River enters the North Sea, begins here.

DAY 3

ALSTON TO STANHOPE (36KM/22 MILES)

Alston may well be England's highest market town, but it's not the highest point on the Coast to Coast. As I ride out the next morning, I'm beginning a day of highs. This day I will pass through Nenthead and Allenheads, two towns that tussle (among a few others) for the title of England's highest settlement. I will also cross Black Hill, which, at 609 metres (1998 feet) above sea level, is the highest point on Britain's vast National Cycle Network.

As that all suggests, it's a hilly day ahead. Though it doesn't have a single sustained ascent like Hartside, it's a tougher day in the saddle, filled with a queue of climbs and descents, but it's also a day that will shatter one of my own preconceived notions about the Coast to Coast. I came expecting to be wowed by the Lake District, but my favourite moments will end up being atop the Pennines.

Past Alston, the moor landscape gets only better – moreish, even, dare I say it. Each town across the top of the range is hidden deep in the folds of valleys, as though sheltering from the notorious weather that sweeps over the Pennines. Each town also heralds the start of another climb, the toughest of which is out of Garrigill, the first town beyond Alston. Here, the ride intersects with the Pennine Way, one of the toughest of the UK's long-distance hikes. Since I'm advancing just 36 kilometres (22 miles) this day, I also take the chance to cycle out from Garrigill to Ashgill Force, a beautiful waterfall hidden beneath a road bridge 2 kilometres (1.25 miles) off the Coast to Coast route.

The climb out of Garrigill scales directly up a ridge, its slopes still scarred by long-gone mining activity, with salt boxes beside the road for when the winter snows come. It's a climb with sting, but it has nothing on the descent, which starts out at a 20 per cent grade and only steepens further as it nears Nenthead, where I stop for snack sustenance. As I ride my brakes down the hill, I'm just glad I'm coming from this direction and not the other.

The climb to the Coast to Coast's highest point atop Black Hill reaches a 'mere' 17 per cent grade, though it's only this steep at the beginning. For most of the ascent, curling up the slopes behind Nenthead, it's nowhere near this steep. Red grouse scatter from among the heather as I pass, and from atop Black Hill, as I cross into Northumberland, the view ahead is vast, looking over the hilltops to come and out across the plains to the east. It's tempting to think I can even see Newcastle upon Tyne and Tynemouth from here, but that's just a cycling fantasy.

No sooner have I entered Northumberland than I seem to leave it. At the top of the climb out of Allenheads I enter County Durham, and a long and glorious descent begins through a virtual museum of mining history. Beside the road stand the forlorn relics of the Grove Rake lead mine, followed by one of the most curious sights of the entire ride – Rookhope Arch, a seemingly misplaced bridge arch (though actually the arch of a horizontal mining chimney) standing beside Rookhope Burn. One final climb to end a day of climbs separates the town of Rookhope from Stanhope, where a short, steep day ends in a riverside B&B.

DAY 4

STANHOPE TO TYNEMOUTH (60KM/37 MILES)

In Stanhope, my final day also begins with the Coast to Coast's final climb. It's not a long ascent – about 4 kilometres (2.5 miles) – but it feels like the steepest hill of the ride, though that could just be my four-day-old legs and the weight of a full English breakfast talking. By the top of the climb, my thoughts are already turning to the second coast in the ride's name, even if it is still almost 60 kilometres (37 miles) away, albeit across the Coast to Coast's easiest and flattest section of riding.

Just as on the other side of the country, a long section of the route here follows the course of an old railway - the Waskerley Way, which is like a ramp that slowly lowers cyclists down from the Pennines. It's a gloriously removed section, with lakes either side and wind turbines chopping at the sky down the valleys. Before I know it, the moors have become fields, and the heather has turned to grasses.

The arrival into Consett (where the ride forks into its two finishes) is stark and abrupt. After 180 kilometres (112 miles) of farms, fells and moors, I'm suddenly pitched among shopping warehouses and emerging housing estates, though soon enough the ride ducks back into a corridor of woodland along another abandoned railway line.

The end is truly nigh when I pedal across the Tyne River at Gateshead and enter the long sprawl of the city of Newcastle upon Tyne. The riverbank path cuts beneath Newcastle's multitude of bridges - seven bridges in just 1.6 kilometres (1 mile) - and continues out of the city towards the river mouth.

It's a curious finish beyond Newcastle, riding through heavily industrial areas, virtually across the top of a set of tollgates on the A19, and past the North Sea ferries port, but among it are Roman baths and the remains of Segedunum Roman Fort, which once guarded the eastern end of Hadrian's Wall, a barrier built by the Romans to shield England from dreaded northerners.

I roll east along the bank of the Tyne River until the North Sea yawns open before me. Soon I'm looking across a beach to the ruined castle and priory that sit crumbled across Tynemouth's easternmost point, with a few hopeful holidaymakers lying on the sand, soaking in the weak autumn sun. I have just one thing left to do - dip the front wheel of my bike into the North Sea - and my Coast to Coast ride is complete.

Riding resources

Sustrans publishes an excellent Sea to Sea Cycle Route map, as well as the *C2C Guide* book. They can be purchased online (shop.sustrans.org.uk).

Coast to Coast sign at the start of the Waskerley Way

PEDALLER

Josie Dew

Josie Dew's life has revolved around cycling. She has cycled more than 850,000 kilometres (528,000 miles) across six continents and 50 countries (some of them by accident). The survivor of several wonky knees and worn-out bottom brackets, she is still firmly fixed in the saddle. She has written seven books about her travels and is in the middle of an eighth. She is a patron of Sustrans and Vice-President of Cycling UK. Josie lives near Portsmouth and is married to Gary (a carpenter) and has three young children (two girls and a boy). Along with the cycle touring and cycling to school and back every day, Josie has pedalled more than 37,000 kilometres (23,000 miles) with her children. For more on bikes and books and bits see: josiedew.com and facebook.com/itsjosiedew.

Where and when was your first cycle tour?

My first cycle tour in the UK was around the Isle of Wight when I was 10. My first cycle tour outside of the UK was to Africa and back after I left school at 16.

What was the biggest lesson your learned on that first trip?

That life on a bike is better than any lesson learnt at school!

What hooked you on cycle touring after that first trip?

The simplicity of cycling and being on the move with that exciting feeling of uncertainty and unpredictability.

What's the main pleasure in a cycle tour for you?

The freedom of going where you want, when you want, under your own steam and at the perfect pace: not too slow that it takes forever to get around the world, but fast enough to move across the map and notice every Tom, Dick and Harry and interesting undulation and sight along the way.

What have been your favourite cycling destinations?

Japan, Iceland, France, Norway, Hawaii, USA, Netherlands, Scotland and the west and north coasts of Ireland.

Where's the one place you'd really like to cycle?

Alaska to Patagonia ... which of course is lots of places. So, if I had to choose one: Patagonia.

Where have you cycled with your children?

I have three children, aged 13, nine and six, and we've cycled in England, France, Belgium, the Netherlands, Germany and Denmark.

Which destinations struck you as particularly good for cycling with children?

The Netherlands for the most elaborate network of cycle paths and cycle facilities in the world. You scarcely have to encounter a motorised vehicle.

What are the extra challenges in cycling with children?

Complaints, tiredness, 'how much further?' moanings, constant hunger, worry about the speed and inconsiderate attitude of some drivers, the amount of extra clobber required, slowness of getting anywhere, and the extra washing (always a challenge when you have to do your washing by hand under a tap – and then try and dry it all in the rain)!

And what are the extra pleasures?

The fun and laughs, the jolly companionship, the multiple silly moments, seeing things through their eyes, and the positive reaction of so many people and strangers when they see us travelling together. Also seeing my children looking healthy, happy and rosy-cheeked while living outside through all weather, and learning and seeing new things in the real world as opposed to the swiping-screen virtual one.

Any tips you'd give to parents cycling with children?

Don't worry about them getting bored. Just pack them on a bike and go. It's the best thing ever. You won't regret it.

Opposite A family affair for Josie Dew
Above Josie Dew in Monument Valley

EUROPE

Lon Las Cymru

WALES

Traverse Wales from south to north on a varied and spectacular route.

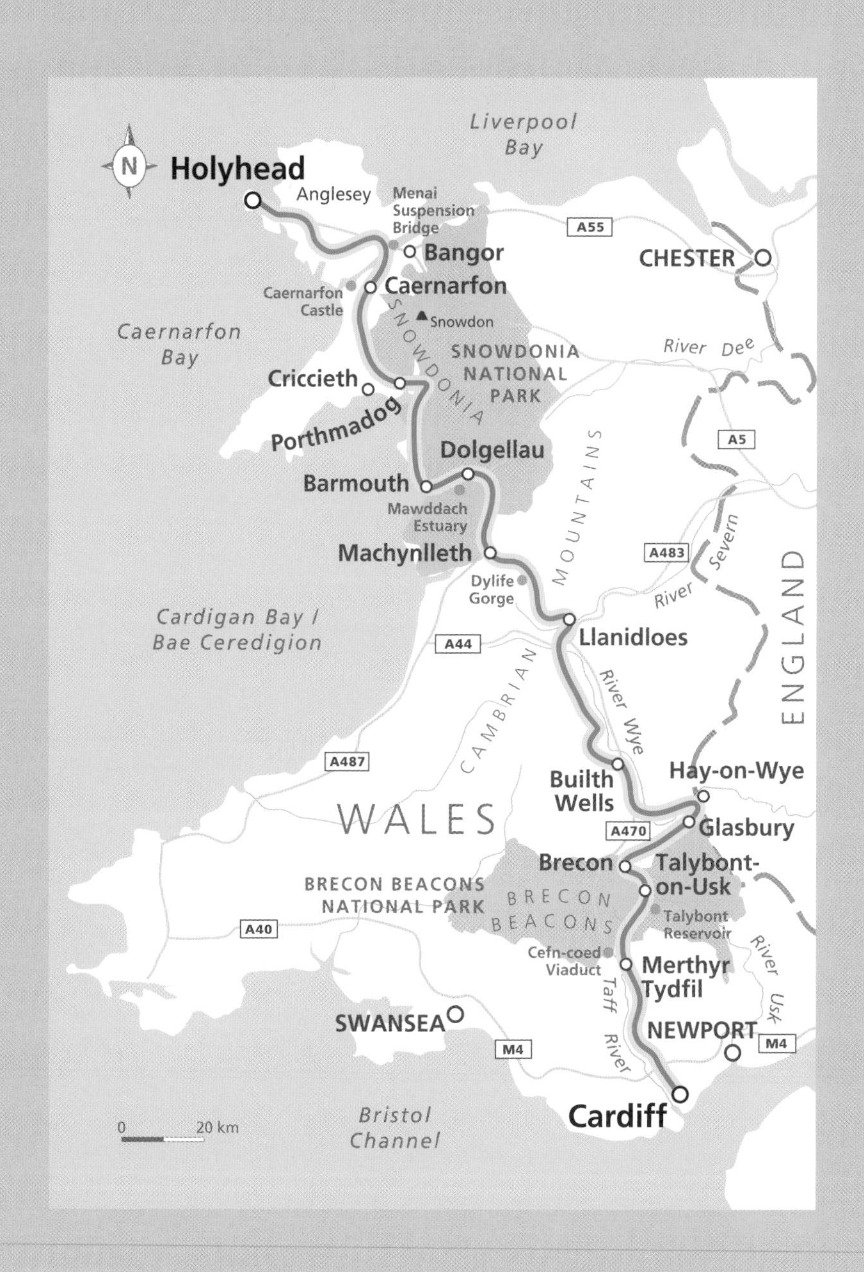
Liverpool Bay
N
Holyhead
Anglesey
Menai Suspension Bridge
A55
Bangor
CHESTER
Caernarfon Castle
Caernarfon
Snowdon
SNOWDONIA
Caernarfon Bay
SNOWDONIA NATIONAL PARK
River Dee
Criccieth
Porthmadog
A5
Dolgellau
Barmouth
Mawddach Estuary
Machynlleth
A483
Dylife Gorge
MOUNTAINS
River Severn
ENGLAND
Cardigan Bay / Bae Ceredigion
Llanidloes
A44
CAMBRIAN
River Wye
A487
Builth Wells
Hay-on-Wye
WALES
A470
Glasbury
Brecon
Talybont-on-Usk
BRECON BEACONS NATIONAL PARK
BRECON BEACONS
Talybont Reservoir
A40
Cefn-coed Viaduct
Merthyr Tydfil
River Usk
Taff River
SWANSEA
NEWPORT
M4
M4
Bristol Channel
Cardiff
0
20 km

Lon Las Cymru

WHY IT'S SPECIAL

This ride traverses an entire country and its surprising anonymity means the way is never crowded and the well-marked route brings a wonderful mix of mountains, coast and history.

Beginning in Cardiff and finishing by Wales's north-west tip in Holyhead, Lon Las Cymru travels the length of Wales on its 410-kilometre (255-mile) journey. Along the way, it crosses the country's mountainous spine, touches the English border on the Wye River and passes through two of Wales's three national parks. Almost one-third of the ride is on traffic-free paths and it somehow manages to cross a country of three million people while barely touching a busy road.

It's a ride that's beautiful at almost every moment – it's the Coast to Coast (*see* p. 47) with more mountains, more coast and bilingual (English and Welsh) road signs. If I could cycle just one of these two British routes, it would be Lon Las Cymru, even if it has almost 5000 metres (16,400 feet) of sometimes steep ascent. They're climbs you can forgive when they lead to such gloriously scenic moments.

BEST TIME TO RIDE

May to September is when you'll get the longest daylight hours and the best of the weather conditions, especially across the changeable Cambrian Mountains.

RIDE IT

Though Lon Las Cymru can be cycled in either direction, I'm starting in Cardiff and riding north with a Londoner friend, Alice. A couple of factors favour this direction of travel: the prevailing winds should be at our backs and the climb over the Cambrian Mountains is more gradual than the straight-up, 500-vertical-metre (1640-vertical-foot) haul out of Machynlleth from the north.

Riding from the south, the towns and villages also seem to materialise in an ascending scale of beauty, culminating in places such as Llanidloes and Dolgellau that are like shortbread tins brought to life. We will spend six days cycling Lon Las Cymru but if time is more pressing, the most spectacular stretch is the 290 kilometres (180 miles) from Cardiff to Porthmadog, abbreviating the ride to four or five days.

The genius of Lon Las Cymru is that even when following quiet roads, it will branch away if even quieter or more beautiful ones exist.

Nuts & bolts

Distance: 410 kilometres (255 miles)
Days: 6
Ascent: 4700 metres (15,400 feet)
Difficulty: Medium-hard
Bike: A mountain bike, hybrid or tourer is suitable. There's some unsealed riding, but it's fairly smooth and hard-packed, so fine on a hybrid or tourer, though the gearing on a mountain bike would be handy on some of the steeper climbs.

Previous Arriving at the sea in Barmouth

LOCAL SNAPSHOT

Hay-on-Wye is known as the 'Town of Books', but if you'd visited the border town in 1960 you wouldn't have found a single bookshop. It was in 1961 that Richard Booth established his first bookshop in the town, creating a snowball effect that would, at its peak, see more than 50 secondhand bookshops lining its streets. In 1977 Booth also proclaimed the town an independent kingdom and named himself as its king. Booth died in 2019 but today Hay-on-Wye is home to around 20 bookshops and hosts the annual Hay Festival, a celebration of literature held over 10 days around the end of May.

Cycling beside the Monmouthshire and Brecon Canal

DAY 1

CARDIFF TO TALYBONT-ON-USK (78KM/48.5 MILES)

Lon Las Cymru begins beside Cardiff's striking Millennium Centre, cruising along the capital city's shores before turning inland along the banks of the Taff River, which cuts a green corridor through Cardiff. Within minutes it's as though there's no city at all, as the trail disappears into woods so thick it feels almost as though the air itself is green.

The Taff River will be our general guiding line through to Merthyr Tydfil, 45 kilometres (28 miles) from Cardiff, where we pause for lunch, since it's here that the ride's first significant climb begins. Across the Cefn-coed Viaduct, an 1866 railway bridge beside the modern bridge of a highway, the ascent begins, rising for 15 kilometres (9.3 miles) past the Pontsticill Reservoir.

The cheat's guide to the climb comes in the shape of the Brecon Mountain Railway, a tourist train that can carry bikes. It departs from beside the route just outside of Merthyr Tydfil, and finishes close to the top of the climb at Torpantau. Hop aboard and it cuts out 8 kilometres (5 miles) of riding and close to 200 metres (650 feet) of ascent.

We pedal on though, entering Brecon Beacons National Park just above the railway's lower station and crossing the dam wall of Pontsticill Reservoir, where the treeless Brecon Beacons – one of my favourite mountain ranges in Britain – peep into view for the first time.

From the pass at Torpantau, a sealed road winds down into a valley to the east, but always searching out minor pathways, Lon Las Cymru turns onto a dirt track that swoops down to the shores of Talybont Reservoir. Here it rejoins the road, curling between hedges that tower overhead – for a few minutes it feels as though we're tunnelling through Wales. It's the most beautiful and most bucolic few minutes of the day as we descend into canal-side Talybont-on-Usk.

DAY 2

TALYBONT-ON-USK TO BUILTH WELLS (62KM/38.5 MILES)

Talybont is about 1 kilometre (0.6 miles) off the marked route, and the next morning we don't immediately return to Lon Las Cymru. Running through Talybont is the Monmouthshire and Brecon Canal, and we turn instead onto a shared-use path running along the edge of the canal. Canal boats come cruising through the early morning ahead of us, and lovely stone bridges arch over the waters. Past a viaduct across the Usk River – a watercourse above a watercourse – the canal path links up with Lon Las Cymru and together they travel the 3 kilometres (1.9 miles) into the town of Brecon. It's been a perfectly gentle warm-up to the day – entirely flat to Brecon and an early coffee stop.

In Brecon, the journey turns north-east, seemingly away from our goal of Holyhead, crossing to Glasbury, just a few kilometres from the English border. The ride out of Brecon takes to narrow country lanes, where we ride once again between high hedges akin to leafy cliffs.

Approaching Glasbury, Lon Las Cymru reaches its easternmost point, turning back west to begin the long crossing to the coast. But from here, it's just 5 kilometres (3 miles) to the English border and Hay-on-Wye (*see* p. 62), the so-called 'Town of Books'. For a cyclist, it's also the town of dilemmas – I could happily lose myself in Hay-on-Wye's secondhand bookshops for hours, but how many books do I really want weighing down my panniers?

In Hay, we turn back west, pointing our front wheels now towards the Irish Sea. It's a quick ride into Glasbury, from where the route runs through thick woods beside the Wye River, which is rarely seen but often heard murmuring over the sound of traffic on the A470 on its opposite bank.

For the first time since leaving Cardiff, we're riding on a road wide enough to require lines down its middle to divide the traffic, but still there are few vehicles and the way is flat on this road built atop a former railway. It's only at the road's end that it cheekily throws in a couple of sharp climbs, before rolling down into Builth Wells where pubs, restaurants and accommodation options are plentiful.

DAY 3

BUILTH WELLS TO MACHYNLLETH (82KM/51 MILES)

Though the ride ostensibly continues along the Wye River all the way to Llangurig, 75 kilometres (47 miles) from Hay, it's beyond Builth Wells that I begin to sense that we're cutting across the grain of this hilly country. From Newbridge-on-Wye, just outside of Builth Wells, Lon Las Cymru rises high up the slopes of the hills, only to return again to the banks of the Wye. Then it climbs once more, only steeper this time, and then back to the Wye again. It's cruelty in the shape of a bicycle. A beautiful section of this ride across the slopes follows an old coach road that can be stony and rutted and provides the roughest surface of the entire trip. If you're not on a mountain bike, there may even be short stretches on which you prefer to push your bike. Each time we return to

the valley, the river has dwindled, until soon it's little more than a stream, even though rain is now falling to top it up.

The wildest and most challenging piece of Lon Las Cymru begins at Llanidloes, with 1200 metres (4000 feet) of climb and two passes separating us from Dolgellau, 60 kilometres (37 miles) to the west. Our plan is to break the climbs into two by staying a night in Machynlleth.

Out of Llanidloes, the ride heads for its highest point in a long and varied climb through stands of pines covered in moss as thick as crash pads and up onto the alpine-like tops of the Cambrian Mountains.

Beside the edge of Dylife Gorge, a deep V-shaped gash in the land carved out by a long-gone glacier, the final climb begins in earnest, rising past a 17th-century drover's inn and towards the bald tops of the range. For the first time, it feels as though we're cycling in the high mountains, though we're barely 500 metres (1640 feet) above sea level.

From the summit of the range, it's a rapid descent into Machynlleth. As we hurtle towards town, rain spits in our faces, and there's a bug or two now swimming in my eyes. The strange thing about cycling, however, is that descents are so prized, you'll put up with anything not to spoil them. There's no way I'm stopping. I will get the bugs out later, down on the flats.

Machynlleth is a little town that thinks big. It claims itself as Wales's ancient capital, and it has its own MoMA art gallery, New York-style. History seems to seep from its pores, right down to the characterful pubs that rescue us from the rain that's pelting down as we arrive into town.

Oppposite Caernarfon Castle *Top* The rainbow connection near Llanidloes *Bottom* Pedalling through the former Welsh capital of Machynlleth

DAY 4

MACHYNLLETH TO BARMOUTH (37KM/23 MILES)

Today's section to Dolgellau, 22 kilometres (13.5 miles) from Machynlleth, is without any food stops, so we grab a full breakfast and top up our panniers with snacks. Out of town, it's another day through a maze of valleys that awaits us, riding through the folds that crease the hilly heart of Wales. The steepest climbs of the entire ride are here, beyond Aberllefenni and a slate mine that sits like a wound in the hills above the village. The ascent through these hills is a series of short, sharp climbs, rising steeply through farmland, then pine forest and then onto the open tops of the mountains as the ride enters Snowdonia National Park. It's a beautiful climb if you can find the ability to look up from your front wheel, while the descent clings to the edge of the slopes before heading out onto farm lanes to again shun main roads as it nears Dolgellau.

Dolgellau is a town seemingly made of more stone even than the mountains. It's also the point at which Lon Las Cymru's toughest section suddenly becomes its easiest section. Here, the ride joins the shared-use Mawddach Trail for 15 ruler-flat kilometres (9.3 miles) along the shores of the Mawddach Estuary to reach the coast, entering the seaside holiday town of Barmouth across a 700-metre (2300-foot) wooden viaduct that's shared between a railway, walkers and cyclists.

On the Barmouth beach at low tide, boats sit high and dry, their keels wedged into the sand. A fierce wind blows sand over the foreshore path and over us, but arriving here will ultimately feel somehow even more significant than arriving in Holyhead – we've just crossed an entire country and its mountains to reach the coast.

DAY 5

BARMOUTH TO CAERNARFON (90KM/56 MILES)

Though it's now ostensibly a coastal ride most of the way to Holyhead, it's not all about coast. After passing a chain of seaside caravan parks north of Barmouth, the ride turns off the coastline and climbs into farmland set to a backdrop of the mountains of Snowdonia.

High up the slopes, the route splits into low and high options. We take the high road, which is no more difficult than the low road anyway, and enter what I think might be the most beautiful section of the whole trail. Through green farmland partitioned by the neatest dry-stone walls I've ever seen, the ride suddenly dips into ancient woods so damp

even the road is carpeted in moss. It's like riding over velvet. A stream pours through the woodland, looking like it's cut straight from the pages of a calendar.

The routes come together again 200 vertical metres (650 vertical feet) above the coast, and together continue north on another beautifully lonely road across the hilltops. Sheep scatter from the road as we ride, while ear-piercing air-force jets and silent gliders provide a contrasting yin and yang in the sky.

A few kilometres, and a bit more climbing, beyond Porthmadog the main trail does a long detouring loop through coastal Criccieth, but a signposted shortcut continues directly ahead, across the Llyn Peninsula. We've spent so much time savouring the hills between Barmouth and Porthmadog that the day is already long and we take the shortcut (trimming around 12 km or 7.5 miles), riding north into Caernarfon, where the waterfront World Heritage-listed castle (open daily for visitors) looks almost bigger than the town itself. Even beyond the imposing visuals, this is no ordinary castle. In 1284, Edward of Caernarfon, the very first English Prince of Wales (and later to become King Edward II), was born here, and the castle is now the investiture site for the Prince of Wales - Prince Charles was invested here in 1969.

If you prefer, there's an even easier way to skip across the peninsula, thanks to another railway, with the West Highland Railway connecting Porthmadog to Caernarfon, cutting out around 45 kilometres (28 miles) of riding.

The tourist drawing power of Caernarfon's castle means that accommodation is abundant in town and easy to find.

DAY 6

CAERNARFON TO HOLYHEAD (61KM/37 MILES)

From Caernarfon, the ride continues north, turning onto Anglesey island - Lon Las Cymru's final stretch - across the Menai Suspension Bridge, built in 1826, and climbing (one of the rare climbs on Anglesey) to Llanfairpwllgwyngyll. If that town's name looks a bit like Scrabble letters tipped straight from the box, consider the fact that it's an abbreviation of the official name, Llanfairpwllgwyngyllgogerychwyrndrobwllllantysiliogogogoch - 58 letters that translate as 'St Mary's Church in the hollow of white hazel near a rapid whirlpool and the Church of St Tysilio with a red cave'. It's worth ducking into the train station where the town name is written in full across station signs.

The early riding across gently undulating, windswept Anglesey is through towns and villages before heading back out into farmland that feels more prosaic, but only in comparison to the gorgeous five days behind us. Roads are more heavily trafficked (which translates as a vehicle every now and then) and the ride changes direction often enough across the island so that you're likely to get a mix of headwinds and tailwinds, which blow violently this day.

As the ride nears the western end of Anglesey, it loops through a marshy area of lakes pooled beside the airstrip for the RAF Valley base, where Prince William served for four years between 2010 and 2013.

Finally, six days after leaving Cardiff, we pedal across the long causeway to Holy Island and into the town of Holyhead, best known as the port for ferries to Ireland. As we roll towards its harbour, the wind almost pins us to the spot, making it an effort even to ride downhill. It's as though nature also doesn't want this glorious Welsh ride to end.

Riding resources

Cicerone publishes a dedicated *Cycling Lon Las Cymru* guidebook, with detailed route descriptions.
For an excellent resource, find downloadable GPS mapping of the ride online (cycle.travel/route/lon_las_cymru).
Sustrans publishes two maps - a southern and northern map - of the ride. Purchase online (shop.sustrans.org.uk).

Bodowyr burial chamber on Anglesey island

EUROPE

Provence

FRANCE

Cycle through the foothills and valleys of France's most romanticised region.

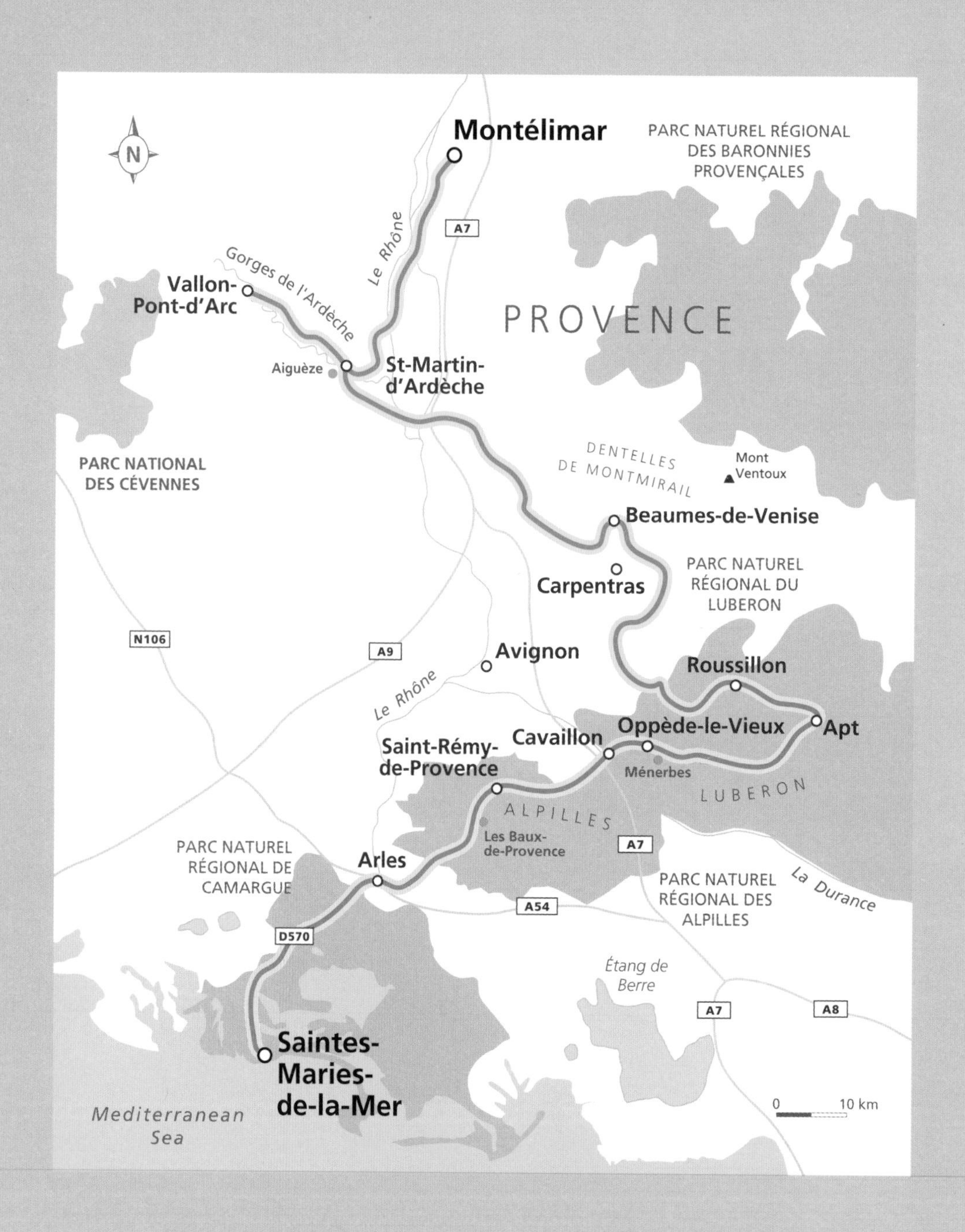
Montélimar
PARC NATUREL RÉGIONAL DES BARONNIES PROVENÇALES
A7
Le Rhône
Gorges de l'Ardèche
Vallon-Pont-d'Arc
PROVENCE
Aiguèze
St-Martin-d'Ardèche
DENTELLES DE MONTMIRAIL
Mont Ventoux
PARC NATIONAL DES CÉVENNES
Beaumes-de-Venise
Carpentras
PARC NATUREL RÉGIONAL DU LUBERON
N106
A9
Avignon
Roussillon
Le Rhône
Apt
Oppède-le-Vieux
Cavaillon
Saint-Rémy-de-Provence
Ménerbes
LUBERON
ALPILLES
Les Baux-de-Provence
A7
PARC NATUREL RÉGIONAL DE CAMARGUE
Arles
PARC NATUREL RÉGIONAL DES ALPILLES
La Durance
A54
D570
Étang de Berre
A7
A8
Saintes-Maries-de-la-Mer
0
10 km
Mediterranean Sea

Provence

WHY IT'S SPECIAL

No country embodies cycling more than France. It's home to the Tour de France, and famed (or infamous) Alpine climbs, such as the Alpe d'Huez, Col du Galibier and Mont Ventoux. Even the cliché of a baguette strapped to a bicycle is real – I have one lying atop my panniers every morning as I pedal across Provence with my family.

One of Europe's most romanticised regions, sun-soaked Provence contains, or sits in easy reach of, many of the famous Alpine ascents, but we're not here seeking big climbs and mountains. We're finding (mostly) the spaces between, as we pedal north from the Mediterranean Sea towards Montélimar, 150 kilometres (93 miles) south of Lyon.

The ubiquitous Provençal dream of lavender and light is founded on the likes of Van Gogh canvases and Peter Mayle's *A Year in Provence*. We will cycle into both – Van Gogh's world and Mayle's village – but the fact that we're towing two young children behind us means that any romance is lost in the underpants that flap from the trailers, drying in the breeze.

BEST TIME TO RIDE

Around April and May Provence gets the literal spring in its step, and roadsides will be coloured with poppies and lavender.

RIDE IT

This ride is dotted with some of France's most beautiful villages (*see* p. 73) and classic Provençal scenery, taking you into the orbit of the Alps and the big-tour pass climbs, but never itself climbing beyond 400 metres (1310 feet) above sea level.

Trains go as far south as Arles, so you might choose to start this ride there, looping out to Saintes-Maries-de-la-Mer, or simply cutting out the first day described here.

Nuts & bolts
Distance: 390 kilometres (242 miles)
Days: 8
Ascent: 5000 metres (16,400 feet)
Difficulty: Medium
Bike: The sealed roads of this ride are well suited to a touring bike or hybrid.

Previous The ochre town of Roussillon

DAY 1

SAINTES-MARIES-DE-LA-MER TO ARLES (38KM/23.5 MILES)

It's the first day of summer in Provence, which sounds like the start of a love story, except that it's raining as we pack our gear – a tent, sleeping bags, a smattering of clothes, a bag of toys for each of the children – into four panniers and two trailers on the shores of the Mediterranean Sea in Saintes-Maries-de-la-Mer. This unadorned town of 2700 people is known for its Roma pilgrimages each May and October, but it's also the capital of the Camargue, a strangely wild place for the busy south coast of France. The Camargue is the marshy delta of the Rhône River, one of Europe's largest rivers, and is a place wandered by wild and native Camargue horses and bulls, with flamingos providing the flair and colour.

'Delta' may well be an ancient cycling word for 'hurrah, it's flat', but there's a foe here that negates any advantage presented by the terrain. It's called the mistral. Generated on the mountains of central France, the mistral is a fierce wind that funnels south through the Rhône Valley and rages into the Mediterranean at speeds of up to 90km/h (56mp/h). In *A Year in Provence*, Peter Mayle described it as a wind that could 'blow the ears off a donkey'. Vincent Van Gogh stated more simply that it 'gets on one's nerves badly'. It's even contended that the mistral blowing over one of Van Gogh's half-finished paintings prompted one of his spirals into depression while he was incarcerated at the asylum in Saint-Rémy-de-Provence.

If the mistral blows, it's something you might expect to contend with for a while. 'Sometimes it can be like this for nine days,' a local man tells me. 'This is the worst wind in France – we say that it's chasing away the clouds for the sun, but that's just how we convince ourselves that it's not so bad.'

Helping distract us from the wind are the flamingo-filled lakes that crowd the road in this delta that's just about more water than land. To the kids these birds are strange pink creatures with ladders for legs, especially as they spear past on the wind with legs, neck and wings spread like crosses.

Opposite Ruins in the Roman city of Glanum, Saint-Rémy-de-Provence
Right Camargue horse

The main D570 road north from Saintes-Maries-de-la-Mer ends in the town of Arles on the banks of the Rhône, home to a Roman amphitheatre and our first brush with Van Gogh (though he did also once spend a week in Saintes-Maries-de-la-Mer, producing a series of paintings). Van Gogh lived in Arles for just over a year in 1888–9, painting the famous *Cafe Terrace at Night* and *Bedroom in Arles* while he was here. In May 1889 he left town, committing himself to an asylum in nearby Saint-Rémy-de-Provence. Suitably, this town is our next goal also, though the only thing to which we're committing ourselves is another day's riding into the mistral.

DAY 2

ARLES TO SAINT-RÉMY-DE-PROVENCE (30KM/18.5 MILES)

The trouble with dodging the mountains in Provence is that it pretty much limits your ride to the busy Rhône Valley, which is not the intention of this ride. So instead, we settle on foothills, weaving across Provence to stitch together much of the best of the region.

Arles and Saint-Rémy-de-Provence are separated by the low Alpilles mountain range, which are the speed bump in this day of riding. It's also the day that Provence truly becomes Provence – cypress trees stand as straight as soldiers at the roads' edges, vineyards spill down limestone slopes, fields are flecked with poppies, and Roman aqueducts cut across the roads.

The slopes of the Alpilles are covered in bare limestone, with the white rock exposed like bones. Through this jumble of boulders and slabs of rock, we ascend the D27 to Les Baux-de-Provence, a ridiculously beautiful village that crowns a spur and gives its name to bauxite, the rock that is the main source of aluminium. Unsurprisingly, Les Baux is listed as a plus beaux, one of France's official Most Beautiful Villages (*see* Local snapshot).

It's a quick descent into our destination of Saint-Rémy-de-Provence, where once again Van Gogh and the Romans vie for top billing. The asylum in which the Dutch artist was committed is open to visitors, and the ruined Roman settlement of Glanum is just a few hundred metres away from the asylum. The fact that you have to ride down the Avenue Vincent Van Gogh to get to Glanum, however, may settle any debate about who really is king here.

DAY 3

SAINT-RÉMY-DE-PROVENCE TO OPPÈDE-LE-VIEUX (33KM/20.5 MILES)

The next morning we continue riding east, as though we really are aiming for the Alps, though our end goal in this direction is a lower set of mountains. The imposing Luberon massif rises to around 1250 metres (4100 feet) above sea level and is a quintessential piece of Provence. For cyclists, the massif is ringed by the 236-kilometre (146-mile) Autour du Luberon, a beautiful ever-hilly ride in its own right, but we are cycling only as far as Apt, less than 50 kilometres (31 miles) along the range from Cavaillon. It means we're riding only on the gently named Petit Luberon; the higher Grand Luberon rises east of Apt.

In our own private version of *Groundhog Day*, the chilly mistral blows on, with gusts forecast to reach 85km/h (53mp/h) as we climb out of Cavaillon onto the massif's

LOCAL SNAPSHOT

It's easy to pick France's most beautiful villages – they are officially classified as such. Les Plus Beaux Villages de France is an association that has painstakingly selected 159 villages as the finest across France, making it easy for visitors to cherry-pick the cutest of the cute. Unsurprisingly, Provence is flush with plus beaux villages, and this ride passes through four of them: Les Baux-de-Provence, Ménerbes, Roussillon and Aiguèze. If too much beauty isn't enough, and you don't mind a few detours, the ride passes near to a number of others also, such as Lourmarin, Gordes, Venasque and La Garde-Adhémar.

northern slopes, following quiet roads that thread between villages, vineyards, wheat fields, olives groves and cherry orchards. The rugged slopes are piebald - grey rock and khaki-coloured bush - and sliced with deep ravines.

Though the Autour du Luberon only truly gets hilly past Apt (we will barely climb beyond 400 metres, or 1310 feet, above sea level, while the Autour tops out at almost 750 metres, or 2460 feet, near the Luberon's eastern end), it still has its moments. Villages here cling to spurs, requiring sudden ascents to reach them - first Robion, then Maubec and finally this day, Oppède-le-Vieux. 'Old' Oppède was gradually emptied of its population from the 16th century on as villagers moved to the more practical centre - and better farming - of 'new' Oppède. It was finally abandoned in 1909 when the town hall joined the residents in new Oppède. Though a few people now live outside the medieval walls of the old town, inside it remains much as it was left more than a century ago. It's here that we stay in a small chambre d'hôte, perfectly positioned for an evening wander through the fascinating ghost town.

DAY 4

OPPÈDE-LE-VIEUX TO ROUSSILLON (45KM/28 MILES)

The climbs beyond Oppède-le-Vieux are gentler than we're expecting, and it's a day that's awash in colour. Cherry trees bulge with fruit, and the fields and vineyards are constellations of flowers. Each time we stop, our four-year-old daughter Kiri climbs from her trailer, picks a bouquet of flowers and hangs it from our panniers so that we now half-resemble Swiss chalets.

We dawdle this day into Ménerbes, the second of the plus beaux villages (*see* p. 73) along our route and the one in which Peter Mayle's *A Year in Provence* was set. Pablo Picasso also spent time here, having bought his mistress Dora Maar a home in the village.

This section of the Autour du Luberon reaches its high point past Bonnieux, before descending to Apt, a town of just 12,000 people that still feels somehow enormous and impersonal after the villages of the Luberon. In Apt, we switch from one cycle route to another, leaving the Autour and doubling back west on the Ochre by Bike trail. The clue to the title of this 50-kilometre (31-mile) bike route comes in Roussillon, 12 kilometres (7.5 miles) from Apt. The third of the ride's plus beaux villages, Roussillon is clustered atop cliffs that form part of Europe's largest deposit of ochre. Its tightly packed homes are painted in ochre colours, making them look almost like extensions of the cliffs.

DAY 5

ROUSSILLON TO BEAUMES-DE-VENISE (70KM/43.5 MILES)

It's from Roussillon that we wash back into the Rhône Valley, returning to the northern journey past Fontaine de Vaucluse, where a spring emerges from cliffs in a brilliant palette of colours, and rounding the outskirts of Carpentras to the foot of bald Mont Ventoux. There are clues in this mighty mountain's name, with Ventoux coming from the French word, venteux, meaning windy. Few cyclists can see the mountain known as the 'Beast of Provence' and not feel some temptation, for it's a peak filled with as much cycling legend as any place on earth. Ten tough stages of the Tour de France have finished on its summit, and British cyclist Tom Simpson died near its top during the 1967 Tour. Amphetamines were found in the pockets of his jersey.

I too feel the temptation to ride to its summit, but I'm weighted down with kids, camping gear, food and toys.

There are people who've towed children to its summit, but I'm not about to become one of them. We cycle on past the mountain, though even on the plains Ventoux is living up to its name, with the mistral continuing to rage.

This night we stay in a town, Beaumes-de-Venise, that shares our pain – it was built into the southern foot of the spiked Dentelles de Montmirail mountain range, supposedly to shield it from the mistral. 'We don't like this wind,' our daughter Kiri has learned to chant from her trailer, even as she continues to fill her hands with flowers and her cheeks with cherries. Her three-year-old brother, Cooper, meanwhile, has filled his trailer with snails – companions for the road.

DAYS 6–8

BEAUMES-DE-VENISE TO ST-MARTIN-D'ARDÈCHE (57KM/35 MILES); VALLON-PONT-D'ARC AND RETURN TO ST-MARTIN-D'ARDÈCHE (80KM/50 MILES); ST-MARTIN-D'ARDÈCHE TO MONTÉLIMAR (37KM/23 MILES)

One more detour beckons as we continue north through the Rhône Valley. Slicing through the mountains for more than 30 kilometres (18.5 miles), the Gorges de l'Ardèche have earned themselves a moniker as the 'European Grand Canyon'. The gorge ends abruptly beside the Rhône River, with the town of St-Martin-d'Ardèche just inside its mouth, less than 5 kilometres (3 miles) from the main roads through the Rhône Valley. It's a pretty little town set right on the banks of the Ardèche, but even more striking is Aiguèze, the fourth and final plus beaux village of the ride, stretching across the very edge of the cliffs on the opposite bank. Aiguèze peers out through the mouth of the gorge, and is a place of narrow cobblestone streets and a quiet air compared to the busier St Martin.

It's a hilly ride through the limestone gorges, so we have decided to treat it as a daytrip, heading out and back, while leaving most of our gear in St Martin. The road's passage along the northern edge of the gorges is as convoluted as the river's, wriggling and wiggling its way west. The scenery is magnificent – high cliffs and wild water – with the river invariably speckled with canoes, since most people come here to paddle rather than pedal.

As we return through the gorge to St Martin, with just one day to ride to our finish in Montélimar, I realise that even though we've come to cycle the general course of the Rhône Valley, we've barely been in the busy valley itself since leaving Arles. Instead we've seen much of the best of Provence – the Alpilles, the Luberon and now one of Europe's most spectacular gorges.

We have avoided the Alps and big alpine climbs, and for this day at least we're riding lighter than usual. It feels almost lazy in comparison to the week that brought us here, though nobody else seems to notice. Passing motorists applaud and honk encouragement, and there's even a call of 'bravo' from one car. The kids wave regally in reply, and we pedal on, with underpants still flapping in the breeze that's building to be the mistral once again.

Opposite Cycling past a lavender field near Roussillon
Above The Gorges de l'Ardeche

Riding resources

Details about the Autour du Luberon section of the ride can be found online (veloloisirprovence.com).
Guided and self-guided trips through Provence are numerous, though don't typically follow the route described here.

EUROPE

French & Italian Riviera

FRANCE, MONACO & ITALY

Combine coast and hinterland on a sunny journey along the Mediterranean's shores.

French & Italian Riviera

WHY IT'S SPECIAL

Is there anything more evocative than the French or Italian Riviera? This ride offers a combination of bike and beach life, framed by sun and sand, with plenty of opportunities to disappear into the sleepy Ligurian hinterland for breaks from the seaside.

It's a journey that shows that a day on a bike can go a long way in Europe, where borders are more like enticements than impediments. As I set out riding from Nice at the start of the week-long ride, I'm beginning a day in which I will breakfast in France, lunch in Monaco and have dinner in Italy ... and yet I'll cycle just 45 kilometres (28 miles). I could easily distil this single day down into the very essence of the joy of cycling in Europe – sections of bike path, towns every few kilometres, quiet roads set apart from highways, and this seamless interchange of countries. And it's just the first day of an extended ride from the French Riviera to the Italian Riviera.

BEST TIME TO RIDE

The full Riviera show comes to life in summer (especially July and Aug), but so does the intense heat and the holiday beach migrations. Aim to ride on the cusp of the high season (May, June, Sept or Oct).

RIDE IT

Over the course of a week I will pedal from Nice to near Genoa, the large city at the eastern end of Italy's Riviera di Ponente. It's a section of coast where it can seem as though every human is born with a beach umbrella, but this ride is far more than just a beach hop. At regular intervals, I'll detour off the coast, rising into the interior to villages that feel several centuries away, rather than several kilometres, from the coast. It's the best of both worlds in a single narrow strip of Mediterranean beauty. The fact that it's a coastal ride might have you anticipating flat riding by the sea, but these roads, especially along the Cote d'Azur, follow a rollercoaster course of headlands and beaches.

Nuts & bolts
Distance: 235 kilometres (146 miles)
Days: 5
Ascent: 3500 metres (11,480 feet)
Difficulty: Medium
Bike: There are almost no off-road sections on this ride, so a tourer or hybrid is the best choice.

Europe

Previous Cycling on the Lungomare Europa near Varazze *Opposite top left* Day's end at Imperia *Top right* Beach life below Cervo *Bottom left* Vine-shaded path in Verezzi *Bottom right* Place Massena in Nice

LOCAL SNAPSHOT

As you pedal into San Remo along the Riviera dei Fiori bike path, you do so through a former railway tunnel that has become a gallery for the history and imagery of the Milan–San Remo, a bike race that was first held in 1907. The longest one-day race in professional cycling, Milan–San Remo covers 298 kilometres (185 miles) and follows much of the general route of the ride described here, in reverse – it begins in Milan and reaches the Riviera coast near Genoa, where it turns west and follows the coastline into San Remo. In the 1500-metre (1640-yard) tunnel through which you enter San Remo, stories and photos hang from the ceiling, telling tales of the great Eddy Merckx, who won the race seven times (more than any other cyclist in history) and other famous winners, such as Erik Zabel, Óscar Freire and Sean Kelly. It's a ride through the history of the race, and the perfect welcome to one of the world's great cycling towns.

Above Riviera dei Fiori bike path tunnel in San Remo
Opposite Catching rays on the stony beach at Ventimiglia

DAY 1

NICE TO VENTIMIGLIA (45KM/28 MILES)

In Nice, the sun pours down on another Côte d'Azur day, and even in the early morning the city's long beach is a mosaic of beach umbrellas and sun-seeking bodies. Running immediately behind the beach is a long cycle path that continues around the narrow incision of Nice's port, where millions of euros float about in the shape of super-yachts.

The bike path quickly ends, but roads with minimal traffic continue to wrap tightly along the coast, staying as near to the sea as roads can get along these hilly shores (for cars, there are more direct and faster roads - and tunnels - to get almost anywhere). Below me, the shore is lined with stony bays and terracotta-coloured villages, strung across the toes of the white, limestone hills that rise directly from the sea.

The approach to each town brings a swooping descent (is this where I confess that I broke road speed limits a couple of times on the bike?) matched by the handbrake effect of a slow grind back out and over another headland or hill. By the time I cross into Italy late in the day, I will already have climbed around 700 metres (2300 feet), despite barely topping more than 100 metres (330 feet) above sea level.

With the sun bathing my shoulders, I feel as though I'm solar-powered as I ride next to, through and under the coastal cliffs. The sea is peppered with super-yachts, and the bays and beaches are sequined with umbrellas. There's no such thing as a bad view here.

From Nice, it's just 20 kilometres (12.5 miles) to Monaco, that great grail of wealth that hides from view until I'm deep inside it, weaving through its maze of road tunnels and suddenly down at the edge of its princely port. Cycling feels like such an uncharacteristic way to arrive in this principality, more noted for its luxury vehicles, Formula One racing cars and mega-yachts. I feel akin to a thief sneaking into Fort Knox.

The cliffs that tower above me now are no longer rock. They are instead the apartments of Monaco, as I follow the coastline beneath the principality's Vegas-sized resorts and hotels back into France. Here, roads creep up the slopes to Cap Martin, with views back into Monaco's harbour, before rolling to the point where France ends in a characteristic burst of beauty in Menton. With its 4-kilometre-long (2.5-mile) beach, Menton is like a slimmed-down version of Nice, with less high-rise apartments, more beach umbrellas,

and a wilder backyard of craggy peaks. At the town's eastern end, beneath great walls of rock, the road rolls into Italy, and I'm into my third country by 3pm.

I stay this night in the first town across the border, Ventimiglia, a settlement split into two distinct and contrasting sections by the Roja River. I arrive first into the old town, which climbs up the slopes in a palette of colours to the inevitable cathedral. Below, across the river, the nondescript new town drapes across the coastal plain like a tail. It could be any out-of-the-way Italian town, rather than part of the glitz and glam of a Riviera. Residents sit out front of unnamed bars in plastic chairs, and the stony beach has an egalitarian atmosphere. I'm 25 kilometres (15.5 miles) from Monaco and in another world.

DAY 2

VENTIMIGLIA TO IMPERIA (50KM/31 MILES)

A border in Europe can mean so little, but the change from France to Italy feels distinct and instantaneous as I ride on from Ventimiglia. Cars appear sprawled more than parked on the roads, the land looks immediately more overgrown and earthy, and in the sea for the first time there's not a single super-yacht in sight. And yet against my own expectation, it's Italy that will prove the most bike-friendly of the countries.

Along a wonderful puzzle of bike paths, coastal carparks and even a road that burrows beneath a hotel, I reach the town of Ospedaletti, 11 kilometres (7 miles) from Ventimiglia. Here I turn onto the Riviera dei Fiori bike path, which follows the former course of the Genoa-to-Ventimiglia railway for 25 kilometres (15.5 miles), which will take up half of my day.

The path cuts through San Remo, the town that's home to one of Italy's four casinos, where Alfred Nobel had a home (where he dreamed up the idea of the Nobel Peace Prize) and Russian Tsars were regular visitors, as evidenced by San Remo's Russian Orthodox Church. The Riviera dei Fiori bike path enters San Remo through a 1.5-kilometre (0.9-mile) tunnel that doubles as a gallery of images and stories about great moments in the world's most prestigious and longest one-day bike race: Milan–San Remo (*see* p. 80).

The bike path runs long and flat past San Remo, and soon I have it almost to myself. San Remo becomes just a smear along the bay behind me, and then as I slip through two more old railway tunnels, it's gone forever.

The hills above me now are crowned with ancient towns that seem to look down in judgment on the hedonistic, sun-worshipping settlements along the coast. I find it impossible to see hilltop Italian towns and not be drawn towards them, and as the bike path ends, I shun the easy finish of an 8-kilometre (5-mile) coastal sprint into Imperia. Instead, I turn up the hill towards the village of Civezza and a chance to change my angle on this beautiful coast.

Within minutes I'm far above the sea, rising through dry slopes dotted with ancient, gnarled olive trees. Apple and pear trees lean over the road, their limbs heavy with fruit, and cats lie in the shade watching me pass. It's as if I've left one Italy and entered another.

Civezza is perched 200 metres (650 feet) above the coast and, like so many towns of its kind, is strung along a high ridge. It's known as the 'circus village' (it hosts a circus festival every May) and the walls along its lanes are dotted with small random mosaics of circus scenes. In the middle of the day, almost nothing moves in the village. An old lady shuffles along on a walking stick, and a radio pours chatter through the open shutters of a window. The scene is almost a caricature of itself – the idyllic Italian village that time forgot – but it's so lovely because of it. I cool my face in a 160-year-old fountain in one of Civezza's squares and cycle on back down.

Just as lovely as Civezza itself is the descent back to Imperia on the coast. The olive trees blur past, and within minutes I'm back riding along the coast into Imperia, where the holidaymakers of the Riviera remain in their natural pose – lying prone on the stones of the beaches. Above them towers the Cathedral of San Maurizio, the largest church in Liguria – so large that it looks as though it too might be holidaying here from Rome or Florence.

DAY 3

IMPERIA TO ALASSIO (42KM/26 MILES)

I leave Imperia on an empty road that overhangs the sea, a piece of infrastructure built for cars but now given over exclusively to cyclists and joggers. A short distance along the coast, I reach Cervo, arguably the most beautiful of the coastal towns along the Riviera di Ponente.

At the base of the town, I park my bike and set out on foot through its steep, cobbled lanes, coiling up to its narrow church and a piazza that's perched like a diving board above the Mediterranean Sea. As I stand at the piazza's walled edge,

Above The old town of Alassio
Opposite Riviera dei Fiori bike path in Ospedaletti

I'm struck by the incongruity of the scene – I'm inside a medieval town, looking down on barely clad beach bodies and pedaloes scooting across the water.

Across another headland, the road swoops down into the town of Andora, where I once again turn off the coast and detour inland, following quiet streets before joining the Via Merula. I'm drawn to the interior this time, not by any particular town, but by the knowledge that I'll be pedalling up part of Liguria's so-called strada (street) of wine and olives, a gourmet tourist route. The idea alone makes me hungry, as does the thought of a long climb about to begin.

At the base of the climb, in Stellanello, I stop at a lone trattoria, where ordering lunch is made simple by the fact that the place serves only one item. I start the climb fuelled by ravioli.

From Stellanello, the ride crosses a line of hills, ascending 350 metres (1150 feet) in double-quick time before plunging into the town of Alassio, where I will stay the night. As I ride across the hills I'm alone again, among cats, blackberry bushes and olive trees – every time I head inland, it's like riding through the aisles of a fruit market.

DAY 4

ALASSIO TO FINALE LIGURIA (43KM/27 MILES)

Alassio is one of the most contemporary and business-minded towns along the Riviera di Ponente (albeit still wrapped around the one-time fishing village at its heart), but it's a town where I have a date with history.

On the slopes immediately above Alassio, I find the remnants of the Via Julia Augusta, a road built by Roman Emperor Augustus in 13 BC, linking Italy's Po Valley to southern France. Its section to Albenga begins beside an 11th-century stone church and archway. For the next 5 kilometres (3 miles) I'll be on a bike, following a pathway of chariots.

The Romans knew their aesthetics, and the Via Julia Augusta is one of the most dramatically beautiful sections of this ride, poised high above the craggy coast, looking back on Alassio's marina and out to the once-monastic Gallinara Island. The way is dotted with the ruins of a Roman necropolis, and soon it's no more than a dirt trail through the forest. Briefly I'm even bouncing across a section of the original 2000-year-old stonework.

At its end, this piece of the Via Julia Augusta descends into Albenga, a settlement with a skyline that makes obvious its moniker as the 'Town of 100 Towers'. Though I'm back on the coast, I will not stay here. This day I'll make two detours inland: from Borghetto Santo Spirito through the Varatella Valley to the village of Toirano; and then, most spectacularly, high up the slopes to the Riviera di Ponente's most enticing hinterland village, Verezzi.

Verezzi sits around 200 metres (650 feet) above its more boisterous sibling, the coastal holiday town of Borgio Verezzi, atop one of the steepest climbs of the ride. It's a tiny hillside village, unadorned in almost every way, and yet listed as one of Italy's I Borghi piu belli (Most Beautiful Villages). From the village entrance, it looks a lot like a Mexican pueblo, but once you start wandering through its narrow lanes, it transforms into a town of quiet osterias, medieval drinking fountains tucked into grottoes, and grape-vines that shroud dining terraces, creating both shade and thoughts of wine. I have only a downhill ride into Finale Ligure to come; I think I'll have a glass, but only one because I want time to explore Finale Ligure, which is a beautiful place to spend a night. It's a sprawling coastal town, but with perhaps the most classically beautiful old town along the Riviera di Ponente coast. The old town is unusually tucked into the foot of a castle-crowned hill, instead of sitting atop the hill like most of its neighbours. Even more unusually, every second store inside the old town seems to be an outdoors store, highlighting the fact that mountain-biking and rock-climbing are huge here.

DAY 5

FINALE LIGURE TO ARENZANO (55KM/34 MILES)

Another day, another detour, though as I leave Finale Ligure I'm drawn inland more by practicality than beauty, avoiding the busy Via Aurelia main road that runs squeezed between the hills and the sea. Instead, I rise into the Altipiano hills at Finale Ligure's eastern edge, making a winding, gradual ascent, with olives, grapes and figs – the very things I'm consuming each night – overhanging the road.

After 4 kilometres (2.5 miles) of climbing, the road flattens out across the table-topped Altipiano. Without effort my speed triples, and the forest becomes my own beach umbrella. There are silhouettes of mountains around me, but I roll along, just 300 metres (980 feet) above sea level, in some kind of Middle-earth between coast and Alps. It's pure riding pleasure.

I hit the coast again at Noli, a town pressed into the mouth of a narrow valley, with medieval architecture that's matched by a medieval regulation banning the wearing of swimsuits through the old town. It's a town that warrants exploration, with its web of ancient lanes and a gorgeous vaulted arcade running inside the town walls. On the stony beach, wooden fishing boats seem almost to sun themselves among the holidaymakers.

The ride's final climb is now behind me, and a wind pushes me east. Roads bend with the shape of the coast, and each town tempts me with gelaterias. The packed city of Savona is the only real barrier to my progress now, but even here a bike path curls along the coast, guiding me through the city.

From Savona, an abandoned train line wriggles along the shore. Some of its tunnels are now decrepit and blocked, but others are open as bike paths.

In Varazze, the old railway becomes the Lungomare Europa bike path, offering 10 kilometres (6 miles) of traffic-free riding, so close to the sea that my bike is almost a boat. Soon Genoa rises ahead like a mirage, but I will be finishing in Arenzano, at the bike path's end, 30 kilometres (18.5 miles) before Genoa, and hopping on a train into the city to cut out any fight with its traffic. Beside the bike path, sunbakers lie out on rocks, looking for all the world like seal colonies, and the Riviera sun continues to bore down. I park my bike and head for a cooling swim.

Riding resources

Bike Trip (rent-bike.fr) hires out a range of bikes, including ebikes and touring bikes with racks, and has offices in Nice, Monaco and Menton.
It's about a 3-hour train ride back to Nice from Genoa.

Opposite Palazzo Nazionale in Finale Ligure

EUROPE

Camino de Santiago

SPAIN

Europe's most famous pilgrimage on wheels across northern Spain.

Camino de Santiago

WHY IT'S SPECIAL

There's a scene in the 2010 movie *The Way* where Martin Sheen and his small posse of pilgrims crest the Alto del Perdón mountains on the Camino de Santiago through northern Spain. Behind them come two bikes loaded with panniers, their bells ringing like mockery as they pass the foot-sore walkers.

'What, you can do this on a bike?' one hiker blusters. 'Why the hell are we walking?'

It is indeed true that Spain's famed pilgrimage can be made on a bike, complete with all the spiritual kudos and credentials that come with hiking it. There's an immense spiritual beauty and fraternity that comes with this pilgrimage on wheels, enhanced by the natural beauty of northern Spain's mountains and the green landscape of Galicia.

While it has traditionally only been a walking route, growing numbers of cyclists are riding it - modern pilgrims clothed not in robes, but in lycra. In 2018, more than 20,000 people cycled the Camino, or about six per cent of the total number of pilgrims. Cyclists on the pilgrim path now even have their own title: bicigrinos.

BEST TIME TO RIDE

Winter and summer can be equally brutal across the heights of the meseta (high plateau) and mountains. The months bracketing summer (Apr, May, Sept and Oct) are the best riding times.

RIDE IT

The main arm of the Camino - the so-called Camino Frances route - stretches across northern Spain from St Jean Pied de Port, just across the border in France, to Santiago de Compostela, a journey of almost 800 kilometres (500 miles). For cyclists, the complete journey is likely to take around two weeks, pedalling about 50 kilometres (31 miles) a day.

There are rules to this pilgrimage that, in turn, create other, shorter options. To be accredited as a pilgrim by the official Pilgrim's Office in Santiago, a cyclist needs only ride the final 200 kilometres (124 miles) into Santiago (hikers must walk the final 100 kilometres/62 miles). It means you can begin riding from as near as Ponferrada, approaching the mountainous climb into Galicia, though most cyclists on abbreviated pilgrimages begin in the city of León, as I'm doing.

Nuts & bolts

Distance: 330 kilometres (205 miles)
Days: 5
Ascent: 4000 metres (13,100 feet)
Difficulty: Medium
Bike: There's a road route that can be cycled on any type of bike, but the more interesting journey is to follow the paths of the walkers' Camino (occasionally branching away into separate trails), which is best suited to mountain bikes.

Previous The pilgrimage's end at Santiago de Compostela Cathedral *Opposite top left* Misty morning near Arzua *Top right* Cycling across the meseta near León *Bottom left* Pilgrims resting in Hospital de Órbigo *Bottom right* León Cathedral

From León, it's 330 beautiful hilly kilometres (205 miles) to Santiago, with the bulk of the infamous meseta already behind your back. This high, dry plain, stretching for more than 200 kilometres (124 miles) between Burgos and Astorga, is the purgatory of the Camino, an empty brown landscape that many pilgrims choose to skip with the unholy option of a bus. León sits near the western end of the meseta, just a day's ride from its finish in Astorga. By starting here, I will get to experience the meseta, but not have to endure its tedium.

LOCAL SNAPSHOT

Spain didn't feature in the Bible, so how did the bones of the martyred Apostle James come to be interred in Santiago de Compostela? As you'd expect, there are various legends about the journey James's body took to reach Santiago after he was beheaded at the order of King Herod Agrippa I of Judaea. The predominant story has James's followers travelling with his body on a rudderless ship to what is now the town of Padrón, south-west of Santiago de Compostela. He was buried 20 kilometres away, in what is now the city of Santiago. The burial site was discovered in the 9th century and the cathedral built around it, almost instantly creating a site of pilgrimage. For more than a millennium, pilgrims have walked - and now cycled - the paths of the Camino de Santiago (the Way of St James) to pay homage to the Apostle and his journey to Santiago.

ITINERARY

DAY 1

LEÓN TO ASTORGA (55KM/34 MILES)

In the early morning in León, I make my way to the plaza that surrounds the city's soaring 13th-century cathedral. León's most striking feature will be my starting point on what's effectively to be a cathedral-to-cathedral ride. I'm far from alone in my impending task. In the plaza, I count at least 20 bikes, most weighed down with panniers, and many with scallop shells - the ubiquitous symbol of a Camino pilgrim - hanging from the panniers.

I weave through the streets of León and out onto the meseta (high plateau), where the city fades to a silhouette behind me. The earth is dry, brown and stubbled with recently harvested crops. Even the storks seem to be nesting high on bell towers in hope of seeing something beyond the plain. But it's also flat enough that I will climb little more than 200 metres (650 feet) across this day to Astorga. Sometimes, especially at the start of a ride, that sort of gentle terrain is all you really need.

Yellow arrows unfailingly point the way west - this may be one of the best-marked long-distance trails in the world - and past the town of Villar de Mazarife, the meseta rolls out so billiard-table flat that the road can be seen ahead for kilometres, without a single bend.

Soon I'm rolling across a beautiful medieval bridge over the Rio Orbigo into the town of Hospital de Orbigo. I've arrived in time for lunch, and yet the walkers who set out from León this morning won't be here until tomorrow. It's a thought that initially gives me a sense of misgiving about this pilgrimage that I'm making at speed. When I cycle past walkers with 10 or 15 kilograms (22 to 33 pounds) on their backs, and their feet at times so heavily bandaged they almost look mummified, I sometimes feel guilty. It's a feeling that quickly blows away each time I barrel down a descent.

Most of the day's climbing comes beyond Hospital de Orbigo, where the route takes to dirt tracks, ascending and descending until I reach a large cross overlooking Astorga. Visible beyond the city is the first big obstacle of my ride - the Montes de León, which form the mountainous end of the meseta, as well as the highest point of the entire Camino. I delay my Montes moment until tomorrow by stopping the night in the beautiful town of Astorga, though even then it takes a rudely steep final climb to reach the town.

It's worth planning an early arrival into Astorga, or intending to set out late the next morning, for it's one of the most beautiful towns along the ride, with a couple of its finest

architectural creations. Astorga's cathedral is so elaborate it looks almost like confectionery. Taking three centuries to build, it finished up in a puzzle of styles – Gothic, Baroque, Renaissance, neo-Classical. And yet it's still almost outdone for ornamentation by the adjacent Episcopal Palace, a typically fantastic design by Antoni Gaudi, the creator of Barcelona's tentacle-like Sagrada Familia church.

DAY 2

ASTORGA TO VILLAFRANCA DEL BIERZO (80KM/50 MILES)

The extra pace of a bike has other advantages on the Camino. At seven o'clock the next morning, hikers are streaming out of Astorga, even as I'm just about to sit down to breakfast. It won't be long until I'm passing them, even though I'm slowed by the abrupt rise of the Montes de León. From Astorga, it's a climb of more than 600 metres (1970 feet) to the top of the range and the Cruz de Fierro, the 'Iron Cross' that is one of the Camino's landmark features.

Before the climb begins, however, I briefly veer away into the village of Castrillo de los Polvazares. It's just 1 kilometre (0.6 miles) off the Camino route, which for walkers is typically a step too far, but for cyclists it's an easy detour. Soon I'm bouncing over large cobblestones in hushed narrow lanes, enclosed by stone homes with brightly painted green doors and window frames. I'm just a kilometre from a mass human migration, yet I'm all alone.

At around 1500 metres (4920 feet), the Cruz de Fierro is the literal high point of the Camino, but it's not the pilgrimage's toughest climb. Through the ascent's steepest section, near the top of the Montes de León range, it averages only about a 4.5 per cent grade. The tall cross stands like a stake atop the range, and it's a pilgrimage site within a pilgrimage. A small crowd has already gathered when I arrive, and I join them in placing a pebble atop the enormous pile of stones around the base of the cross. It's a ritual act performed by almost every pilgrim, symbolic of leaving behind a burden. Many have carried a stone with them from home, lugging it in their backpack or panniers since setting out from France more than 500 kilometres (310 miles) back.

Though there are off-road tracks leading down from the Cruz de Fierro for bikes, I take to the road, swooping down to Molinaseca, 20 kilometres (12.5 miles) along the road, in half an hour with barely a turn of the pedals. Despite my

Top Pilgrim traditions - signatures on a trail marker
Bottom The old town of Ponferrada

early misgivings about the fact of being a pilgrim on wheels (is it cheating?) I'm soon sipping coffee on the banks of the Rio Meruelo and certain that I wouldn't trade this for blisters and aching feet.

Things remain civilised for me, as the descent continues to Ponferrada - the closest point to Santiago at which a cycling pilgrimage can begin - before undulating through the wine country of the Bierzo. Unlike an earlier section of the Camino through the town of Irache, there are no fountains here dispensing wine for pilgrims, which is a pity because after 80 kilometres (50 miles) and 1000 metres (3280 feet) of climbing this day, I could do with a nice, crisp white before the final few kilometres into Villafranca del Bierzo.

DAY 3

VILLAFRANCA DEL BIERZO TO PORTOMARIN (100KM/62 MILES)

I've fallen into riding with a Spanish cyclist who raced with a pro team for five years, so when he tells me that the climb facing us out of Villafranca del Bierzo will be 'very tough', I believe him. The climb to O Cebreiro, the cobblestoned town that sits astride the Galician border, is the most notorious on the Camino, and with a long day spooling out ahead of us, we set out at a more pilgrim-like time. Sunrise is still half an hour away as we pedal out of Villafranca del Bierzo beneath a salmon-coloured sky, but even here we're weaving through walkers who've beaten us out of bed.

Temporarily the route is fairly flat, following the Rio Valcarce as it pours out of the mountains, but as we leave the village of Las Herrerías, fortified by caffeine, the feared climb awaits. In around 10 kilometres (6 miles) the road will ascend more than 650 metres (2130 feet), and within a kilometre we're passing cyclists who've stopped to push their bikes - they're in for a long day.

Partway up the slopes, the cyclists' route diverges from the walkers' route - sensibly the former sticks to the quiet road and soon we're inching our way near to O Cebreiro, marking my arrival into Galicia, the region at Spain's north-west tip that houses Santiago de Compostela. Out of town, we pass a large statue of a pilgrim holding his hat against the wind. On the heel of the pilgrim, somebody has stuck a bandage, as if covering a blister.

The statue's buffered pose betrays the fact that these hills are notoriously windy. Fortunately, the wind blows at our backs, propelling us across the top of the range, where only the final steep climb into Alto do Poio defeats us. We push to the top of the climb, where we sit in a cafe and watch every other cyclist behind us do the same. 'It's impossible,' one mutters as he passes.

The big range may be conquered, but in no way is the Camino's climbing done. Galicia is hilly, washed with rain, and so green it seems to gleam – it feels like the Garden of Eden compared to the meseta. Distance markers suddenly tick off the kilometres to Santiago – 150 (93 miles) to go, as the ride dips into valleys and rises steeply over hills. Even the towns offer little respite.

When cycling in Spain, you come to rue the fact that the country has so many hilltop towns, and late in the day we struggle up a steep hill into Sarria only to learn that our day's goal, Portomarin, 25 kilometres (15.5 miles) ahead, used to be positioned in a valley until Spanish dictator Francisco Franco dammed the river. It was an act that sent the town scurrying up the hill, where it was reconstructed stone by stone, adding one final climb to our day.

DAY 4

PORTOMARIN TO ARZUA (55KM/34 MILES)

After two long days with big climbs, I wake with my own version of pilgrim legs – weary and sore. But Santiago is just 95 kilometres (59 miles) away; I'd just about push the bike all the way now, if that's what it took.

Portomarin is the nearest point to Santiago at which walkers can begin a pilgrimage, and suddenly there seem to be thousands, rather than hundreds, walking the route. It's raining and everybody looks tired – Santiago feels close, but for walkers it's still a few days away. They now mutter rather than chirp *buen camino*, the shared greeting among pilgrims, and the bell on my bike begins to sound almost like unintended scorn as I weave through them.

It's a beautiful stretch of riding towards Arzua on a shorter day that switches between the bucolic openness of dairy farms and deep, vine-tangled forest. All the while, Galicia's well-earned reputation for rain is borne out in the greenery of the landscape.

In the middle of the day, as we pedal into the town of Melide, 40 kilometres (25 miles) from Portomarin, it becomes apparent that this most modern of pilgrimages is no longer about deprivation. Melide is home to several traditional pulperias (octopus restaurants) and each one is filled with pilgrims. We squeeze into empty seats at one called Pulperia a Garnacha, and are quickly lunching on fried octopus sprinkled with paprika. By the time we've washed it down with a beer and a brandy I'm just about ready to stop for the day, but the pilgrimage must go on. At least Arzua, tonight's stop, is only 15 kilometres (9 miles) away.

DAY 5

ARZUA TO SANTIAGO DE COMPOSTELA (40KM/25 MILES)

On this religious pilgrimage, the end is nigh and anticipation is high. Santiago feels almost in sight as we leave Arzúa on my final morning, though it's an elusive destination, hidden among a surround of hills. We thread once again through forest and farmland, interspersed with eucalyptus plantations.

It's only as we rise to the summit of Monte do Gozo, the final hill along the Camino, 5 kilometres (3 miles) from Santiago, that the city finally comes into view. Pilgrims gather on the hilltop, seeing for the first time the spires of the cathedral that has drawn us all forward. Equally blessed is the idea that all of the climbing is now behind us, and we roll on, excited now, heading downhill into Santiago and the busiest streets since I set out from León.

The heart of Santiago's old town is the vast Praza do Obradoiro square, wrapped around the cathedral. I park my bike and head down into the crypt of the cathedral to pay a pilgrim's respects to the remains of St James. Returning to the square, I'm struck by a sense of loss that seems to pervade everybody here – the pilgrimage is over. Hikers lay sprawled across the square, as though too exhausted to consider anything beyond this moment – is it any wonder when it's estimated that the average pilgrim will have taken one million steps since leaving St Jean Pied de Port?

I too am a pilgrim, but my journey has involved barely a step. I have completed my pilgrimage, and my feet don't hurt a bit.

Riding resources

The Confraternity of Saint James (csj.org.uk) publishes a handy, 36-page *The Cycling Pilgrim* booklet featuring route descriptions and bike advice.
Bicigrino (bicigrino.com/en) rents out bikes, fitted and ready for the Camino, that can be delivered to various start points along the route. It also has workshops dotted along the way.

EUROPE

Lakes Route

SWITZERLAND

Weave past the Swiss Alps on a lake-to-lake journey.

Lakes Route

WHY IT'S SPECIAL

Switzerland may well have the world's best cycling network, and this ride takes you past the Alps without climbing them, threading instead between the country's lovely lakes.

It's a ride through and into the heart of Switzerland, where lakes, rural valleys, alpine peaks and chalets, and copious amounts of cheese await, with a few unexpected and quirky treats included, such as the world's hot-air-ballooning capital, a famous fictional death, and one of Europe's holiest pilgrimage sites.

Towns are plentiful along the route, making it easy to break the days into manageable blocks. My longest day is 81 kilometres (50 miles) from Spiez to Sarnen, with two days that are less than 50 kilometres (31 miles), allowing plenty of time to explore and indulge in this land of mountains, cheese and chocolate.

BEST TIME TO RIDE

The best conditions come in summer and early autumn (June to Oct) when lake swims beckon. September and October appeal because the heavy tourist season is over and the heat is beginning to wane, making the climbs more comfortable.

RIDE IT

Switzerland is the mountain country by which all other nations judge themselves. Kashmir calls itself the Switzerland of the east, and the Australian state of Tasmania once billed itself as the Switzerland of the south. More than 60 per cent of Switzerland is covered by mountains, and it has more peaks higher than 4000 metres (13,120 feet) than any other country in Europe.

But Switzerland also does a fine line in lakes, with more than 1500 of them sprinkled across the landlocked country, and it's these bodies of water that can be the true lure for cyclists, courtesy of the Lakes Route. One of nine national cycling trails that zig and zag across the country, the Lakes Route begins in the west, on the shores of Lake Geneva, and traverses the country to finish 510 kilometres (317 miles) later on the shores of Lake Constance. Along the way it passes another 10 major lakes, while having the profound common sense to almost entirely avoid all of the country's mountains, even as it stays in sight of them for much of the journey.

The most spectacular section of the ride is the 343-kilometre (213-mile) stretch between Lake Geneva and Lake Zurich, where it darts around gorgeous lakes, such as Brienz, Thun and Lucerne, and in sight of some of the Alps's most famous peaks. It's this stretch that I've come to ride.

Nuts & bolts
Distance: 343 kilometres (213 miles)
Days: 6
Ascent: 5000 metres (16,400 feet)
Difficulty: Medium
Bike: Only 30 kilometres (18.5 miles) of the ride to Lake Zurich is on unsealed surfaces, making it possible to do the ride on any bike except a road bike.

Previous Lake Sarnen *Opposite* A curious Simmental cow in the Simmental valley

Though the ascents between Lake Geneva and Lake Zurich total an intimidating 5000 metres (16,400 feet) – about the equivalent of cycling up the Alps's highest mountain, Mont Blanc, from sea level – there are few climbs that are steep, and the two toughest can be circumvented on public transport, if you lack the willpower or leg-power on the day.

The Lakes Route, which is marked by '9' signs throughout (it's national cycling route No. 9), is just one small part of Switzerland's national, regional and local cycle-route network that stretches across more than 8000 kilometres (4970 miles). There's an app (SwitzerlandMobility) that covers every kilometre of the network, and the Lakes Route adheres to quiet roads as much as possible. It's all an indication of one likely fact: Switzerland may be the most bike-friendly country on earth.

LOCAL SNAPSHOT

For anybody with a love of cheese, Gruyères (day one, *see* p. 99) is a mouthwatering stop, with the eponymous Gruyère cheese said to have been made here for almost 1000 years. Suitably, Gruyères knows how to milk a theme. Cheese shops ring its cobblestoned medieval main square, while fondue and raclette dominate restaurant offerings.

In complete contrast, just a few steps from the square, is the HR Giger Museum, celebrating the otherworldly creations of Hans Ruedi Giger, the Oscar-winning designer of the movie *Alien* – curiously, if you stop here and at Chaplin's World (*see* p. 99), you can see three Oscars statues (two at Chaplin's World, one in the Giger Museum) in a single day of cycling.

Opposite St Theodul Church in Gruyères

DAY 1

VEVEY TO GRUYÈRES (41KM/25.5 MILES)

On the shores of Lake Geneva, Switzerland's largest lake, on a summer's day there's the atmosphere of a Riviera, even though the nearest coastline is more than 250 kilometres (155 miles) away to the south. Paddle-steamers, stand-up paddleboards and kayaks jostle for space. Children splash in the shallows, as white swans cruise the shores. In the lakeside town of Vevey, where I begin pedalling, the tines of a giant, sculpted fork pierce the water, watched over by a bronze statue of Charlie Chaplin, the great comedian who spent the final 25 years of his life in Vevey.

Immediately I pick up the trail of the Lakes Route's '9' markers that will become my unfailing guides to Lake Zurich, with this ride signed as meticulously well as all others in precise Switzerland. The way out from Lake Geneva is up – a 400-metre (1310-foot) climb through the slopes that cup the lake – ascending to ever-widening views over the lake to distant Mont Blanc. It's not the kindest start to a ride, though you can choose to warm up your legs on the route's official opening 7-kilometre (4.3-mile) stretch along the lakeshore between Montreux and Vevey. Even kinder is the possibility of cutting out the climb altogether, by catching the Mont Pèlerin funicular railway from Vevey, knocking off the ascent without the turn of a pedal.

I have shunned the very real temptation of the funicular to pedal my way out of Vevey, which has the added attraction of taking me past the doors of Chaplin's World, the mansion-turned-museum where comedian Charlie Chaplin resided after being exiled from the United States for his supposed communist sympathies during the McCarthy era. I've cycled less than 10 kilometres (6 miles) and I'm already off the bike, delaying the climb by wandering the rooms of Chaplin's home and watching clips from his slapstick oeuvre.

Soon the lake is far behind me, and rural Switzerland rolls out ahead of me. Cowbells chime as if signalling the final lap in a velodrome, and out here, by the French border, the farmhouses are not the alpine chalets of the Swiss mountain regions, but more a grand French-stucco-style. Only the pots of geraniums hanging from the windows bestow a Swiss alpine touch.

As I roll into Châtel-Saint-Denis, the first town above Vevey, I also cross the European divide. From here, waters flow down one side to the Rhine, and down the other to the Rhône.

Outside of the town, the ride follows farm roads that would be no wider than bike paths in other countries. At times, they edge to within metres of the highway, and yet I feel aeons away, rolling through cornfields and tiny, timeless farming villages.

Near Bulle, the route does a U-turn, swinging back on itself and entering the Gruyère valley, where I stay this night in the gorgeous hilltop town of Gruyères – famed for its cheese (*see* p. 98) – 41 kilometres (25.5 miles) from Vevey.

Above Cycling through the Simmental *Opposite* Spiez Castle rising above the town and marina

DAY 2

GRUYÈRES TO GSTAAD (39KM/24 MILES)

I begin this morning with my panniers filled with the day's essentials - bread, salami, Gruyère cheese - as the Lakes Route continues turning back on itself. The ride heads south through the Gruyère valley, which is so green it seems to glow beneath its serrated rim of mountains. Cows trail in and out of milking sheds, and as the ride follows empty farm roads near and, yet, so far from the main road through the valley, it's hard to believe I'm cycling through the heart of one of the most densely populated countries in Europe.

Eventually the valley narrows to the point that there's only space for one road, and among the traffic - patchy as it is in this rural area - I squeeze between mountains and out of the Gruyère valley. I'm now less than 15 straight-line kilometres (9 miles) from Vevey, yet I've cycled more than 60 kilometres (37 miles).

The next valley - the Saane - climbs higher than the Gruyère, rising through Château-d'Oex, the world's hot-air-ballooning capital, complete with a ballooning museum to prove it. At the town's edges, the slopes are getting buzz-cuts, as farmers gather up hay for the winter, and it feels as though I've crossed more than valleys since leaving Gruyères. Suddenly, here in the pre-Alps, the architecture has turned alpine, with Switzerland's trademark wooden chalets dotting the fields and towns. It's as though I've finally arrived in the right country. I stay a night in fashionable Gstaad, ahead of a day in which the ride will climb to enter the Simmental, the valley that gives its name to a breed of cow.

DAY 3

GSTAAD TO SPIEZ (52KM/32 MILES)

The Simmental valley is the ultimate in bucolic - the fields are as green as emeralds, and the namesake cows stare curiously as I pass - and it's a downhill roll through the valley, following the course of the river on more superb farm roads, where the only things I have to move aside for are occasional tractors.

Just as I'm picturing meadows and cowbells all the way to Lake Zurich, however, the valley ends abruptly at an incongruous cluster of industry. It comes like an earth tremor, sudden and shocking, but it also signals a change in the very character of the ride. It's here that the Lakes Route begins to truly resemble its name. As I emerge into sight of arguably the grandest mountain trio in the Alps - the

Eiger, Monch and Jungfrau – the trail drops to the shores of Lake Thun and the castle-topped town of Spiez, where I sleep this night in a hotel pinched between the castle and the busy marina.

DAY 4

SPIEZ TO SARNEN (81KM/50 MILES)

I set out early this morning to enjoy dawn along an odd couple of alpine lakes. Lake Thun is the beautiful green of the ocean, sitting side-by-side with the gleaming blue Lake Brienz, the pair separated by just a flat shelf of land across which sprawls the popular tourist town of Interlaken.

I roll around the rim of Lake Thun, and then around the rim of Lake Brienz, beginning what will be my biggest day by any measure – time, distance and lakes. It's a day in which I'll cycle along four lakes: Thun, Brienz, Lungern and Sarnen.

In the early morning it's almost as though you could cycle across the flat surface of Lake Brienz, instead of having to go around it. But alas, you do have to go around it. The route clings to the lake's southern shores, far removed from the main road that hurries past above, and it's the most peaceful cycling imaginable – just me, the ducks and the sunlight inching down the slopes.

The otherwise flat shores are interrupted by steep climbs through a pair of bluffs broken by the beauty of Iseltwald, a small town with a fairytale castle crowning a finger of land that pokes into the lake. The greatest treat along these shores, however, comes near their end, as the route cuts right past the base of Giessbach waterfall. A walk of just a few minutes ends up in behind the pouring falls.

This waterfall is popular enough to have attracted a luxury hotel at its base, but that still only makes it the second-most famous waterfall of my day. Above the town of Meiringen, my lunch stop this day (and an appropriate food stop, since this town gave its name to the meringue), the 120-metre (395-foot) Reichenbach Falls plummet out of the Alps. It was at these falls that Sherlock Holmes met his fictional end, pushed to his death by Professor Moriarty. You can detour from your ride and pay tribute to the great detective, via a funicular railway that runs from the edge of Meiringen to the falls. Or you can visit the Sherlock Holmes Museum, stay in the Sherlock Holmes Hotel, or have a night out at the Sherlock Lounge Club.

If Sherlock fell here, however, I'm hoping that I don't, because Meiringen also marks the start of the Lakes Route's most challenging climb. Brünigpass is the only pass that the ride crosses in this country of mountains, and it stands 450 metres (1475 feet) above Meiringen. It's possible to pretend that it's not even here by taking a train from Meiringen to Brünig-Hasliberg atop the pass, but I pedal on, rising on a tiny track - sometimes dirt, sometimes sealed - that switchbacks above Meiringen, before flattening out across the slopes to Brünigpass. For most of the climb there's not a vehicle to be seen, for there are easier roads to Brünigpass in a car.

From Brünigpass, it's a rapid descent to Lake Lungern, then a second descent to Lake Sarnen, as the ride changes character once again, turning its back now on the Alps, riding away from them instead of along them as it swings towards Lake Zurich and Lake Constance - but not before a welcome night's stop in the town of Sarnen at the end of a long day.

DAYS 5–6

SARNEN TO ZUG (60KM/37 MILES); ZUG TO RAPPERSWIL-JONA (70KM/43.5 MILES)

Past another chain of lakes beyond Sarnen, the ride wriggles around the bays of Lake Lucerne and into the city of Lucerne. Here, it crosses the Reuss River between the city's two famous wooden bridges and follows the waterway out of the city and long beyond.

Lucerne marks the point at which the ride gains a more urban edge, with towns becoming larger and more business-minded, but out of wealthy Zug, at the start of my final day, I ride for an hour, heading east through the sort of dense forest you forget still exists in Europe. The woods are lit golden by the sunlight that leaks through the canopy, and main roads rumble past on bridges so high overhead they look like something from science fiction.

Though the convoluted landscape of the Alps is behind me, it's only now that the ride itself begins a convoluted course, swinging up to ridge-tops and winding down to lakes. Approaching the shores of Lake Sihl, the final body of water before Lake Zurich, I enter Einsiedeln, which feels like any other small town until suddenly an abbey rises from within that somehow looks almost bigger than Einsiedeln itself. This 10th-century Benedictine abbey is part of the multi-armed network of Camino de Santiago (*see* p. 87) walking paths across Europe, and is Switzerland's most magnetic pilgrimage site, with half a million people said to come here each year to pay homage to its wooden Black Madonna statue.

One climb remains beyond Lake Sihl, and though the mountains are just memories behind me, it's strangely one of the steepest ascents of all. From its top come views of Lake Zurich, with the city of Zurich itself gleaming at its far northern end. I switch up into a high gear and let the bike do its thing, freewheeling almost 600 metres (1970 feet) down to the shores of Lake Zurich, where the ride funnels onto the Seedam Causeway across the lake. My final pedal strokes before I finish in the castle-topped town of Rapperswil-Jona will be across this causeway. It's the most fitting of ends - riding atop a lake to complete the Lakes Route.

Riding resources

Geneva-based Cycle Classic Tours (cctbikerentals.com) hires out a range of bikes, including ebikes and hybrids with racks and panniers. Delivery of your bike can be arranged to Lausanne near Vevey.
For complete mapping of Switzerland's entire cycling network, download the SwitzerlandMobility app.
Head online for more information about the Lakes Route (myswitzerland.com/en-au/experiences/route/lakes-route).

Opposite Pause on the shores of Lake Brienz

EUROPE

Bavarian Beer Route

GERMANY

A gentle ride through German valleys packed with breweries.

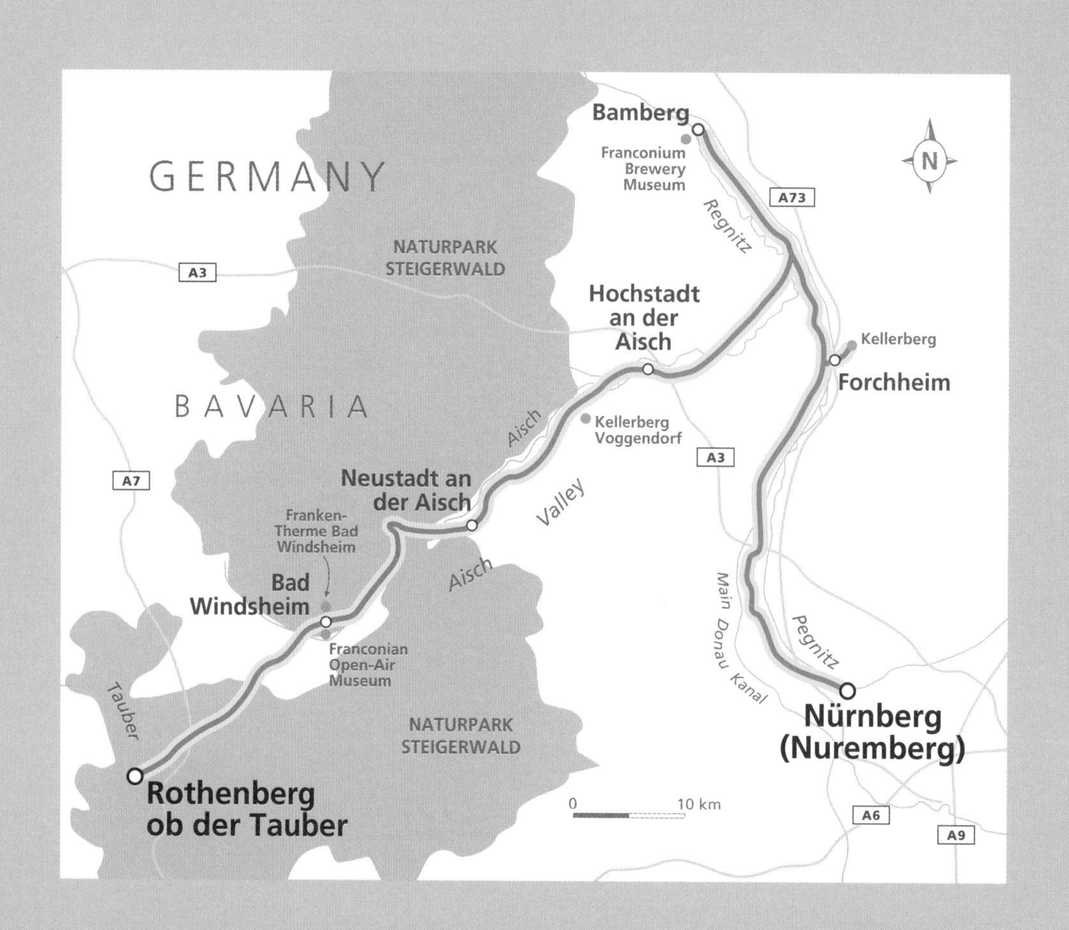
GERMANY
BAVARIA
NATURPARK STEIGERWALD
NATURPARK STEIGERWALD
Bamberg
Franconium Brewery Museum
A73
Regnitz
A3
Hochstadt an der Aisch
Kellerberg
Forchheim
Aisch
Kellerberg Voggendorf
A3
A7
Neustadt an der Aisch
Valley
Franken-Therme Bad Windsheim
Bad Windsheim
Aisch
Main Donau Kanal
Pegnitz
Franconian Open-Air Museum
Tauber
Nürnberg (Nuremberg)
Rothenberg ob der Tauber
0
10 km
A6
A9
N

Bavarian Beer Route

WHY IT'S SPECIAL

Watch the patterns of any morning cycling peloton and you'll quickly discover that the ride is as much about coffee as cadence. For touring cyclists, however, journeys tend to revolve more around bakeries and beer, a fact that makes Bavaria heaven-sent as a cycling destination.

On this ride, you'll get to discover European canal-towpath riding on a flat route through perhaps the greatest concentration of breweries on the planet.

In the north of the southern German state of Bavaria, the region of Franconia is said to be home to a full one-third of Germany's breweries. Within Franconia, pinched between a triangle of beautiful cities – Nürnberg (Nuremberg), Bamberg and Rothenburg ob der Tauber – the Aisch Valley alone is said to have an average of one brewery every kilometre. It's been called the greatest concentration of breweries on earth.

What's particularly great about this region is a string of bike routes that can turn these small breweries, and their multitude of associated beer gardens, into drink stops along a fine cycle journey between the three cities. The riding is easy and mostly flat, leaving plenty of energy and time to explore the beer heritage of the area and the beauty of its old cities.

BEST TIME TO RIDE

This route can be comfortably cycled from around April to October. The height of summer (July and Aug) might add sweat, but it's good weather in which to pedal up a thirst for a beer.

RIDE IT

I've come to Franconia to cycle for three days, beginning in Nürnberg (Nuremberg) and finishing in Rothenburg via Bamberg and the Aisch Valley. It's just as simple to add a fourth day, completing the loop with an 80-kilometre (50-mile) ride back into Nürnberg, but Rothenburg provides such a glorious finish (and Germany's rail system such an easy exit) that I'm content to leave the triangle unclosed.

The 200-kilometre (124-mile) ride to Rothenburg follows canal towpaths most of the way to Bamberg before joining the Aisch Valley Cycle Route along minor roads that are as quiet as a Sunday hangover. These towpaths are a classically European cycling tradition, and they're unfailingly flat, while the Aisch Valley also has few climbs of note. The carbohydrates I'll be imbibing are purely for pleasure's sake.

Nuts & bolts
Distance: 200 kilometres (124 miles)
Days: 3
Ascent: 950 metres (3115 feet)
Difficulty: Easy
Bike: Sealed roads and hard-packed trails make a tourer or hybrid bike ideal for this ride.

Previous The colours of the Franconian Open-Air Museum

LOCAL SNAPSHOT

At one point in the 19th century, Bamberg boasted 65 breweries, nine of which remain today. Beer festivals fill its cultural calendar, and you can quietly nurse a hangover through the Franconian Brewery Museum. Residents are so fervent about their ale that they staged the so-called Bamberg Beer War in 1907, boycotting breweries after they increased the price of beer by a pfennig. The drinkers won the battle: prices were lowered again.

The beer speciality in Bamberg is Rauchbier (smoked beer), which has a smoky flavour that comes from drying malted barley over an open flame. The best bars in which to try Rauchbier are Schlenkerla in the old town, and Spezial to its north.

Below Drinking crowds at Schlenkerla in Bamberg *Oppsoite top* The Main Danube Canal towpath *Bottom* Cycling signs on the approach to Rothenburg ob der Tauber

DAY 1

NÜRNBERG (NUREMBERG) TO BAMBERG (70KM/43.5 MILES)

In Nürnberg (Nuremberg), I set out west, riding along the banks of the Pegnitz, the river that forms a green corridor where the city typically comes out to play. This morning, though, I'm almost alone, as rain washes over the city and the river. Within a few kilometres, I find my guiding line to Bamberg, the Main Danube Canal, which runs soberly straight between the towpaths atop its banks. Enormous canal boats cruise along beside me, rising and falling on elevators of water through the locks, and canola fields bloom as brightly as flares beside the path.

There couldn't be a simpler way to start a ride than along this canal. Navigation is no issue, with the canal running steadfastly all the way into Bamberg, and climbs are non-existent. Liquid temptations, however, are plentiful, with my map showing more than 50 beer gardens along this stretch of canal riding. Some are a few kilometres from the trail, while others are right beside it.

I resist the amber lure until the town of Forchheim, around 45 kilometres (28 miles) from Nürnberg and the perfect lunch stop. I bump along its cobblestoned streets – Europe's classic cycling massage – and rise onto a hill known as Kellerberg.

There's a saying in Forchheim that to drink is to go 'auf die Keller' (into the cellar). At the edge of the town, the forested slopes of Kellerberg are punctured with more than a dozen cellar pubs, originally cut into the hill for the town's breweries (which once numbered 33) to store their beer at a constant temperature of 6–10°C (42–50°F) – natural refrigeration. Today they house restaurant-bars, where I seize the vague excuse of replenishing my energy reserves for the short afternoon ride into Bamberg with a schnitzel and a stein of beer.

I pedal out an hour later mysteriously cheerier than when I cycled in. I weave back through Forchheim, past a pair of breweries that stand cheek-by-jowl along the cobblestones of the once-royal town, and return to the canal, which points north like a compass needle. Another 90 minutes of flat cycling and I reach the outskirts of Bamberg, a city where beauty and beer vie for top billing.

Bamberg's entire old town is World Heritage–listed, and the 15th-century town hall, with its traditional criss-cross fachwerk panelling, sits astride an island in the middle of the Regnitz River as it pours through Bamberg's heart.

I barely have to deviate as I ride into Bamberg, for I'm staying in a hotel right beside the Main Danube Canal, connected to the old town by Bamberg's famous bridge of love locks. It's Saturday night and I'll have to pace myself even more in this city than on the bike, because Bamberg is about as beery and cheery as this sudsy region gets.

I do my civic duty and trawl through a few bars in search of Bamberg's signature smoked beer (*see* p. 108), including, at the heart of it all, the ever-popular Schlenkerla, which has been brewing in Bamberg since at least 1405.

DAY 2

BAMBERG TO NEUSTADT AN DER AISCH (70KM/43.5 MILES)

The second day of the ride isn't difficult, but while almost every village along the way has a brewery, there are few stores other than in Hochstadt an der Aisch, so it's worth carrying some snacks for the day.

From Bamberg, I retrace my ride along the canal towpath for an hour until I'm almost back in Forchheim, where the Aisch River pours into the Regnitz. I turn west, off the canal towpath and onto the small, narrow roads and bike paths that clip together to form the Aisch Valley Cycle Route.

For the first time, there are bumps in the land, though they're no more than gentle undulations – just enough in the climbs to alert my legs to the fact that I'm cycling. The Aisch carves through the valley below me, though only occasionally does it come into view. Mostly it's a ride through a rural idyll of tiny villages and crops of corn and canola.

I lunch in Hochstadt an der Aisch, the largest town along this day's ride, but my eye is really ahead to Voggendorf, about 10 kilometres (6 miles) further down the road. Little more than a cluster of farm buildings, it's a place where I feel immediately welcome as I pedal in past a metal sculpture of a cyclist (albeit with its bum being bitten by a fish). On a rise behind the sculpture is Kellerberg Voggendorf, the beer garden attached to the village's Prechtel Brewery.

From the beer garden, I stare out over fields and surrounding towns, enjoying a stein before returning to my task. Neustadt an der Aisch is just 16 kilometres (10 miles) ahead, and I'm in the company of nature for the hour that remains in my cycling day. Squirrels bounce about the trail, their jaws locked around acorns, while small birds of prey hover hopefully above ploughed fields.

The Aisch is now just a trickle in the landscape, a squiggled line that leads me into Neustadt. This town of 12,000 people is framed around a gorgeous town square, and I'm suitably staying the night inside a brewery, Kohlenmuhle. Sitting right beside the trail, Kohlenmuhle started brewing the good stuff in 1401 and today occupies a former mill on the banks of the Aisch River. It combines a brewery with a bustling, wood-lined restaurant and a guesthouse. The rooms are tiny, but it's the shortest of walks home after a few beers.

DAY 3

NEUSTADT AN DER AISCH TO ROTHENBURG OB DER TAUBER (60KM/37 MILES)

From Neustadt, it's a beautiful ride into Rothenburg ob der Tauber, a city where beauty finally and unquestionably trumps beer – the intersection of lanes at Plönlein inside Rothenburg's old town is said to be one of the most photographed spots in Germany.

It's another easy ride, meandering gently beside the Aisch River for the first half of the day into the town of Bad Windsheim, which is the logical lunch stop. Unlike the proliferation of breweries and beer gardens over the two previous days, Bad Windsheim also contains the only real connection to beer on this day's ride. At one edge of town is Franken-Therme Bad Windsheim, the mineral salt baths (bad) that gives Bad Windsheim its name, providing the opportunity to soak away a few days of cycling aches, but it's a museum on the other side of town that has my attention.

On the banks of the Aisch River, the Franconian Open-Air Museum may sound dry, but it's not. Literally. Inside this collection of around 100 historic homes and buildings from around Middle Franconia, steam pours from a chimney and a wonderful malty aroma fills the air. It comes from Wirsthaus am Freilandmuseum, one of two working breweries inside the museum. Inside, bags of malt are piled against the walls, and a kettle drum from the 1850s brews up beer four times a week.

As I leave the museum, I cross the Aisch River for the final time and begin the slow ascent towards Rothenburg. Though it's a climb of about 200 metres (655 feet) over the next couple of hours, it may also be the most beautiful stretch of riding of all, crossing from the Aisch Valley into the Tauber Valley. The land is covered in swatches of yellow canola and green forest, with the spires of churches rising above tiny villages. More beautiful still is the tailwind that propels me forward.

As I approach Rothenburg, beams of sunlight bore through the cloud cover like spotlights, and the city's rooftops glitter like gold. It feels like some sort of heavenly welcome at the end of a cycling pilgrimage, though my thoughts are more grounded, because really I'm just fancying another beer to celebrate the end of my ride.

Riding resources

Bikes can be hired in Nürnberg. Rent a Bike Nürnberg (rentabike-nuernberg.de) has good touring bikes with panniers.
This isn't a common ride offered by cycling tour companies, but UTracks (utracks.com) operates a self-guided itinerary, supplying you with a bike, maps, notes, accommodation and luggage transfers along the way.

Opposite View over Rothenburg from the town hall tower

PEDALLER

Charlie Walker

Charlie Walker is a London-based travel writer. Over the last decade he has cycled 80,000 kilometres (50,000 miles) through 65 countries, including Afghanistan and the Democratic Republic of the Congo (DRC). His longest tour began at the age of 22 and lasted for more than four years. He has written two books about his bicycle adventures: *Through Sand & Snow* and *On Roads That Echo*.

Find him at charliewalker.org or on Instagram: @cwexplore

What was your first bike trip?

A few weeks after leaving university I flew to Beijing and spent a couple of weeks cycling roughly 1600 kilometres (994 miles) across the Gobi Desert and up to the capital of Mongolia, Ulaanbaatar.

What impact did that trip have on you and your life, and how did it help create your passion for cycle travel?

If I'm completely honest, I didn't much enjoy it! I was ill-prepared and injured at the start (broken wrist and recently snapped quadriceps). The ride was hot and painful and often on sandy tracks, which made for slow-going. There were times, however, when I got the sense that cycle touring could be truly great, particularly in peaceful evenings camped in the desert and the encounters with remote people that I would never have had if I was simply backpacking.

What to you is the special quality about cycle travel over other forms of travel?

The combination of speed (not too fast, not too slow), affordability, and the access to otherwise overlooked places.

Where have been your favourite places to cycle?

Katanga Province in the Democratic Republic of the Congo – in the dry season it's cool and peaceful, while feeling otherworldly and intrepid. Western Mongolia has aggressively rugged landscape and it's impossible to not get off-the-beaten path, as it's pretty much all off-road anyway. Iran is vast, varied, fascinating and home to the friendliest people I've encountered anywhere in the world.

What's your one essential bit of kit on a cycle trip?

Books. One of the greatest joys of cycle touring is the richness of time. I like long, slow tours where I take naps under trees after lunch and read in the tent long after breakfast. I used to carry as many as 10 paperbacks but I now just take a Kindle.

What tips would you give to someone preparing for a bike trip?

Don't get too bogged down in planning and preparation. Pick a destination that piques your curiosity, work out how to get a bike there, book a flight, pack a tent, and GO! You'll figure the rest out as you go along. Necessity is a great facilitator of resourcefulness.

Given the choice – panniers or bikepacking?

Panniers. I don't like to rush and so don't need to pack particularly light. I don't carry very much, but I also don't like spending half an hour trying to stuff kit into undersized bags.

Is cycle travel also a really good excuse to eat and drink well and guilt-free?

Absolutely! On my longest tour (four years, 69,000 kilometres/43,000 miles) my weight fluctuated constantly and drastically. I lost a quarter of my body weight crossing Tibet (illegally) in winter, but then relished indulging the limitless appetite that cycling engenders and piling the pounds back on once I reached civilisation again.

Where's the one place you'd really like to cycle?

I'd like to spend a few months taking in a cross-section of South American mountains, jungles and high-altitude deserts. I've never visited the continent and it feels like the obvious next destination to me.

Opposite Charlie Walker in Katanga Province, Democratic Republic of the Congo *Left* Cycling through the mountains of Kyrgyzstan *Right* Overlooking Fish River Canyon, Namibia

Murray to Mountains Rail Trail

AUSTRALIA

A gentle gourmet ride into Australia's High Country.

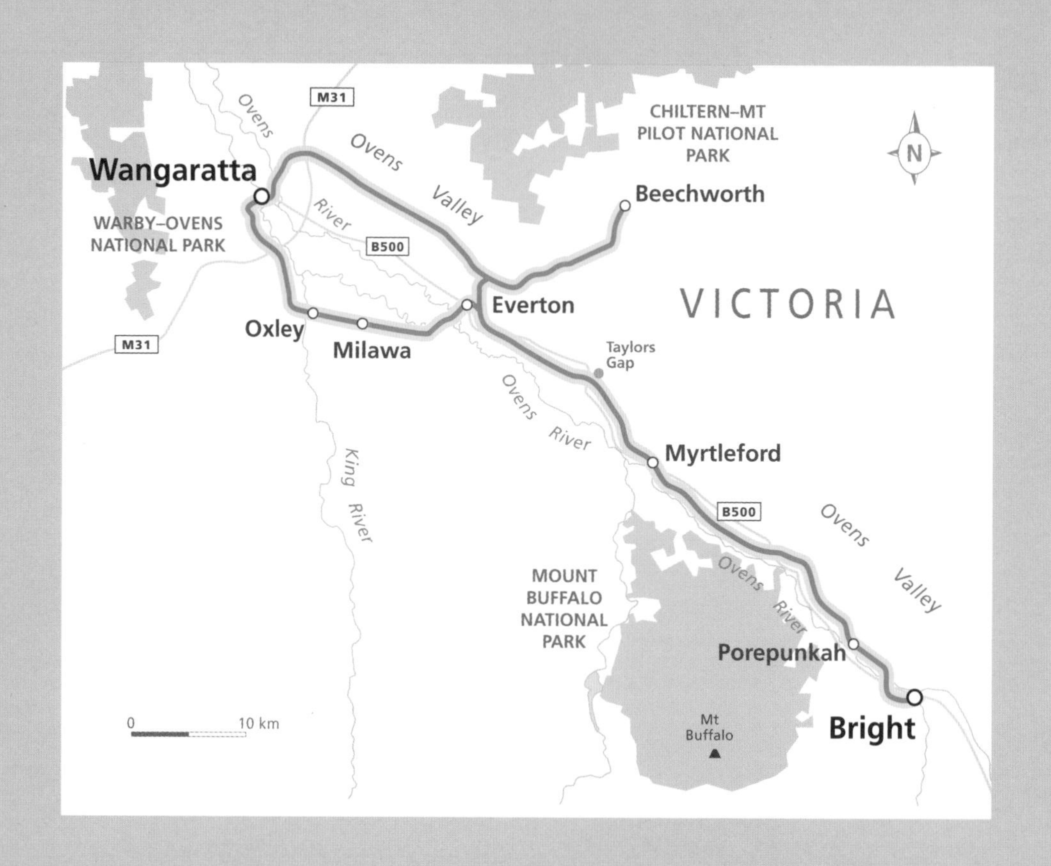
M31
Ovens
CHILTERN–MT
PILOT NATIONAL
PARK
N
Ovens
Wangaratta
Valley
Beechworth
WARBY–OVENS
NATIONAL PARK
River
B500
Everton
VICTORIA
Oxley
Milawa
M31
Taylors
Gap
Ovens
River
King
River
Myrtleford
B500
Ovens
Valley
MOUNT
BUFFALO
NATIONAL
PARK
Ovens
River
Porepunkah
0
10 km
Mt
Buffalo
Bright

Murray to Mountains Rail Trail

Nuts & bolts
Distance: 206 kilometres (128 miles)
Days: 5
Ascent: 1200 metres (3940 feet)
Difficulty: Easy
Bike: The rail trail is unsealed but the surface is smooth and wide, so is suited to any bike - a tourer or hybrid will roll best.

WHY IT'S SPECIAL

The Murray to Mountains Rail Trail in north-eastern Victoria is Australia's premier rail trail and a perfect introduction to cycle touring, with gentle gradients and an abundance of wine and food stops. It's lovely as an easy ride, but even for experienced cyclists it's a good excuse for an indulgent few days on wheels.

The trail, which opened in 2002, follows the course of an old railway along the edge of Australia's High Country, near to the highest mountains in Victoria. The main thread of the trail stretches 84 kilometres (52 miles) between the towns of Wangaratta and Bright, with side trails radiating like spokes to Beechworth, Wandiligong and the Milawa Gourmet Region.

BEST TIME TO RIDE

In April and May, Bright and Beechworth get their glow on with golden displays of autumn colour. Bright hosts a 10-day Autumn Festival (brightautumnfestival.org.au), celebrating its deciduous delights.

Spring (Sept to Nov) is also a nice, mild time to ride.

Winter and summer are times of climate extremes and best avoided.

RIDE IT

Though the trail is in the mountains, it's not through the mountains, because railway builders share one ambition with most cyclists - they seek to find the flattest route possible. It's this that makes trails such as Murray to Mountains so enticing, especially for novice bike tourers or those, like me, with kids in literal tow.

It's my first cycling trip with my two preschool-age children, and a carefully chosen one. I've pedalled the Murray to Mountains Rail Trail several times without kids, and know that the distances between distractions are short and that there are things to please both tall and small along the journey. Few compromises are needed to ensure the kids' enjoyment.

It's possible to ride Murray to Mountains out and back in two days, but we've come for five days - two days from Wangaratta to Bright and three days back, including a day on the side trail up to Beechworth.

Previous Ovens River near Porepunkah

DAY 1

WANGARATTA TO MYRTLEFORD (57KM/35 MILES)

We begin on one of Murray to Mountains's side trails, setting out from the trailhead in Apex Park in the regional town of Wangaratta, at the trail's western end, towards Milawa. It's a fine way to start; a section that proves that cycling, gastronomy and children can happily coexist. Even by the standards of this easy rail trail, it's a flat ride to Milawa, following the King River south. Without the anchor of the child trailers, and the distraction of the treats of the gourmet region around Milawa and Oxley, it's a 20-kilometre (12.5-mile) stretch that could easily be cycled in an hour. But on a trip this leisurely, time is elastic, and this short ride fills an entire morning, especially since it begins beside a playground in Apex Park – our bikes are parked and the kids are scrambling out of their trailers before we've even started – and it's surrounded by vineyards for much of its length. More time is spent cycling between cellar doors than in actually getting to Milawa itself.

In a morning that will set the tone for the week, we stop at three vineyards before we've even reached Milawa. Each one has toys to amuse the kids, while we're being amused by tastings. There are dogs to pat, and tricycles to ride at one of the vineyards. It's a promising start.

When we leave Milawa in the afternoon, we set out riding on roads for the only time in the trip, following first the Snow Road and then Markwood-Everton Road, heading north to meet the main rail trail outside the small town of Everton. It's a ride through a landscape that's almost monochrome, with gum trees rising like florets above dry plains that shimmer in the heat haze.

From within the trailers, there's barely a murmur of discontent as we ride through this snapshot of classic Australiana. Songs and nursery rhymes are our soundtrack, every cow and galah draws comment, and the trailers slowly fill with stones, flowers and other treasures gathered each time we stop.

At Everton, we swing onto the main rail trail for the first time, and in the heat of the day the trail hazards are those common to Australia – snakes warming their bellies on the hot path. It's a strange form of traffic jam, stopping us each time, but it's not the snakes that occupy my mind. Towing a child behind me for the first time, I'm more concerned about Taylors Gap, the most significant of the two discernible climbs on the main section of the rail trail.

When we arrive at the base of the climb, which ascends little more than 100 metres (330 feet), one child is singing songs and the other is asleep. I almost envy my own children at this moment.

As I pedal up the hill, my daughter Kiri pushes at the inside of her trailer – helpful in her mind, if not in reality. 'I'm pushing you up the hill, Dad,' she calls, though there are few things as heavy, or as determinedly helpful, as a child in a bicycle trailer during an uphill ride. Somewhere just behind me I hear my son Cooper, suddenly and instantaneously awake, ask a straightforward question from the trailer of his mum's bike.

'Where are we going?' he calls. 'Uphill,' she answers, though the truthful answer is Myrtleford.

LOCAL SNAPSHOT

Murray to Mountains is the most famous of Australia's rail trails, and the one that has popularised rail trails in the country. If you enjoy this ride, there are many similar possibilities in Australia. Rail trails exist in every Australian state, though Victoria has the most extensive rail-trail network. Close to Melbourne, you can set out on the 40-kilometre (25-mile) Lilydale to Warburton Rail Trail, or perhaps stretch things out on the 134-kilometre (83-mile) Great Victorian Rail Trail, which noses into the foot of the state's High Country from beside the main highway between Melbourne and Sydney.

The longest rail trail in the country is the Brisbane Valley Rail Trail, which stretches for 161 kilometres (100 miles) through south-east Queensland. If you happen to be cycling the East Coast Tasmania ride (*see* p. 123), there's an option to ride the North East Rail Trail out of Scottsdale.

The Rail Trails Australia website (railtrails.org.au) is a good resource, covering all rail trails.

The steepest moment on Taylors Gap comes at its top, though thankfully it's a short pinch before the trail crosses the Great Alpine Road, the main thoroughfare between Wangaratta and Bright, and begins its descent to Gapsted Wines, where we stop to graze again, sitting out on a deck overlooking the lines of vines.

From here, the ride gets positively civilised, with a queue of vineyards and primary producers dotted along the trail all the way into Bright. But it's not as if all the fun is in the stops. This side of Taylors Gap, the landscape seems decidedly brighter, and the rail trail passes through a rural landscape populated by cows, horses, goats, kookaburras and cockatoos, and for children on a bicycle it all seems within view and touch.

From the winery, it's just 7 kilometres (4.5 miles) to our night's stop in Myrtleford, a rural town long regarded as little more than a gateway into the mountain grandeur of Victoria's High Country, but which is now sprinkled with good cafes, restaurants and a wine bar.

Cycling past Gapsted Wines

DAY 2

MYRTLEFORD TO BRIGHT (32KM/20 MILES)

Past Myrtleford, as Mount Buffalo begins to fill the view, there are signs of what might be called the Ovens Valley's misspent youth. Tobacco once grew all through this valley, and it's still dotted with tobacco kilns, including one that's been converted into a cafe just outside of Myrtleford.

Today the tobacco is gone, but its natural companion – beer – remains, with the rail trail rolling past the fields of one of Australia's major hop-growing areas. Cycle past at harvest time, as I've done before, and the scent can be intoxicating. Luckily, there are fine and inviting craft breweries in both Bright and Beechworth, though the kids, of course, are far more interested in the valley's berries and the possibility of an ice-cream or three.

The ride from Myrtleford to Bright is gentle, almost always climbing but imperceptibly. The Great Alpine Road is right beside us now, but so beautiful is the landscape that I barely even notice it. It's unquestionably the most attractive section of the rail trail. The bare granite walls of a deep gorge on Mount Buffalo rise above the foothills, the hop fields look like hanging gardens, Mount Hotham peeps through a break in the mountains and, as the trail nears Bright, our home for the night, it becomes lined with poplars that turn to ingots of gold in autumn.

Bright has long been the mountain town of choice for Victorian holidaymakers, drawn here by the nearby ski fields in winter and the mountain access in summer, though the town has an inviting beauty of its own, with parks (and the brewery) lining the Ovens River, and quality eateries lining the streets.

Below Overlooking Bright *Oppsoite* Rolling downhill from Beechworth

DAY 3

BRIGHT TO MYRTLEFORD (32KM/20 MILES)

In Bright, we pause before turning back on our own tracks along the rail trail. Instead of riding directly back to Wangaratta, however, we will detour (on day four) up into the hills to Beechworth.

The first day on the return ride is as leisurely as it's possible to get, retracing our route to Myrtleford. From Bright, the rail trail slopes ever so slightly downhill, so time is abundant, allowing us even more indulgence in winery and ice-cream stops. There's a strong chance that by the time we roll into Myrtleford, more calories have gone into our bodies than have gone out.

DAYS 4–5

MYRTLEFORD TO BEECHWORTH (41KM/25.5 MILES); BEECHWORTH TO WANGARATTA (43KM/27 MILES)

As we leave Myrtleford the next morning the forecast is for rain, and there are comforting words from my passenger.

'It doesn't matter if it rains,' Kiri chirps. 'It's only water.' Easy words from someone who will be cocooned inside a trailer.

Our other passenger is more conspiratorial about the conditions. 'Mum and Dad are going to get soooo wet,' Cooper says to Kiri in those toddler whispers that aren't whispers at all.

In nearby Albury, 25 millimetres (one inch) of rain will fall this day, but we ride as if in a rain shadow, remaining dry all the way to the base of the climb to Beechworth, which starts around 25 kilometres (15.5 miles) from Myrtleford.

This detour to Beechworth – the most demanding section of the rail trail's various tentacles – rises up the hills that enclose the northern edge of the Ovens Valley. It's not steep, but it is persistent, climbing almost 400 metres (1310 feet) over 16 kilometres (10 miles).

But at least I have help for the climb, or so I think. As we begin the ascent, moving slower than even the I-think-I-can locomotives of days gone by, I look behind me, expecting to see Kiri pushing in earnest from within her trailer. But she is asleep. I will have to shoulder the burden of this climb alone.

Beechworth is a welcome reward atop the climb. The popular tourist town is famed for its gold rush, bakery, lolly shop

and the prison time of Australia's favourite bushranger, Ned Kelly. The vast golden wealth of the 19th century also helped furnish the streets with enough grand architecture to turn Beechworth into one of Victoria's most beautiful heritage towns.

The other beauty about Beechworth is the very thing that awaits us the next morning – the long descent back down the hill, before we turn west and return along the rail trail to Wangaratta. We roll off the hill, gathering momentum, and there are no offers of help coming from within the trailer now. I can only hear squeals of delight.

Helpful resources

Full details about Murray to Mountains, including accommodation and other services and a downloadable map, can be found online (ridehighcountry.com.au).
At the rail trail's ends, Rock and Road Cycles (Wangaratta, rockandroadcycles.com.au) and Cyclepath (Bright, cyclepath.com.au) hire out bikes, including ebikes. The Beechworth-based Bike Hire Company (thebikehirecompany.com.au) also rents out bikes that can be delivered to you anywhere along the trail, and operates self-guided tours.

East Coast Tasmania

AUSTRALIA

Cross rainforested hills to reach a vibrantly coloured coastline and Maria Island, rich in wildlife.

CYCLISTS

East Coast Tasmania

WHY IT'S SPECIAL

Constructing a long bike tour in Australia isn't always a simple task. Distances are large, landscapes can be fierce, and often the only feasible road option is Highway 1, which makes a 13,500-kilometre (8388-mile) circuit of the country. With all that in mind, Tasmania is undoubtedly the country's most enticing cycling destination.

Tasmania's east coast is as colourful and stunning as any in the world, and this ride runs as close to shore as it's possible to get, while also passing through one of the world's great mountain-biking towns, Derby. You won't find quieter highways in too many other parts of the world.

The east is adorned with dazzling white beaches and turquoise waters, fewer climbs than in the west of the state, and a summer swarm of cyclists. It is dotted with holiday towns and the wild glory of the Freycinet Peninsula and Maria Island.

BEST TIME TO RIDE

Early to mid-autumn (Mar and Apr) is prime time to be cycling in Tasmania, with stable weather conditions and the lightest winds. Summer (Dec through Feb) is also good for cycling, albeit peppered with a very hot day here and there. Spring (Sept to Nov) can be windy.

RIDE IT

The thread that connects Hobart to Launceston along the east coast is the Tasman Highway (A3, now branded as the Great Eastern Drive). It's a highway only in name, being generally light on traffic, though it does get narrow and tight at times, and traffic volumes do ramp up during the state's summer holidays (Christmas and Jan) and around Easter. There's no compelling reason to cycle in one specific direction, but I've decided to begin in Launceston so that I'll be on the ocean side of the road as I pedal, and the toughest of the climbs will be out of the way early.

Tasmania is the most mountainous state in Australia, and the roads on the hinterland crossings - from Launceston to St Helens, and from Orford to Hobart - get particularly tight and hilly. Whichever direction you ride means starting through the hills, so you'll want to have done some training for this trip, though there's also the option of shortening the daily distances, with the entire route liberally sprinkled with towns and accommodation options.

Nuts & bolts
Distance: 550 kilometres (341 miles)
Days: 10
Ascent: 5500 metres (18,050 feet)
Difficulty: Medium
Bike: Though this ride can be done entirely on sealed roads, a mountain bike is recommended if you want to get the best of the experience, riding the North East Rail Trail, exploring the mountain-bike tracks at Derby and venturing out to Maria Island.

Previous Lilydale Falls *Opposite top left* Vineyard in the Tamar Valley *Top right* Mountain-biking at Derby *Bottom left* The Gardens in the Bay of Fires *Bottom right* Cycling sign on Freycinet Peninsula

Another thing to prepare yourself for is the presence of roadkill. It's been estimated that around 500,000 animals are killed on Tasmanian roads every year, which is in part a reflection on the vast quantity of wildlife in the state. It's inevitable that you'll see plenty of roadkill - wallabies and possums, mostly - though by the slow and unenclosed nature of cycling, you're likely to smell it before you see it.

You can feasibly cycle between Launceston and Hobart along either the east coast or west coast, but the east coast, as described here, is very much the cyclists' coast. The west coast is a place of mountain roads, swathes of World Heritage–listed wilderness and the lion's share of Tasmania's rainfall. In comparison to the ride described here, the west coast stacks on an extra 3000 metres (9850 feet) of climbing along the way.

Below Trailside mushrooms on the Derby mountain bike network *Opposite* The North East Rail Trail

ITINERARY

DAY 1

LAUNCESTON TO SCOTTSDALE (68KM/42 MILES)

As I pack my panniers in the small city of Launceston, a couple of options present for the ride to Scottsdale. I can set straight out along the Tasman Highway, but that is to inflict the east coast's most difficult climb - up and over a line of hills known as the Sideling - onto fresh legs. Instead, I choose the B81 road that skirts to the north, where I climb more gently through tall forest to Lilydale, pausing for a short stroll into Lilydale Falls, before skirting the edge of the Tamar Valley wine region and out into open farmland. By the time I reach the former forestry town of workaday Scottsdale, I've done much the same amount of climbing as if I'd pedalled the highway, but in a gentler, more prolonged fashion.

DAYS 2–3

SCOTTSDALE TO DERBY (42KM/26 MILES); DERBY TO ST HELENS (65KM/40 MILES)

My route merges with the highway in Scottsdale, but I don't need to continue on roads. In the centre of town, I find the trailhead for the North East Rail Trail and for the next 26 kilometres (16 miles) I ride without seeing a car or even another bike, curling along the course of the former Launceston-to-Branxholm railway. The rail trail stays close to the highway for the first 9 kilometres (5.5 miles), then disappears into blissful, fern-lined isolation, squeezing at one stage between the 10-metre-high (33-foot) granite walls of a cutting blasted through the rock. Momentarily, it feels more like a gorge than a railway.

The rail trail ends at Billycock Hill, the second of the high points along the highway, from where it's a cruise down into Branxholm and to the newest member of Tasmanian cycling royalty - the former tin-mining town of Derby. If you're on a mountain bike (or if you want to hire one from one of the bike stores in town), Derby could happily delay your journey by a day or two (or three ... or four). As recently as 2014, Derby was a forlorn, dying town, with the tin and most of its life stripped away. Then in 2015, the Blue Derby mountain-bike trail network opened, earning such raps that the town is now considered among the world's best mountain-bike destinations. If mountain biking is in any way in your cycling arsenal, you'll want to pause and ride some trails here, or at the very least, delay the final climb before the coast.

Having skipped the Sideling, it's the Blue Tier immediately beyond Derby that presents my ride's toughest climb, with

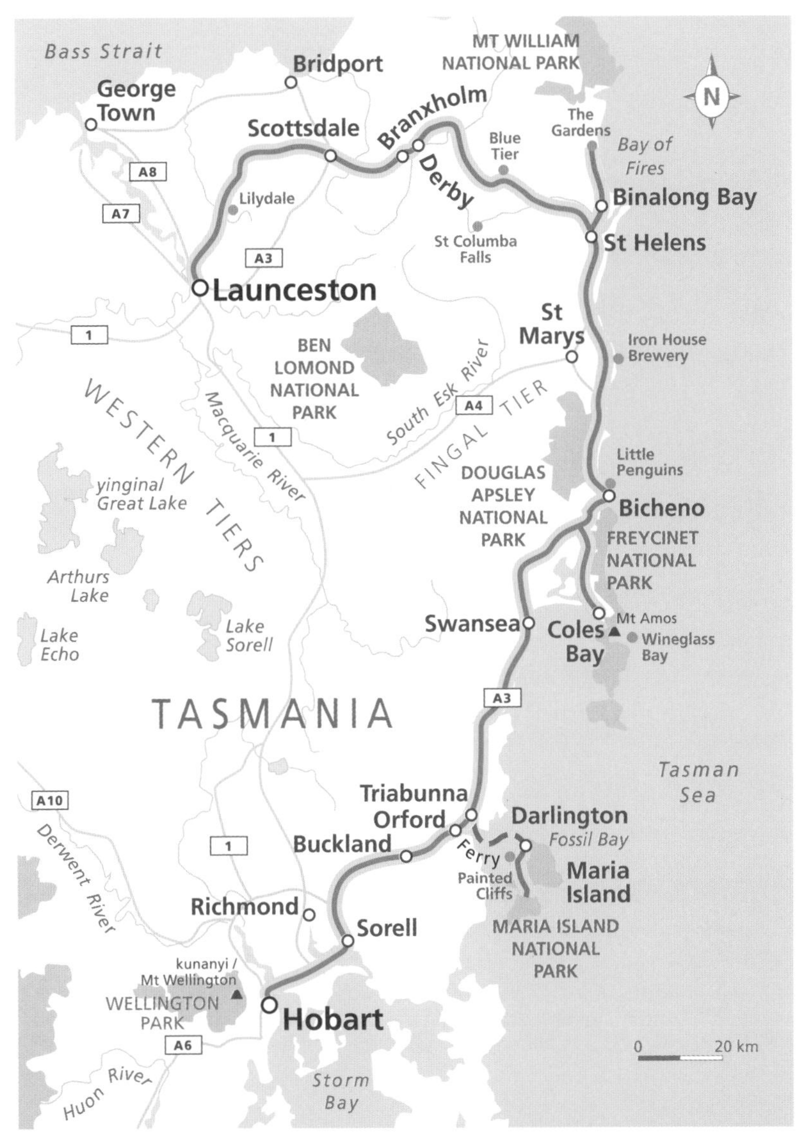

LOCAL SNAPSHOT

Mountainous Maria Island is entirely national park, but it has a human history that's just as fascinating as its natural history. At its northern end is the former settlement of Darlington, which was established as a convict station in 1825 in a location of such beauty that one political prisoner wrote, 'To find a gaol in one of the loveliest spots formed by the hand of nature in one of her loneliest solitudes creates a revulsion of feeling I cannot describe'. Darlington had such a reputation for laxity and escape attempts that it was replaced by the infamous Port Arthur convict station in 1833 (though Darlington later served as a probation station in the 1840s).

In the 1880s, an entrepreneur named Diego Bernacchi leased the island and tried to transform Darlington into a flourishing industrial and tourist centre. He built a cement works, planted grape vines, started silk production and immodestly renamed the place San Diego. To tourists he spruiked the island as the 'Riviera of Australia'. By 1896 it had all gone pear-shaped and Bernacchi left the island, only to return in 1925 for another short and failed attempt at cement production.

Bernacchi's son, Louis was one of Australia's first Antarctic expeditioners, including as a member of Robert Scott's first expedition – Scott was best man at Louis Bernacchi's wedding.

the highway ascending around 450 metres (1475 feet) through thickly rainforested slopes. I advance about as slowly as the trees grow, though fortunately Derby's main street has a couple of good cafes for a carb load to sustain me over the range.

The Blue Tier climb tops out at around 600 metres (1970 feet) above sea level, creating a hurtling descent to the coast, 35 kilometres (22 miles) away in St Helens. The northernmost of the holiday towns on Tasmania's east coast, St Helens is also home to the state's largest fishing fleet. If the adrenaline of Derby's mountain biking is still coursing through your system, St Helens opened its own network of mountain-bike trails immediately south of town in 2019.

DAY 4

RETURN DAY RIDE TO THE GARDENS (43KM/27 MILES)

An enticing detour awaits in St Helens. Running north from the town is the Bay of Fires, with a coastline as bright as its name suggests. The beaches are white and the seas are turquoise, but the most striking feature is the orange lichen that seems almost airbrushed across the granite headlands that divide the bay's beaches. Behind the bay, there's a quiet no-through road from St Helens to the holiday settlement of The Gardens, and this is a coast so spectacular that it's worth adding a day just to explore it. It's a day that's like a seaside holiday on wheels.

From St Helens, the road climbs over Humbug Hill, before flattening out behind the beaches. I dart down tracks to discover campgrounds and perfect slices of beach, before turning around at The Gardens and returning over Humbug Hill to St Helens.

DAYS 5–6

ST HELENS TO BICHENO (75KM/46.5 MILES); BICHENO TO COLES BAY (35KM/22 MILES)

My journey south begins along what is inarguably one of the most beautiful coastlines in Australia. If you could dial the water temperature up a few degrees, it might be one of the country's great seaside holiday coasts, and yet often the only infrastructure in sight is a few fishing rods staked into empty stretches of sand.

For these few days, I will ride largely in view of this coastline, which unspools as a string of long beaches separated by clusters of boulders.

So perfect are the distances between towns along this coast that they might have been placed by a cyclist. No day is too long; no day is too short. The day of cycling from St Helens will be my longest along the coast – especially when I factor in a necessary beer stop at the Iron House Brewery on a remote slice of coast 40 kilometres (25 miles) from St Helens – and yet it's pure seaside pleasure all the way to Bicheno, which is probably my favourite of the east coast towns. This fishing town, about half the size of St Helens, goes about its local life barely disturbed by the regular flow of holidaymakers, or by the little penguins that march ashore across its beach every night. Bicheno sits pressed against a rocky, rugged shoreline where a blowhole shoots like a geyser with each arriving wave. It could look like a harsh, brutal coast were it not also for the presence of glorious white beaches.

The custom-made design of the cycling days is most evident the next day as I detour off the highway along the C302 road onto Freycinet Peninsula and Coles Bay. It's just 35 kilometres (22 miles) to Tasmania's most cherished coastal holiday town – a couple of hours of riding, allowing ample time for a walk to one of Tasmania's most emblematic natural scenes: Wineglass Bay.

This beach, shaped like the glassware of its name (but actually named because of the whale hunting that used to turn the water red like wine), is separated from roads by the low Hazards mountains, so can only be seen on foot. There's an easy-to-reach lookout in a low pass through the mountains, with a track that then continues down to the bay's coarse white sands. The best view, however, comes at the end of a more challenging walk to the summit of Mt Amos, scrambling up granite slabs to a boulder-strewn mountaintop that's like an opera box above the beach.

DAY 7

COLES BAY TO SWANSEA (50KM/31 MILES)

The next morning, I return along the peninsula road (C302) and rejoin the Tasman Highway. Though I'm briefly retracing my route, the beauty of cycling remains as ever in the detail – those things that you see from a bike that you never see from a car. Things like the echidnas scratching at the roadside, and the lingering glimpses of Moulting Lagoon, a large shallow lake that's like a marina for black swans.

Back on the highway, the ride turns off the coast for a time to climb through low hills, snaking through beautiful farmland, with just a hint of ocean in the breeze. As I roll down the hills towards the small town of Swansea, vineyards appear again – would a cheeky morning wine be okay? – and the coast and highway reunite as I enter town.

DAY 8

SWANSEA TO TRIABUNNA (50KM/31 MILES)

Swansea heralds the start of the highway's most spectacular section. It's the hilliest bit of the coastal section of the ride, but each time it rises over crests, it seems to reveal new beaches and rocky shores, with the peaks of the Freycinet Peninsula seeming to bubble up out of the ocean. A convict bridge spiked with sharp stones stands immediately beside the highway, and on Tasmania's driest edge, yellow plains

Above Wineglass Bay *Opposite* Cycling the Tasman Highway

end at white beaches and pure blue seas. I stop at one empty beach where the high-tide line is marked by a strip of scallop shells hundred of metres long, and when the road edges away from the coast, the landscape is dotted with lagoons that are in turn dotted with black swans.

This night's stop – the one-time wood-chipping town of Triabunna – is a prelude to greater things, with wild and car-free Maria Island rising steeply offshore and beckoning me.

DAY 9

DAY RIDE ON MARIA ISLAND (37KM/23 MILES)

In a direct line, Maria Island is just 7 kilometres (4 miles) off the Tasmanian coast, rising from the sea like a giant green whale. The World Heritage–listed Darlington convict settlement at its northern end is wrapped inside national park lands and 700-metre-high (2300-foot) mountains. Maria's gift to cyclists is a network of roads and tracks, where the only traffic is the island's copious wildlife, since vehicles are banned here (except for park ranger vehicles).

In Triabunna, I roll my bike onto the island ferry, which crosses to the island five times a day in summer, and soon I'm pedalling off the pier at Darlington and into the convict settlement, where the buildings remain remarkably intact.

Dirt roads radiate out from Darlington, heading north to the edge of the Fossil Cliffs, which are composed of millions of ancient marine fossils, and south to the wider island – follow these roads and it's possible to ride 20 kilometres (12.5 miles) to Haunted Bay on the island's south coast.

My goal is the island's isthmus, the filament of sand that effectively ties two islands together as one. The road to the isthmus leaves through Darlington's extensive lawns, which are nibbled to putting-green perfection by the wallabies, wombats and Cape Barren geese that even now wander casually about. Come evening, these lawns are about the most reliable place in the world to sight a wild Tasmanian devil, the threatened creature that is the unofficial symbol of Tasmania.

Even before the lawns have ended, the road passes above Maria's most striking sight, the Painted Cliffs, a line of low sandstone cliffs seemingly hand-painted with natural patterns. Try to be here around low tide, when you can wander along the base of the cliffs, taking in the natural gallery of its rock.

Past Frenchs Farm, where the French family were among the island's last farmers before it was declared a national park in 1972, the island constricts into McRaes Isthmus, which feels about as thin as a chicken bone – at its centre you need walk less than 100 metres (330 feet) left or right to find beaches. By the time I return to Triabunna on the ferry, I'm just one solid day of riding from Hobart.

DAY 10

TRIABUNNA TO HOBART (85KM/53 MILES)

It's a long day in the saddle today, among building traffic on narrow, hilly roads, so settle into a groove and look forward to the sight of Tasmania's beautiful capital city crouched beneath the 1270-metre (4167-foot) kunanyi/Mt Wellington.

The highway leaves the coast at the holiday town of Orford, 6 kilometres (4 miles) south of Triabunna, and I begin rising up the Prosser Valley on the Tasman Highway. Faintly visible across the valley is an old convict road scratching through the bush.

This inland crossing returns hills to the journey, at least until the highway rolls down into the town of Sorell near Hobart's edge, from where it's an easy ride past Hobart's airport and over the Tasman Bridge to my finish in Tasmania's largest city, a place that is the perfect marriage of water and mountain.

With more than a week of cycling in my legs, these hills feel nowhere near as challenging as the climbs between Launceston and St Helens, but someone before me clearly disagreed. West of Buckland, the highway rises over climbs with the disgruntled names of Bust-Me-Gall Hill and Break-Me-Neck Hill. There's a fair chance they were named by cyclists.

Helpful resources

Touring bikes and panniers can be hired in Launceston and dropped off in Hobart (or vice versa) through Long Haul Tasmania (longhaultasmania.com.au).
A touring bike will be okay on the North East Rail Trail and Maria Island. If you want to ride the trails at Derby, however, you will need to hire a mountain bike from Vertigo MTB (vertigomtb.com.au) or Evolution Biking (ebiketasmania.com.au).

Opposite Cycling out of Darlington, Maria Island

Kate Leeming

One of Australia's most accomplished explorers, Kate has cycled a distance greater than twice the world's circumference on her major expeditions through Europe, Russia, Australia and Africa. For the last five years, Kate has been preparing to make the first bicycle crossing of the Antarctic continent via the South Pole. Kate has published two books, *Out There and Back*, the story of her 25,000-kilometre (15,500-mile) Great Australian Cycle Expedition and *Njinga, Breaking the Cycle in Africa*. In 2014, Kate's first feature documentary, also titled *Njinga*, won several awards at the Action on Film International Film Festival in LA. She is producing her second film about her world-first ride down Namibia's notorious Skeleton Coast. See: breakingthecycle.education

What was your first bike trip?

Cycling in France or Italy seemed an unattainable dream, until 1990 when I first travelled to the UK to play hockey for my university. After the tour, I did my first little trip with a friend in Ireland, hiring some mountain bikes from a local fisherman and cycling for five days through counties Cork and Kerry. I was immediately sold on this form of travel. Back in London, I set myself up for bicycle touring and planned a longer journey through France and Spain. Over the next two years, I rode a total of 15,000 kilometres (9300 miles) in Europe, through the Mediterranean countries to Turkey, the Alps and through Norway to Nord Kapp, Europe's most northerly tip.

What impact did that trip have on you and your life?

My European cycle journeys enabled me to discover my passion and learn what I could achieve on a bike. I loved bringing a line on a map to life. Cycling from one destination to another under my own steam gave me great personal satisfaction and also fired my motivation to explore further. Pedalling through constantly changing landscapes in all sorts of conditions while taking in the sights, sounds and smells, I felt I was travelling harmoniously within the environment.

What to you is the unique special quality about cycle travel?

The bicycle is a simple yet humble tool for adventure that provides a wonderfully close connection with the people and the land. My bikes always feel like an extension of me. Bicycle travel enables me to better understand how each region, country and, subsequently, the world fits together.

Where have been your favourite places to cycle?

West Sayan Mountains, Russia

In 1993, I completed my first major expedition, the Trans-Siberian Cycle Expedition, in aid of the children of Chernobyl. In addition to pedalling a continuous line from St Petersburg to Vladivostok, I chose to cycle a 1200-kilometre (745-mile) loop around the West Sayan Mountains. It is always the extra effort that brings the greatest rewards. Crossing the spectacular 2200-metre (7217-foot) West Sayan Pass, the highest on the circuit, we left the grasslands and forests of Khakasia and entered Tuva, a land of yaks and yurts. Alpine meadows carpeted with dainty purple, yellow and white wildflowers soon gave way to the stark, rugged mountains that flank the mighty Yenisei River.

Ladakh, Indian Himalaya

I have done two different cycle journeys through Ladakh and will no doubt return again in the near-future. I find it a very spiritual place, located at the junction of the Himalayan and Karakoram ranges. It is a high-altitude desert where the only vegetation is found as ribbons of greenery along the banks of glacial rivers that carve paths through the bare, mineral-rich mountains. Cycling in Ladakh (*see* p. 183) is challenging due to the altitudes involved, with many passes between 4500 metres and 5400 metres (14,000 to 18,000 feet), but the effort is always incredibly rewarding.

The Skeleton Coast, Namibia

In 2019, I made the first ever cycle journey down Namibia's entire coastline, 1600 kilometres (994 miles) from the mouth of the Kunene River on the Angolan border to the Orange River mouth on the South African border. This is one of the harshest environments on Earth – the Namib Desert is the world's oldest and one of the driest deserts. The San people called the coast 'the land that God made in anger'. But out of the harshest of environments comes beauty. I love the challenges of learning to adapt and cope in such unforgiving places. It builds resolve and I get to learn much more about myself, as well as the incredible history and natural features of this largely pristine land.

What's your one essential bit of kit on a cycle trip?

The kit I use varies a lot, depending on the type of journey – unsupported or supported, mountain bike or fat bike, remoteness, polar or warm climate. Perhaps a constant requirement is decent mountain-bike shoes or boots with hard soles and cleats to clip into pedals for efficiency and to protect your feet but also enable you to walk freely off the bike.

If you could pick one place to cycle, where would it be?

I still have many places on my bucket-list. The next expedition is called 'The Andes, the Altiplano and the Atacama', a 3500-kilometre (2200-mile) altitude expedition though South America (Peru, Bolivia, Argentina, Chile). I plan to pedal to altitudes of around 5700 metres (18,700 feet), before finishing on Ojos del Salado, the world's highest volcano in Chile. This is one of six expeditions helping me prepare physically and mentally for Breaking the Cycle South Pole, my planned bicycle crossing of Antarctica via the South Pole.

Below Kate Leeming at the origin of the Finke River, Northern Territory *Opposite* Cycling the Canning Stock Route in Western Australia

Alps 2 Ocean
NEW ZEALAND

A mountains-to-sea ride on New Zealand's longest cycling trail.

Alps 2 Ocean

WHY IT'S SPECIAL

During the Global Financial Crisis in 2008, New Zealand hatched a genius idea – invest $50 million in building cycle routes across the country. Already arguably the world's best and most varied adventure destination, the country set about creating a network of cycling trails that has now also elevated it among the finest places on the planet to ride.

New Zealand is now home to 22 listed Great Rides, covering more than 2500 kilometres (1550 miles). Alps 2 Ocean is one of the Great Rides, as well as being New Zealand's longest dedicated cycling trail. Riding it brings the kudos of cycling from the foot of the country's highest mountain to the sea, almost entirely away from busy roads.

BEST TIME TO RIDE

Autumn (Mar to May) and spring (Sept to Nov) are the finest times on Alps 2 Ocean, away from the summer tourist crowds and the chilly winters around Mt Cook Village and Lake Ohau.

RIDE IT

Alps 2 Ocean begins on the South Island at the foot of the country's highest mountain, 3724-metre (12,217-foot) Aoraki/Mt Cook, and ends 306 kilometres (190 miles) later on the coast in the town of Oamaru. As that description sweetly suggests, the trail's trend is downhill (overall, a 750-metre, or 2460-foot, difference in altitude from start to finish), but this is no bobsled ride to the bottom. Along the way there's also around 2500 metres (8200 feet) of ascent, including a couple of sharp climbs.

Though Alps 2 Ocean begins in Aoraki/Mt Cook Village, the tourist centre that's almost in touching distance of Aoraki/Mt Cook, there's one complication. To ride the trail in its entirety, you have to somehow get across the Tasman River, which is unbridged and impassable from ground level. To combat this, a helicopter ride from Aoraki/Mt Cook Village's airport to the opposite bank of the Tasman River is officially part of the ride. It can be considered either a bonus bit of flight-seeing, or a drain on your wallet. Or you can do what most cyclists do and begin the trail across the Tasman River, cutting out the first 8 kilometres (4.9 miles), or in the town of Tekapo at the end of a 30-kilometre (18.5-mile) spur trail.

I've cycled Alps 2 Ocean twice, and on my most recent ride I decided to pedal it from go to whoa, complete with helicopter shuttle. But in this alpine environment, the best-laid plans are at the mercy of nature.

Nuts & bolts

Distance: 306 kilometres (190 miles)
Days: 5
Ascent: 2500 metres (8200 feet)
Difficulty: Medium
Bike: For most of its journey, the ride is on hard-packed trails, providing easy surfaces for anything but a road bike, although there's one section between Lake Ohau and Quailburn Road that's best suited to a mountain bike. Given the choice of bikes, a hardtail mountain bike would be the ideal.

Previous Lake Pukaki *Opposite* The Hooker Valley and Aoraki/Mt Cook

DAY 1

AORAKI/MT COOK VILLAGE TO TWIZEL (77KM/48 MILES)

When I arrive in Aoraki/Mt Cook Village on the afternoon before I begin riding, the landscape is aglow in sunshine. By the next morning, however, the mountains have been devoured by cloud, and furious winds roar through the Hooker Valley, gusting to around 100km/h (62mp/h). All helicopter flights have been grounded. I will be starting across the other side of the Tasman River, after all.

Just a few kilometres from this pseudo-start, the Tasman River pours into Lake Pukaki. A corrugated unsealed road runs along this lake's eastern edge, forming this initial section of the Alps 2 Ocean trail. Traffic is minimal – two cars pass in an hour, creating a welcome counterbalance to the main road into Aoraki/Mt Cook Village, which runs along the lake's opposite shore, often in view across the water as I ride. The pyramid-like summit of Aoraki/Mt Cook sits over my shoulder, albeit erased by cloud and storms this day, and the fjord-like Lake Pukaki is the impossible blue that is unique to glacier-fed lakes, with their waters coloured by the fine particles of rock ground down by moving ice.

Approaching the head of the lake, 40 kilometres (25 miles) along the road, the ride turns away onto the sort of wide and wonderful bike path that defines Alps 2 Ocean, winding its way around the shores to the lake's southern point. On fine days, a large carpark here is treated to one of New Zealand's most famous views – a mirror-perfect reflection of Aoraki/ Mt Cook and the Southern Alps – but on stormy days like this one, the water is a marauding mess of white-capped waves and the view is menacing. The only thing that's flat right now is the way ahead, with the trail crossing the well-named Pukaki Flats that stretch improbably between the mountains to my first night's stop in Twizel.

DAY 2

TWIZEL TO LAKE OHAU (38KM/23.5 MILES)

Twizel is an unprepossessing town that was built in the late 1960s to house workers on a hydroelectric scheme being carved through the Waitaki Valley. Dams were built and canals sliced into the alpine landscape. Fifty years after their construction, the canals have become a belated blessing for cyclists. From Twizel to Lake Ohau, Alps 2 Ocean predominantly follows the canals, riding on roads as unfailingly flat as rail trails. The waterways are blue lines

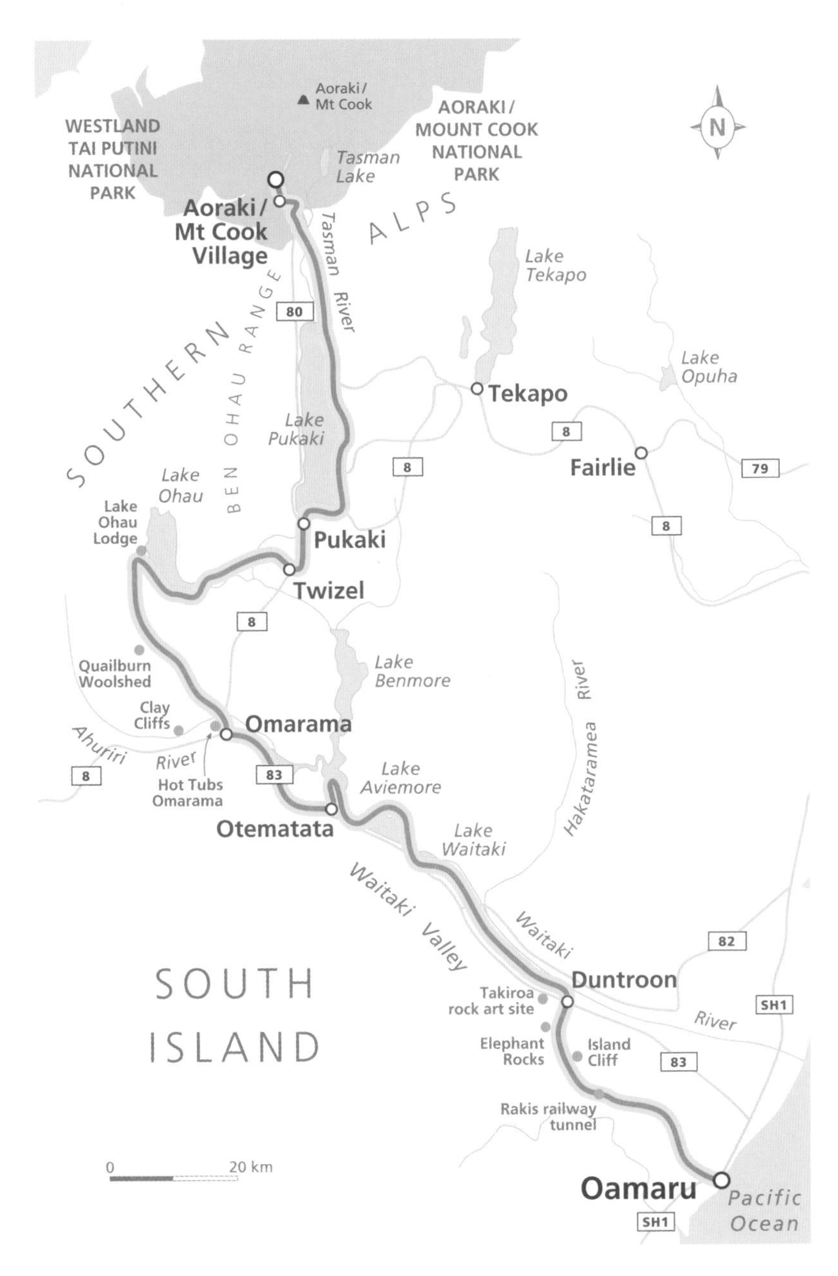

Opposite Suspension bridge over the Hooker River
Right Cycling along the shores of Lake Pukaki
Overleaf Trail above Lake Ohau

LOCAL SNAPSHOT

In some ways, Alps 2 Ocean is a modern incarnation of a traditional pathway. The Waitaki Valley, which forms the backbone of this ride, was used by Māori as a corridor from the Southern Alps to the sea, long before it was popularised by bikes. The Ngāi Tahu people would travel the river in rafts, connecting coastal areas to the Mackenzie Basin, where eels and weka (a flightless New Zealand bird) were abundant – three tonnes of birds were collected in the final recorded harvest in 1870. Today, the most visible reminder of this history is the Takiroa rock art site, which you'll cycle past just before reaching Duntroon. Many other rock art sites were flooded during the creation of Benmore and Aviemore Lakes in the 1960s.

through a yellow landscape, and the roads are free of vehicles, creating a wonderful sense of remoteness, but all the while on smooth and flat roads. The Pukaki Canal becomes the Ohau Canal, which is lined with salmon pens. As I pass the pens, anglers stand at their edges, tossing in lines in hope of snaring escapees for dinner.

The canal ends at Lake Ohau, where the trail crosses a weir and wraps around the lake's southern edge, heading far up its shores to the base of the road to the Ohau ski fields, which is deathly quiet outside the winter ski season. The singletrack trail runs tight against the water, where the pebbly shores are covered in lupins and driftwood washed down from the valleys. The lake itself is like another blue tile laid across the floor of the mountains, which are now slowly untangling themselves from cloud. White glaciers are finally replacing white cloud.

Like most Alps 2 Ocean cyclists, I'm staying this night at Lake Ohau Lodge, which is propped above the lake at the end of a driveway lined with tall ponderosa pines. When I first cycled Alps 2 Ocean during its construction in 2012, I sat here alone, eating with the lodge owners, but such is the ride's ever-growing popularity that on this night, seven years later, bikes stand outside almost every room, waiting for their moment on Alps 2 Ocean's biggest climb first thing in the morning.

DAY 3

LAKE OHAU TO OMARAMA (45KM/28 MILES)

'Ohau' means place of wind, but all is still and calm as the climb begins this morning. The lake is rolled out like tin, and Aoraki/Mt Cook peeps over the Ben Ohau Range across its opposite shore. The 300-metre (985-foot) climb begins immediately, cutting a straight line across the slopes - always up, but never too steep. Even though it's the climb that occupied everybody's thoughts in the lodge last night, it's the descent that packs the bigger punch. The downhill track is lumpy and bumpy, with tight turns at the top and splashing through streams at the bottom, where it turns upstream to the remains of the Quailburn Woolshed, hidden high up a valley. This shearing shed, built of beech poles in the 1920s, is now dilapidated, but it provides a snapshot of a time when 80,000 sheep a year would be sheared here.

From the woolshed, a dirt road rolls almost all the way to the town of Omarama, 26 kilometres (16 miles) away, but a good side trip beckons as Omarama nears. Just 7 kilometres (4.3 miles) off the trail, along an often-corrugated road, the

Clay Cliffs are a line of fluted clay pinnacles rising above the Ahuriri River - they look like something from Cappadocia (Turkey), with a southern hemisphere address. Bring a bike lock, as you'll need to park your bike and walk the final section to the cliffs.

Omarama is the point at which Alps 2 Ocean turns its back on the mountains, which are now just a pigment on the horizon, and heads for the coast. The town is just 30 kilometres (18.5 miles) by road from Twizel, and yet I've cycled more than 80 kilometres (50 miles) from Twizel to get here - such has been the circuitous nature of the ride until now. Relief doesn't come so much in the arrival of the Waitaki Valley and the direct course to the coast, however, but in the presence of Hot Tubs Omarama, where outdoor tubs filled with mountain water are heated by wood-fires. They provide a chance to soak away cycling aches under a sky ablaze with stars.

DAY 4

OMARAMA TO DUNTROON (96KM/59.5 MILES)

From Omarama, the Waitaki Valley steps down towards the coast past a series of lakes, beginning with Lake Benmore, where the trail all but overhangs the water, with just a low fence preventing a cycle becoming a swim.

The lakes will dominate this day's riding, which is mostly a cruise downstream, with long sections of freewheeling broken by a climb to a saddle between lakes Benmore and Aviemore. It's one of the few sections on a busy road - Highway 83 - along the entire trail. The prevailing winds are at least typically behind you through this valley, although a growing headwind anchors me into a long, slow grind over the saddle. I'm more than ready for the coffee van that awaits at its base in the small town of Otematata.

In Otematata, the ride leaves the highway again, rounding the shores of Lake Aviemore and making a sharp climb to the top of Benmore Dam, where there's a grandstand view of the lake, enclosed by barren hills, with water-skiers and jet-skiers skimming across the waters.

For the next 70 kilometres (43.5 miles), the riding is simplicity itself, following roads, trails and briefly the highway again as Alps 2 Ocean descends through the Waitaki Valley, losing 200 metres (650 feet) in altitude.

Around 5 kilometres (3 miles) before Duntroon, I stop at a Māori rock art site tucked into low limestone cliffs across the highway from the trail. The 19th-century drawings

portray people riding horses, European sailing ships and the red figures of Taniwha, the large water creatures of Māori tradition, though much of the art was cut away by early archaeologists and carted away to museums.

I ride on and in a few minutes come to my night's stop in Duntroon.

DAY 5

DUNTROON TO OAMARU (54KM/33.5 MILES)

Takiroa is the first of a pair of rock stars either side of Duntroon. As the ride leaves the Waitaki Valley from the small town, it scales the slopes to the evocatively named Elephant Rocks. The last 2 kilometres (1.2 miles) to the rocks is uphill, so that I'm almost bellowing like the said elephants when I arrive into one of those fantasy landscapes that New Zealand does so well – there's a reason the country made such a good Middle-earth in Peter Jackson's *Lord of the Rings* film trilogy. Sitting among some of the most fertile farmland imaginable are knuckles of limestone that protrude in myriad shapes – it's rock moulded like pottery.

The trail climbs on past the rocks, which end only in name rather than nature. Shortly after leaving Elephant Rocks, it's as though I'm right back in them again, as the trail ducks intermittently into narrow limestone gorges, with rock walls eroded in a wonderland of shapes.

It's hilly terrain on this section of riding above the Waitaki Valley, but for a time the trail weaves through the folds in the land, so that even though I'm riding through a lumpy landscape framed with limestone escarpments, the way is flat. That ends abruptly as the trail comes to a switchbacking climb that only gets steeper as the ride continues up dirt roads to finally crest the hills at Island Cliff, around 350 metres (1150 feet) above sea level. The Pacific Ocean is suddenly in sight beyond another glorious descent and the 100-metre (328-foot) Rakis railway tunnel, where day will momentarily turn to night before I set off across the coastal plains to Oamaru and the trail's end. I roll off the top of the hills and let gravity finish the work for me.

Above The trail near Kurow *Opposite top* Elephant Rocks
Bottom Cycling through the Rakis Tunnel

Riding resources

Alps 2 Ocean's official website (alps2ocean.com) is a wealth of information, dishing up everything from daily trail descriptions to accommodation and eating options. Self-guided and guided ride options are plentiful; local operator Adventure South (adventuresouth.co.nz) is one of the few that runs an end-to-end trip that includes the helicopter transfer over the Tasman River.

AUSTRALIA & NEW ZEALAND

Old Ghost Road

NEW ZEALAND

Mountain-biking magic across the rugged peaks of New Zealand's South Island.

THE OLD GHOST ROAD

Old Ghost Road

WHY IT'S SPECIAL

New Zealand's longest singletrack ride provides a rare sense of journey on a mountain bike, rising through both the mountains and a golden history. The ride's alpine sections are as exhilarating as any cycling route in the world.

Sometimes across the open tops of the Lyell Range, it's not clear whether the ghosts are past or present. As one end of your handlebars all but scrapes against the cliffs, and the other seems to overhang a drop of hundreds of metres, the Old Ghost Road may well play haunting games with your mind, but you only need look up to view the mountain scenery and the track cutting across the slopes ahead to be reminded of the full magnificence of this ride.

BEST TIME TO RIDE

The warmer season (Nov to Apr) provides the best conditions - there's likely to be snow over the mountains at other times. The ride is near to some of the wettest areas in the country, and can get doused in rain at any time of year, so come prepared for a drenching.

RIDE IT

Stretching for 85 kilometres (53 miles) across the mountainous hinterland of the South Island's north-west coast, the Old Ghost Road is the longest stretch of continuous singletrack in New Zealand. It's that rare treat of a mountain-bike ride and a cycle journey in one, rising out of Buller Gorge and across the high slopes of the Lyell Range to finish near the wild west coast at Seddonville.

It's easily one of the most enjoyable mountain-bike rides I've ever done, though it doesn't yield easily. It has several technical and exposed sections, but hopping off and pushing through them is an option.

The trail can be cycled in either direction, but the best option is to ride from south to north - Buller Gorge to Seddonville. Though it begins with a 1200-metre (3940-foot) climb from this direction, it's a far friendlier gradient than you'll encounter if you try to pedal up Skyline Ridge and the switchbacking trail to Ghost Lake Hut, if you come from the north. Just don't expect to breeze across in either direction if you haven't prepared for the ride with plenty of hill climbs.

In Buller Gorge, the Old Ghost Road begins at the Lyell campsite, where a large archway announces the start of the ride. I'm doing the ride as a bikepacking trip, eschewing panniers and strapping my gear to various parts of the bike. A saddlebag hangs from the seat of my bike, and a roll of gear dangles off the front of the handlebars. I meet one cyclist along the

Nuts & bolts
Distance: 85 kilometres (53 miles)
Days: 2
Ascent: 2200 metres (7200 feet)
Difficulty: Hard
Bike: Mountain bike only; throw on a good set of 2.1- to 2.4-inch tyres.

Previous Riding atop the Lyell Range *Opposite top left* The Old Ghost Road trailhead at Lyell campsite *Top right* Ghost Lake Hut above Ghost Lake *Bottom left* Cycling through rainforest on the climb above Lyell campsite *Bottom right* South Island robin

trail who's gone the traditional way of panniers, but on this narrow and often tight trail, it's far better to avoid the extra width and bulk that comes with these bags. Bikepacking (*see* p. xi) is by far the better option.

As always with bikepacking, the limitations come mostly around packing. I will be out for just one night, so I carry a single change of clothes, a sleeping bag and raingear – the latter is vital considering that nearby Greymouth averages around 2.5 metres (8.2 feet) of rain a year.

There are no stores or other facilities along the Old Ghost Road, so it's essential to carry all of your food. Six huts have been built along the trail. All have mattresses, and the four largest huts – Lyell Saddle, Ghost Lake, Stern Valley and Specimen Point – have gas cookers and crockery, eliminating the need to carry any cooking gear. These four huts need to be booked before you ride. The four large huts also have a separate, more private, summer-only 'sleepout' hut, each containing two double mattresses. Sleepouts can only be booked by one person or group at a time. The other two huts – the small and basic Goat Creek and Mokihinui Forks – operate on a first-come, first-served basis. There's a bike workstation at Lyell Saddle Hut.

Miners' dray track out of Lyell campsite

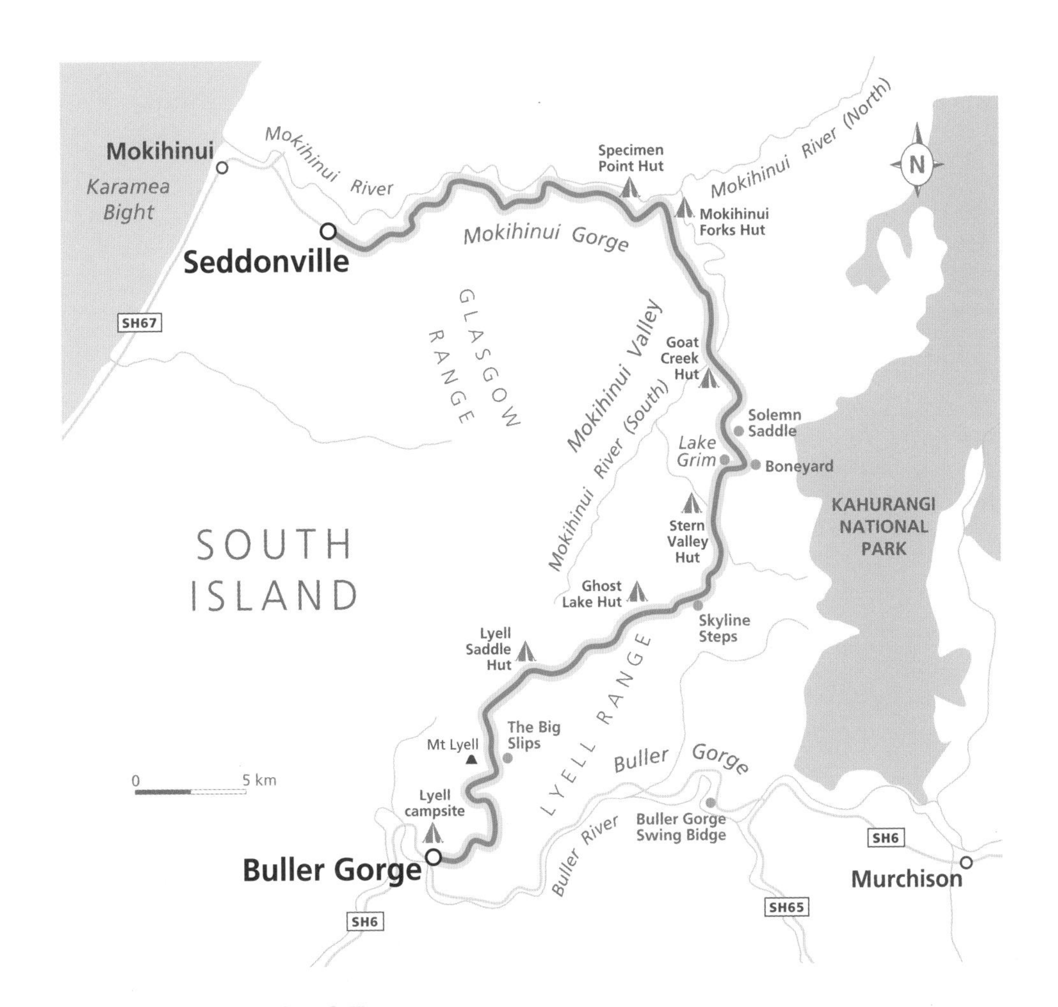

LOCAL SNAPSHOT

The Old Ghost Road is a new trail with a long history that tells tales about the rough nature of the terrain, the remoteness and the challenge of the ride. The track has its origins in the 19th-century gold rush that flooded the west coast of New Zealand's South Island with miners. Tracks were built to connect goldfields in the Buller Gorge and the Mokihinui Valley, but so brutal was the mountainous landscape in between that the tracks were never completed.

More than 100 years later, somebody stumbled across an old map with the proposed track marked on it, seeding an idea to revive the path and open it to mountain-bikers and hikers. Remnants of track existed at either end, but 50 kilometres (31 miles) of new trail was needed to stitch the two ends together. It took more than 100,000 hours of labour to do so, but it was finally opened at the end of 2015 and the result is stunning. The track takes its name because it effectively follows what had become a ghost of a road.

ITINERARY

DAY 1

LYELL CAMPSITE TO GHOST LAKE HUT (30KM/18.5 MILES)

The Lyell campsite, inside Buller Gorge, is an appropriate start to this historic track. The grassy camp was once the gold rush town of Lyell, which briefly boasted banks, several pubs, a post office, a brewery, a newspaper and a school with more than 80 students. Stand here now, surrounded by thick forest and steep mountain slopes, and it's difficult to imagine where trails could possibly lead, but for the gold miners attempting to create that first path to the Mokihinui Valley in the 1870s, this section was the easy bit.

Across a bridge over Lyell Creek, the Old Ghost Road begins on an old miners dray track, rising steadily through thick rainforest and past the remnants of former mining settlements, such as Gibbstown and Zalatown. Despite a smattering of debris, it's incongruous that settlements ever existed in these remote reaches – these long-gone towns are the true ghosts of the Old Ghost Road.

The climb from Lyell is continuous but on a steady, manageable gradient, and while the track can seem intimidatingly narrow at first, it soon begins to feel normal and comfortable. In retrospect, as I traverse far-more exposed sections across the top of the range, these early kilometres will come to seem about as wide as a six-lane highway.

Inside the rainforest, my companions are mostly avian. Fantails flit about behind my bike, feasting on the bugs disturbed by my wheels. When I stop for a rest, a South Island robin hops onto my shoe and starts picking grass seeds from my sock.

For more than an hour, there's only this rainforest and the effort of rising through it, but after 11 kilometres (6.8 miles) the track crosses the so-called Big Slips, where an entire hillside sheared away during a huge earthquake in 1929. Nearly a century on, it remains a deep wound through the rainforest, and presented even the modern trail-builders with an obstacle that took two years to overcome. Signs ask cyclists to dismount and push through the slips, but warn against stopping anywhere within them.

Past the slips, after 700 metres (2300 feet) of relentless climbing, the trail flattens, running just below the crest of the ridge and into Lyell Saddle, where the first of the Old Ghost Road's huts – Lyell Saddle Hut – is situated. I've covered just 18 kilometres (11 miles), but it's time for lunch.

The hut, which comes complete with a bike workstation, peers across the top of the rainforest to adjacent mountains. Also visible are the yellow tops of the Lyell Range high above, and it's here that I'm heading next.

The miners who set out to carve the path to the Mokihinui Valley gave up just beyond Lyell Saddle, where it all became too difficult. Take that bit of knowledge as a warning - even after 700 metres (2300 feet) of climbing from the Lyell campsite, the tough stuff is really only just about to begin.

The ride rises up the range in a succession of short steep pinches - there will be plenty of light-hearted grumbling about this section among cyclists in Ghost Lake Hut this night - before popping out of the rainforest into tussocky alpine grasslands around 7 kilometres (4.5 miles) beyond Lyell Saddle. The contrast to the rainforest is immediate and extreme, from views that extend little more than a few metres one moment, to views that spread wide across valleys and mountains the next.

As I catch my breath, two cyclists come pedalling across the mountains from the opposite direction. The previous day they'd cycled the length of the Old Ghost Road and now they're riding back - 170 kilometres (105 miles) of singletrack riding, with a few thousand metres of ascent, in two days. I'm exhausted just listening to their story.

'I bet there were a few beers in Seddonville last night for you,' I say.

'We only had energy for one,' comes the weary answer.

The Old Ghost Road's longest climb tops out shortly after reaching the alpine section - Lyell campsite is now 1200 metres (3940 feet) below me - and its most spectacular moments begin. Looking ahead, the track appears like a thread of string laid across the slopes, and just beyond the track's high point is the first of two sections marked in red - Danger! - on maps. It's an 800-metre (2620-foot) stretch, where the ever-narrowing track scrapes past cliffs on one side, and the slopes plunge away on the other side. It's an airy few minutes of riding, with my handlebars all but scraping against the cliffs and stones loose under the wheels of my bike. There's even a boulder named the Tombstone, which is not a consoling thought along this stretch that already has me wondering if I might yet become the track's next ghost.

My riding day ends at Ghost Lake Hut, 5 kilometres (3 miles) along the alpine tops, poised on a knoll above its namesake lake, which is a beautiful small pool fringed with red reeds and yellow moss. It's been one of the best and most exciting

Above Exposed terrain on the Lyell Range
Opposite Old Ghost Road trail marker

days of riding I can remember, and the view from the hut promises a whole lot more. Out one window, I look down onto the lake, but out the other is the sight of the start of tomorrow's ride – a dizzying line of squiggles across the ridges of surrounding hills. It's a view of the Old Ghost Road's most technical and tricky section.

Cyclists roll in behind me, filling the hut, and behind them come sheets of rain. The kindest thing that can be said about the weather on New Zealand's west coast is that it's dynamic. This first day I set out in sun, riding through a scene as still as a painting. On the second day, there will be times I half wonder if I might be better off on the track in a kayak.

DAY 2

GHOST LAKE HUT TO SEDDONVILLE (55KM/34 MILES)

From Ghost Lake Hut, the Old Ghost Road dips first to the lake and then plunges off the side of the mountains, writhing down a steep ridgeline through switchbacks so tight they're almost knotted. The rainforest glows fresh in the rain, but the tree roots that grope across the track are as slippery as ice. At one point my handlebars clip a tree and suddenly I'm lying in front of my bike on a soft bed of moss.

As quickly as this descent ends, the toughest climb of the journey begins, swinging up the slopes of Skyline Ridge, where the track is regularly stepped with rocks and tree roots. Other times, it's simply a very steep climb.

Atop the ridge, the track feels as narrow as a slackline at times. If you've ever watched Danny MacAskill mountain bike down the Cuillin Mountains on Skye ... well, it's nothing like that, but it feels like it. As morning mist blows in and out from the valleys below me, the views one moment are endless, and the next I can't even see another bike that's a few metres ahead of me.

It's a short ride along the ridge, which ends in a section of terrain so complicated and so steep that track builders could find no other solution but to build a staircase instead of a trail (as I write this, there are plans to replace the staircase finally with a trail solution). As I climb down the 60 metre high (200 foot) wooden stairs, with my laden bike slung over my shoulder, I begin to truly appreciate why it took a year just to build a 6-kilometre (4-mile) section of this incredible trail.

The stairs mark the point at which the Old Ghost Road leaves the alpine heights and returns to rainforest. Lichen hangs like streamers from the trees, and the trail widens

again as it dips into Stern Valley, where it passes the Stern Valley Hut. Cascades and waterfalls hurry downhill beside the track, which also now flows more smoothly than anything behind me - 15km/h (9mp/h) has never seemed so fast.

Just when I think the ride might stay this gentle, the trail comes through open river flats to Lake Grim (which at least sits right beside Lake Cheerful) and begins another climb, winding through the boulders of the so-called Boneyard, which were shaken from the mountains and dumped here by the same 1929 earthquake that shaved away the Big Slips.

It's the final climb of note on the trail, and by the time I crest at Solemn Saddle, I'm back in rainforest, and the way ahead is primarily downhill, first through enchanting scenes as the Mokihinui River wraps around boulders covered in a pelt of moss and then, beyond the two most basic of the tracks huts - Goat Creek and Mokihinui Forks - into Mokihinui Gorge, immediately below the watchful windows of Specimen Point Hut.

Tiny Seddonville, which is little more than a welcome pub, is now beckoning, but first I must navigate this gorge that is the Old Ghost Road's spectacular dismount. Inside here, rushing green waters brake to a stop in deep pools, narrow swing bridges overhanging deep gulches, and the frighteningly named Suicide Slips - another set of earthquake landslips - test the nerves of cyclists.

It's a fantastically beautiful gorge, made even more exciting by the daring nature of the trail, which is cut hard against - and at times, into - the gorge's cliffs. Signs warn of 'Extreme rockfall' danger, and there are chains beside the most exposed sections to assist and still the hearts of hikers. As a cyclist, you either trust your balance or hop off and push.

As I approach the end of the ride, and one final short climb over County Hill, the rain continues to top up the gorge, and mist rises like steam from the river. It's a ghostly image - nature creating a fitting finish to the Old Ghost Road.

Riding resources

Book huts and campsites through the Old Ghost Road's official website (oldghostroad.org.nz), a detailed source of information. Follow its 'Trail Operators' link to find bike hire, shuttle services and guided-trip operators.

Opposite Steps atop Skyline Ridge

ASIA

Yeongsan & Jeju

SOUTH KOREA

Discover South Korea's riverside bike network and a modern-day wonder of the world.

Yeongsan & Jeju

WHY IT'S SPECIAL

When you think about Asian cycling destinations, South Korea might not automatically spring to mind - but it should. This country, hanging like a stalactite from the eastern edge of Asia, might be one of the most densely populated on earth, but it also has more than 2000 kilometres (1240 miles) of dedicated bike paths outside its cities. These paths have transformed South Korea into arguably the most bike-friendly country in Asia, and while cyclists tend to worry about traffic in Asia, this ride predominantly follows bike paths as good as anywhere in the world.

Even though the route barely touches a road, it's lined with cities and towns, making for uncomplicated riding days. Lunch and refreshment stops are plentiful all the way to Mokpo, and around the fringes of the island of Jeju.

Jeju is the so-called Hawaii of Korea, and the most enticing part of this ride. Compared to the Korean mainland, Jeju is a relatively uncrowded island of just 600,000 people, and there are gloriously quiet sections of riding, even when the route is just a painted blue line or median strip of separation from the traffic. Other times, as it hugs the coast away from all other vehicles, it's a path so smooth that the only bumps come from the gusts of wind that roll off the sea.

BEST TIME TO RIDE

Jeju is noted for its autumn foliage - a spectacular multi-coloured coat - making September and October perfect for this trip. Sitting south of the peninsula and surrounded by sea, Jeju has a warmer and slightly more humid climate than the rest of the country, though this won't impact on your ride.

RIDE IT

The core of the path network is the Four Rivers Project, a multi-billion-dollar scheme, completed in 2011, to rejuvenate the banks of four of the country's largest rivers: the Han, Nakdong, Geum and Yeongsan. As part of the project, towpath-style bike paths were built along each of the four rivers.

In addition to this, a bike route encircles the large, southern island of Jeju, and I think this is the pick of South Korea's cycling options.

The volcano of Hallasan might create a mountainous interior for Jeju, but the island's bike route predominantly adheres to the coastal plains that ring the island. Cyclists will, however, encounter another familiar foe on Jeju - wind. As the clusters of wind turbines around its coast attest, this

Nuts & bolts
Distance: 365 kilometres (227 miles)
Days: 5
Ascent: 2000 metres (6560 feet)
Difficulty: Easy-medium
Bike: Excellent bike paths and roads are well suited to a tourer or hybrid bike.

Previous The Metasequoia-lined Road in Damyang *Opposite top left* Lighthouse on Jeju island *Top right* Hoesan White Lotus Pond *Bottom left* Cycling beside the Yeongsan River in Damyang *Bottom right* Fishing boats in Mokpo

is a gusty island, and any circuit ride inevitably means at least some time battling into headwinds.

When I cycled on Jeju, I came via the Four Rivers Project, beginning my ride on the peninsula, in the southern town of Damyang. This settlement of 50,000 people sits near the source of the Yeongsan River, which I planned to follow south to the port city of Mokpo, from where ferries depart to Jeju.

The Four Rivers bike paths take advantage of centuries-old levees bracketing the rivers, and each route is lined with 'certification centres' – red, phone-box-like places in which you can stamp a cycling passport as a memento of the ride. There are six such stops along the Yeongsan.

From Damyang, it's a 130-kilometre (80-mile) ride to Mokpo, which I will break into two days even though the flat terrain makes it feasible in a day. South Korea might be 80 per cent covered in mountains, but the Four Rivers Project paths have all but flattened the country for cyclists.

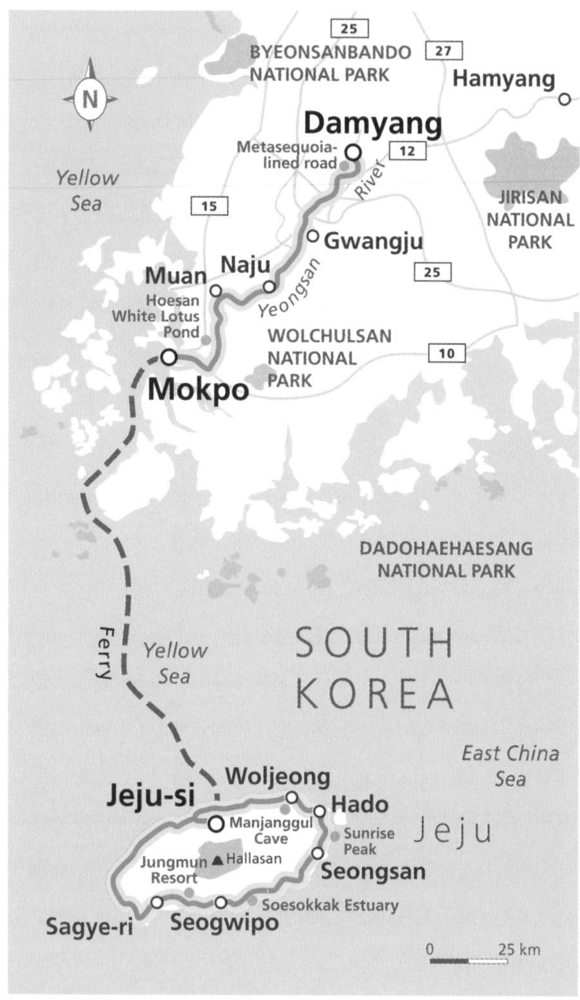

LOCAL SNAPSHOT

South Korea's largest island of Jeju is almost the size of Mauritius, and sits 80 kilometres (50 miles) off the southern tip of the Korean Peninsula. It's effectively a volcano in the sea, with the island wrapped around the 1947-metre (6388-foot) Hallasan mountain and dimpled with more than 300 volcanic hills. It's an island that's both beautiful and barren. Often referred to as the Hawaii of Korea, it's the most popular holiday destination in South Korea. Indeed, when an online poll to select the New Seven Wonders of the World was unveiled in 2011, Jeju was a surprise selection, named among more usual suspects such as Iguazu Falls, the Amazon and Halong Bay.

ITINERARY

DAY 1

DAMYANG TO NAJU (65KM/40 MILES)

Damyang is famed in Korea for its bamboo forest, but I start riding beside another of its floral marvels – the Metasequoia-lined Road, where ruler-straight lines of deciduous trees create a postcard image over a pathway. As I set out, autumn leaves rain over the path, though once I'm out of the town the scene changes dramatically, and soon I'm riding above rice fields in various stages of harvest. The terrain is flat, and the wind is at my back – it's reminiscent of towpath cycling beside European canals, but with kimchi for lunch. The easiest 65 kilometres (40 miles) imaginable rolls out ahead of me for the day.

Even as I ride through Gwangju, South Korea's sixth-largest city, around 35 kilometres (22 miles) from Damyang, the path has been so faithful to the levee and river that I've not encountered a vehicle. It's Sunday and the path is busy with local cyclists, who whoosh past with tinny K-pop blaring from their phones. A boy calls out, 'Welcome to Korea'. Compared to the tyranny of traffic encountered when cycling in many other Asian countries, it's pure delight.

I stop this night in the riverside city of Naju, staying in a hotel on the riverbank among a clutch of restaurants specialising in the local delicacy: raw, aged (ergo, rotten) skate, a fish dish that's said to make durian smell like perfume. Even the out-of-town Koreans I meet won't brave this Naju dish. 'I've worked in a lot of Asian countries and can eat pretty much anything, except this,' one man tells me. I leave Naju in cowardly fashion, without having tried the local dish.

DAY 2

NAJU TO MOKPO (65KM/40 MILES)

Past Naju, the Yeongsan River begins to widen as it approaches the sea. The path is empty – hello Monday! – and in the rice fields, mechanical harvesters shatter the romance of the scene.

It's a beautiful day of riding, winding through small rural villages removed from any form of tourism – the sort of places so wonderfully isolated that you'd stumble into them through no other way of travel but cycling. Old women sit on the roads, beating beans from the harvested bushes.

I lunch beside the Hoesan White Lotus Pond, carpeted in a beautiful small forest of lotuses. It's said to be the largest lotus pond in Asia, and is just a few minutes' detour off the track in Muan County. From here, the flat run continues to the sea, broken only by the occasional, rudely steep pinch to shred the thighs – 13 per cent gradient on one climb.

Approaching the port city of Mokpo, I'm one moment among rice fields and the next surrounded by apartment buildings. Beyond here, there is only sea, but my ride has really only just begun.

Above Bridge crossing over the Yeongsan River *Opposite* Rice field along the Yeongsan River *Overleaf* Beach at Sagye-ri

DAY 3

JEJU CITY TO SAGYE-RI (85KM/53 MILES)

For the next three days, the beautiful island of Jeju will be my cycling home as I make the lap around its perimeter. Jeju is an oval-shaped island, and with its bike route completed in 2015, the place is now like a velodrome in the sea.

In Mokpo, I board the *Santa Lucino* ferry and head across the Yellow Sea to Jeju. The day is as grey and wet as the ocean, but in four-and-a-half hours I'm rolling ashore in Jeju-si (Jeju City). I set out anti-clockwise, staying as close to the coast as possible as I ride west along the island's north coast.

This day the wind blows from behind me, propelling me towards Jeju's western tip. I cruise along at 30km/h (18.5 mp/h), with barely a turn of the pedals. I know there will be a price to pay later – a contrary headwind somewhere – but for the moment, with the wind at my back and the waves by my feet, life couldn't be any better.

For the first time since leaving Damyang, there are climbs, though none of them are large. Fishermen stand on rocks, waves breaking around them, and the fertile volcanic soil is so chocolate-brown in colour that it looks almost edible itself. Lighthouses around seemingly every bend testify to the power and potential brutality of this coast. I stay the night in the south-coast town of Sagye-ri.

DAY 4

SAGYE-RI TO SEONGSAN (88KM/55 MILES)

Today I begin looping back east, heading first into Jungmun Resort, 20 kilometres (12.5 miles) from Sagye-ri, following the path as it adheres to the island's main circuit road, separated from the traffic by a median strip.

Almost every holiday island or coastal strip has one place it sacrifices to mass and crass tourism, and on Jeju it's Jungmun Resort. A Ripley's Believe It or Not museum sits beside one of the town's two teddy bear museums. There's a safari park, a K-pop theme park, and a Museum of Sex and Health, with vast gardens filled with erotic statues. But it's worth stopping in just to see the Jusangjeollidae columnar joint, a 2-kilometre-long (1.2-mile) volcanic spectacle formed along the coast when an ancient lava flow from the now-dormant Hallasan mountain cracked as it cooled on entering the sea. It now stands like a Giant's Causeway, with hexagonal columns of rock up to 25 metres (80 feet) in height.

Asia

Beyond Jungmun Resort, the ride along the south coast passes through Jeju's second-largest city, Seogwipo, with the ominous summit of Hallasan now sliding by to my left. If you have a day to spare, it's well worth heading inland and joining the Korean hiking crowds on one of the many trails on South Korea's highest peak. On this southern side of the volcano, the various trails climb to a shelter at Witsae Oreum, 230 metres (750 feet) below the summit, where most people turn around and descend the mountain.

As I ride on, the scene somehow looks more rugged every time the route touches the coast, where black shores occasionally burst into brilliant beaches. Inland, fields are delineated by Jeju's ever-present stone walls, built with the surfeit of rock discharged from Hallasan. There are said to be more than 6000 kilometres (3730 miles) of these dry-stone walls on the island. Known as the Black Dragons, they have been collectively listed as a Globally Important Agricultural Heritage System by the United Nations Food and Agriculture Organization.

Another stop worth making on this south-coast ride is the Soesokkak estuary, just beyond Seogwipo. This estuary is pooled inside a narrow coastal slot, with low basalt cliffs topped with a canopy of forest and vines. It fades into the sea across a brown-sand beach enclosed by a pair of lighthouses. Pedalos and glass-bottomed canoes paddle and pedal up and down the estuary's short pools, or there's a boat trip that involves the 'captain' pulling the boat up the river by a fixed rope.

This day I finish riding in Seongsan, at the foot of Sunrise Peak on the island's eastern tip, arriving perhaps ironically just on sunset.

DAY 5

SEONGSAN TO JEJU CITY (62KM/38 MILES)

There's a pilgrimage quality about Sunrise Peak, which protrudes like a large thumb from the peninsula on which Seongsan sprawls. The peak is a low, round volcanic crater, and in the darkness of the next morning I set out on foot rather than bicycle, joining a mob on the climb to its summit for the eponymous sunrise. Such is the popularity of this morning ritual that there's grandstand seating atop the peak, but nature is fickle and on this cloudy morning the sun never arrives on Sunrise Peak.

What I do find here, however, at the end of a coarse, black-sand beach scratched into the base of Sunrise Peak, are Jeju's

most famous inhabitants: the haenyeo. Across the island, statues and museums immortalise these women, who are as tough as volcanoes themselves. They are both mermaids and marvels, free-diving up to 20 metres (65 feet) below the ocean surface, holding their breath for up to two minutes, to fish for the likes of sea cucumbers, sea urchins and squid. From the beach at Seongsan they dive for their catch, selling it at the beach's edge.

My last day of riding will take me back along the north coast to Jeju City. It's a simple ride, once more along the coastal plains, but complicated by the thing I've been expecting since I first arrived on the island and blew along with the wind behind me: I must face my headwind.

Overnight my hotel has been shuddering in the wind, and on the bike I hunch over the handlebars, making myself as small as possible against the wind. Kite-surfers skim across the bays, waves and sand blow over the bike path, and wind turbines chop at the sky like propellers, turning, turning, turning as the wind blows relentlessly across Jeju.

Wind aside, this may be the finest day of riding of all. The bike route, which is a mix of paths and roads, is pressed hard against the coast, and passes through little pockets of stylish seaside towns, such as Hado and Woljeong, where wind-worn cafes line the road, often with their seats spread into the bike lane. The landscape here is softer, and there are suddenly as many white beaches as black sections of coast. Briefly, I turn inland, rising to Manjanggul, a perfectly arched cave, hollowed inside an old lava flow, complete with the world's largest-known lava column, formed when lava poured through a hole in the ceiling of the cave and solidified.

With all this to accessorise a cycling day, even a fierce headwind seems less of a concern.

Opposite Hiking trail on Hallasan

Riding resources

Local tour operator bikeOasis (bikeoasiskorea.com) runs a guided trip along the Yeongsan River and around Jeju. Hire bikes can be found in Seoul and transported with you to Damyang. Damyang is three-and-a-half hours by bus from Seoul. It's easier to get bikes onto buses than trains in South Korea.

ASIA

Guangxi & Guizhou

CHINA

Pedal through rice fields and among a fantasy karst landscape in southern China.

G320
Kaili
Xijiang
Leishan Pass
GUIZHOU
Yongle
S15
HUNAN
N
G65
G59
G76
Rongjiang
Zhaoxing
Basha Miao
G76
G72
S31
High-speed train
Li River
CHINA
Guilin
Lijiang Gudong Scenic Area
G65
Yangdi
River raft
Yulong Bridge
Xingping
GUANGXI
Hechi
0
50 km
G72
Yangshuo
G78
G78

Guangxi & Guizhou

WHY IT'S SPECIAL

There are few more striking mountain landscapes on earth than the bristling karst peaks around Yangshuo and Xingping in China's Guangxi province. They are truly extraordinary, and unexpectedly kind to cyclists – there are few mountain regions in the world that yield so easily to a bicycle. Running between the peaks, which stand like forests of rock, are valleys as flat as pages. It's a natural design that has made day rides on bikes a big feature of Yangshuo's tourism landscape, so you'll be in plenty of cycling company here. In contrast, as you pedal across Guizhou on the approach to Yangshuo, you'll encounter few other cyclists or even international tourists.

BEST TIME TO RIDE

Dodge the summer crowds and the winter chill by riding in spring (Mar to May) or autumn (Sept to Nov).

The professional Tour of Guangxi is raced in October, if you want to combine your ride with some tour action.

RIDE IT

The flat ease of the valleys around the city of Yangshuo has made cycling one of the most popular ways to tour the surrounding countryside, which is among the most recognisable in China. Few people cycle to get here, however, though to do so is to truly be wowed by these mountains known throughout China as the 'best under heaven'.

The impact of arriving among these Guangxi mountains is further heightened if you pedal here from little-visited Guizhou, the neighbouring province to the north-west. Pinched between the tourism giants of Yunnan and Guangxi, Guizhou has traditionally had little tourism of its own, and is one of China's poorest regions. Cycling through Guizhou also provides a glimpse along the way into some of the beauty and culture of the Miao and Dong minority groups.

To reach the limestone mountains from this direction you must climb through other mountains. Little here is flat, but neither is anything huge – the highest point I'll reach on my approach to Guangxi is around 1300 metres (4260 feet) above sea level. It's the accumulation of climbs rather than any single ascent that provides any sting.

Nuts & bolts

Distance: 390 kilometres (242 miles)
Days: 7
Ascent: 5000 metres (16,400 feet)
Difficulty: Medium
Bike: The hilly terrain lends itself well to a mountain bike, and the road surfaces mostly suit a hybrid or tourer, so anything but a road bike is good.

Previous The Guizhou town of Xijiang

LOCAL SNAPSHOT

The Miao are the fifth-largest of China's 55 minority groups, with a population of almost 10 million people. On day one of this ride, you'll cycle to Xijiang, which is the largest Miao village in China. It's a place that well knows its tourist value. There's ticketed, turnstile admission into the town, and with its dark wooden homes seeming almost to rise in mounds along both banks of a stream, it has the feeling of a medieval European town, but with Chinese design and Miao faces. It's a town of great beauty and great contrast, where tradition intersects with modern life – teenagers play basketball beside a square filled with traditionally dressed women, and there's the unexpected find of a nightclub among its traditional wooden buildings.

Below Cycling through rice fields above Yongle *Opposite top* The Miao minority village of Xijiang *Bottom* Miao traditional dress in Xijiang

DAY 1

KAILI TO XIJIANG (30KM/18.5 MILES)

I begin riding in the Guizhou city of Kaili, about a three-hour drive east of the provincial capital of Guiyang. In my mind, it's just far enough from this city of three million people to remove the tyranny of traffic. And sure enough, the ride begins gently, on quiet roads that wind along the banks of a river, the waters of which are almost luminously green, with the lush bush only shades behind. Down here, it's as though I've disappeared from the world, though I only have to look up to see it in motion on the enormous motorway bridges that span the valley overhead, but still I'm struck by the happy paradox that in the world's most populous country, I'm alone.

It's a short first day into the Miao village of Xijiang. It would be easy to ride further, but Xijiang is a perfect first window into the the life of the Miao minority people (*see* p. 168).

DAY 2

XIJIANG TO YONGLE (80KM/50 MILES)

The next morning, I wake to the knowledge that the biggest climb of the ride is about to begin. Over 40 kilometres (25 miles) the ride will roll south, ascending to its highest point atop Leishan Pass, around 1300 metres (4260 feet) above sea level, before it descends into Yongle, a town so little visited that when I arrive I will see only one hotel. Briefly, I'm going to be cycling off the tourist map.

I head out of Xijiang on undulating dirt roads, with highways still suspended overhead like a parallel universe. Down here on the earth, any flat bit of land has been converted into crops.

I roll into the town of Leishan for an early lunch – rice noodles on the footpath, taking on energy for a big afternoon ahead because it's here that the climb truly begins.

Leishan Pass is around 500 vertical metres (1640 feet) above Leishan, and my pace slows as the climb takes grip. Vehicles pass in a chatter of horns, though it's purely conversational and not aggressive. Caged birds twitter from the verandahs of homes, and there seem to be more trees than people, even in this land of 1.3 billion souls. Finally, the road contours across to the pass, staring down into a deep, blue sea of mountains fading away to the horizon.

The descent – the sort of long, curling bends that barely require braking – is over in minutes; too quickly, as they always are. No sooner does it end across a river, than the next climb begins.

The finest part of the day – the moment in which all climbing is forgiven and forgotten – comes at its end. As the road summits this second climb, the descent to Yongle begins, curling through rice terraces that are like rungs on a ladder into the valley. The rice is just being planted as I pass, so that each terrace is a flat, reflective pool of water and the entire landscape looks like the sky cut into the pieces of a jigsaw puzzle. Women stand up to their knees in the water, planting the rice for the next season and breaking into laughter as I pass. It's as though my passage is purely for comedic distraction. I feel as though I've cycled into every postcard ever made of China's famous rice terraces, but with life and laughter added to the picture.

DAYS 3–4

YONGLE TO RONGJIANG (75KM/46.5 MILES); RONGJIANG TO BASHA MIAO VILLAGE (70KM/43.5 MILES)

For the next two days, I continue east across Guizhou, connecting the dots of some of the province's most beautiful minority villages. Along the way there are scenes seemingly cut from another dynasty. Dugout canoes are tied to riverbanks beside tiny villages, and a worker hangs in a makeshift swing from power lines, precariously repairing them.

After a night that's more just a pit-stop in Rongjiang, I stay the next night in the Basha Miao village, which is actually a string of interlocked villages rolling across the top of a ridge. Basha is noteworthy as the last village in China where residents are allowed to carry guns – part of the Basha Miao tradition. Past the short main street, lined with shops, the beautifully kept village gets more rural and the homes more basic than in Xijiang. Drying racks loaded with rice stalks rise high above the wooden stilt houses, and stone pathways wind between the sections of the village and the bamboo forest that separates them.

Above Cycling across a forested ridge in Guizhou *Opposite* The Li River at Xingping

DAY 5

BASHA MIAO VILLAGE TO ZHAOXING (45KM/28 MILES)

The next day brings the first hint of the landscape that's ahead. Through bush as unruly as the road's traffic, white cliffs emerge. It's an outlier of limestone, not the start of the ranges, but still it's like a road sign: Karst Country Ahead.

My final stop in Guizhou is the most pleasant surprise of all. As the road winds up through hills and crosses a low pass, the 2000-year-old Dong village of Zhaoxing suddenly materialises below. Drum towers stand tall over rice fields at the entrance to the village, which snakes through a narrow valley, and there's a vague sense of having stumbled into some sort of Shangri-la.

The drum towers, which housed drums to signal messages, are the very symbol of Zhaoxing. Throughout China there are said to be now only around 630 drum towers, and five of them are in this village of 4000 people. As I wheel my bike beneath one of the drum towers and into the village, the first few hundred metres of the wide main street feel pre-packaged and made for tourism, but in just a few steps, history swamps the place. The main street fragments into lanes, the streams become like canals that flow between the houses, and all the polish and lustre is gone for the better.

As I keep walking, the village comes to an abrupt end, with a sheer line of homes yielding to rice fields, where kids are playing with firecrackers and women are again planting rice. The tourist shops just a few hundred metres back suddenly seem kilometres away.

Zhaoxing sits near to Guizhou's border with Guangxi and the karst mountains now beckon.

DAY 6

TRAIN TO YANGSHUO, CYCLE YANGSHUO TO XINGPING (30KM/18.5 MILES)

Having crossed Guizhou by bike, the best plan from Zhaoxing is to skip the messy, traffic-filled approaches through Guilin to Yangshuo, and instead head direct to Yangshuo by train to commence riding. The Congjiang train station is just a handful of kilometres from Zhaoxing, and it's little more than an hour by high-speed train to Yangshuo, the busy city at the heart of the karst landscape.

Though my ride will end in Yangshuo, the best is only beginning when I arrive here. From the city, I will make a varied loop out to the even more spectacular town of Xingping, a trip that itself would make for a fine two- to three-day ride if you wanted only to cycle among the limestone mountains.

Yangshuo is a small city that pulses with visitors. At its heart, West Street is just a few hundred metres long but it can be shoulder-to-shoulder with thousands of people. And yet the city is also webbed with quiet lanes too narrow for most vehicles, and it's through these that I weave peacefully out of the city.

The thread that connects Yangshuo to Xingping to its north is the Li River, a waterway that was listed by National Geographic in 2010 as one of the world's 10 watery wonders. Along the river, karst peaks close around the water like teeth. Orange groves cover the slopes as I rise slowly out of Yangshuo to a lookout over the river and a host of

fantastically shaped peaks etched into the haze. There are mountains around here with quixotic names, such as Lion Watching the Nine Horses, Tortoise Climbing the Hill and Grandpa Guarding the Apple. It's like a ride into Chinese mythology.

When I turn corners out here, blades of rock spear up from ridges and hills - China's original high-rises - until I eventually weave down to the riverbank on narrow dirt roads that are almost too tight for cars. Directly across the river from Xingping, on a peninsula with a rare shelf of wide, flat land, is a passenger ferry that transports me into town.

Xingping sits at a point where the Li River takes the tightest of turns, banking below lines of limestone spires. It's an impossibly beautiful place. It's here that string-bearded old men use cormorants to fish - a classic image of China - and a 10-minute walk from town is the riverside spot that appears on China's 20 yuan banknote.

DAY 7

BAMBOO RAFT TO YANGDI, CYCLE YANGDI TO YANGSHUO (60KM/37 MILES)

Xingping is surrounded by hundreds, if not thousands, of peaks and it offers the chance to climb one, so I delay my departure this morning. From beside the ferry dock, a walking trail rises to the summit of a peak towering above the town. In 30 minutes, I'm standing atop the mountain, peering over other mountains that appear to have no end as they recede to the horizon. Far below me, the Li River bends so sharply it almost cuts a peninsula (the same one on which I'd cycled to the ferry yesterday) into an island.

Xingping's docks are crowded with river-cruise boats and bamboo rafts, and it's onto one of the latter that I'm taking the next part of my trip. These traditional bamboo rafts with long-tail motors are ubiquitous on the Li River, though many are now made from PVC piping, rather than bamboo. I strap my bike onto a raft and I'm soon weaving through an armada of boats as I'm transported upstream.

The river twists and turns around the karst peaks, and tangles of forest climb up the slopes, bursting open into rocky summits - there are spires and domes by the dozens and yet, like fingerprints, no two look the same.

It's a two-hour raft trip upstream to Yangdi, where I unload my bike and begin the ride back to Yangshuo. It's a steep climb out from the river, but then a glorious roll towards Yangshuo.

I follow rural lanes, where dogs and ducks outnumber cars and trucks, and pull aside for the only form of traffic jam here - old men ambling down the roads leading buffaloes. Framed by lumpy mountains, the crops of potatoes, rice and even grapes create the very picture of agricultural fertility.

I pedal south-east until I meet the Yulong River and Yulong Bridge - the so-called Dragon Bridge - a 600-year-old arching bridge hung with wispy vines. Located around 20 kilometres (12.5 miles) from Yangshuo, it's one of the most popular cycling goals for visitors to the city, so suddenly I'm riding in a virtual peloton of bikes. Like the river and the bamboo rafts that crowd its surface, we all flow towards Yangshuo, pedalling beneath this most extraordinary skyline of mountains.

Riding resources

If you are taking the train between Congjiang and Yangshuo, the best source for tickets is online (china-diy-travel.com). Train tickets go on sale 30 days before departure date.

Opposite The karst landscape at Xingping

ASIA

Central Vietnam

VIETNAM

Roll over high roads and low roads through the beauty of central Vietnam.

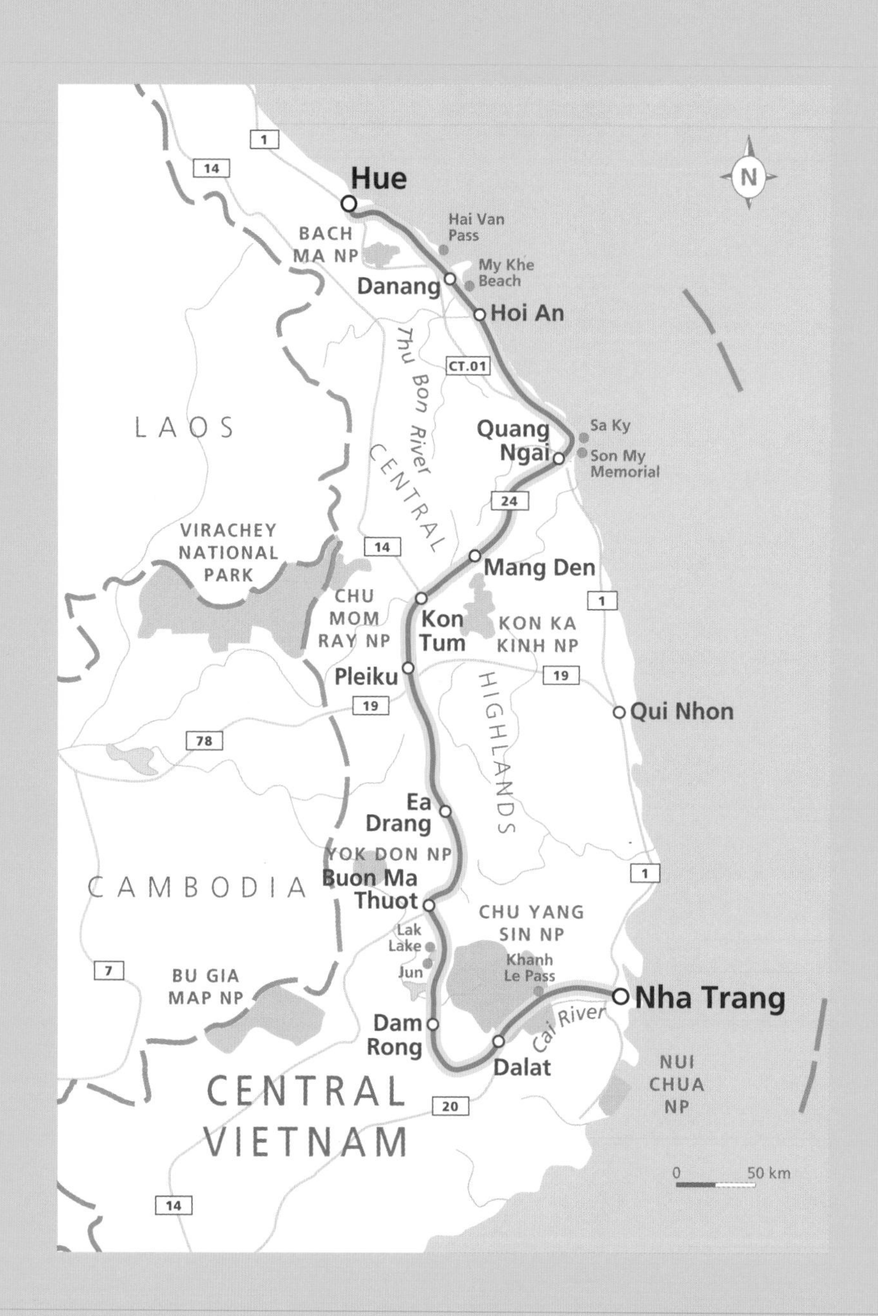

Hue
BACH MA NP
Hai Van Pass
My Khe Beach
Danang
Hoi An
Thu Bon River
CT.01
LAOS
Quang Ngai
Sa Ky
Son My Memorial
CENTRAL
24
VIRACHEY NATIONAL PARK
14
Mang Den
CHU MOM RAY NP
Kon Tum
KON KA KINH NP
1
Pleiku
19
HIGHLANDS
Qui Nhon
78
Ea Drang
YOK DON NP
CAMBODIA
Buon Ma Thuot
CHU YANG SIN NP
Lak Lake
Jun
Khanh Le Pass
7
BU GIA MAP NP
Nha Trang
Dam Rong
Cai River
Dalat
NUI CHUA NP
CENTRAL VIETNAM
20
0
50 km

Central Vietnam

WHY IT'S SPECIAL

The longest ride in this book provides a real sense of journey, first along the coast and then into the lush highlands of narrow Vietnam. Your reception in towns and along the roads may be the friendliest you've ever encountered. It's this quality - the unadulterated welcome of the people wherever you pedal - that might become the strongest memory of your ride. You'll pedal over hills and through history, coffee plantations and rice-terraces cut as perfectly as palace staircases. And somehow there's always a wave and a friendly face wherever you cycle.

The ride goes from the former imperial capital city of Hue to the seaside resort city of Nha Trang - old Vietnam to new Vietnam - and is far removed from the country's bookending metropolises of Hanoi and Ho Chi Minh City. Though Hue and Nha Trang are connected by the country's main highway, it explores coastal areas pinched between the highway and the South China Sea, and climbs into the lush highlands that stand suspended above this narrow strip of a country.

BEST TIME TO RIDE

The months following the monsoon (about Nov to Feb) provide the coolest and most pleasant riding.

Vietnam's wet season (around May to Oct) can create testing conditions in the highlands and is best avoided.

RIDE IT

There are some long days in this ride, so prepare and train well. For the sake of the first day alone, you should begin this ride as fit and strong as possible.

At a glance, Vietnam's roads are a chaotic swarm, abuzz with energy, impatience and anarchy. And yet this nation of almost 100 million people is the very image of Asian cycling, and perhaps the most popular country on the continent for touring cyclists. Even beyond the ride described here, the options are manifold - from bucolic jaunts among the rice fields and limestone peaks around Mai Chau, to flat-as-mirror riding through the Mekong Delta, to an epic 1700-kilometre (1056-mile) journey along the spine of the country on the legendary Ho Chi Minh Highway between Hanoi and Ho Chi Minh City.

Nuts & bolts
Distance: 1030 kilometres (640 miles)
Days: 12
Ascent: 14,000 metres (46,000 feet)
Difficulty: Medium-hard
Bike: Preference will be personal on this ride - tourers and hybrids will roll best, but mountain-bike gearing will be a treat on the highland climbs.

Previous The Imperial City of Hue

LOCAL SNAPSHOT

The coffee plant was introduced into Vietnam in 1857, brought to the country by caffeine-craving French missionaries. Plantations flourished in the early 20th century, but after the Vietnam War, known locally as the American War, privately owned plantations were banned. The ban was overturned in 1986, propelling Vietnam to a position where it is now the second-largest coffee producer in the world, after Brazil. Coffee plantations cover around 6600 square kilometres (2550 square miles) of the country, and output grew from just 18,400 tonnes in 1986 to around 1.76 million tonnes by 2016. Although the first coffee plant introduced to Vietnam was arabica, today robusta coffee accounts for about 97 per cent of the country's production – Vietnam is the world's largest exporter of robusta coffee, which is typically used for instant coffee.

The heartland of Vietnam's coffee production is the area around Buon Ma Thuot, which you will cycle through on this ride.

Top The Thu Bon River in Hoi An *Middle* Fisherman in the fields outside of Hue *Bottom* Street scene in Hoi An *Opposite* Local women cycling through Hoi An

ITINERARY

DAYS 1–2

HUE TO DANANG (100KM/62 MILES); DANANG TO HOI AN (30KM/18.5MILES)

At 5am the traffic in Vietnam's ancient royal city of Hue is already wide awake. I can hear it from the ninth floor of my hotel, honking, swirling, roaring and revving. In just a couple of hours I will be down amongst it – one bike in a storm of traffic. It's like dropping a twig into a flooding river, except that this river of traffic turns out to be surprisingly placid.

In the streets of this city of 450,000 people, I quickly discover that there's order in the seeming disorder of the traffic. Vehicles bear down on each other but somehow never collide. I merge into roundabouts that seem to spin like atoms, and the traffic magically parts around me. I have been absorbed into Vietnam.

With the worry of traffic now gone from my mind, the day's other challenges come into focus. The cycle to Danang, the next city to the south, is no soft start. It's a 100-kilometre (62-mile) ride that includes Vietnam's most famous hill climb – Hai Van Pass.

Hue ends in a sea of rice fields, which are awash with recent rains. Here the traffic also ends as I wind through the fields on village paths that have room only for bikes and scooters. Men punt narrow boats through the fields, fishing their waters, and school children rush to high-five me as I pedal past.

As the ride first touches the coast, the climb to Hai Van Pass begins. Popularised by the TV motoring show *Top Gear*, which described it as 'one of the best coast roads in the world', Hai Van Pass sits astride a hill that intrudes into the sea as a peninsula. The 500-metre (1640-foot) climb, with about a 7 per cent average gradient, bends and buckles its way up the slopes, blissfully removed from the main flow of traffic, which digs its way through the hills inside Vietnam's longest road tunnel instead.

As the road climbs, the view widens, taking in beaches, headlands, the country's main railway, and a coastline matted with forest. At the pass, there's a cluster of stores selling food and drink, and the ruins of an old French bunker that was also used by US forces during the Vietnam War.

It's a predictably good descent into Danang, where I spend the night before pedalling out the next morning behind the long strip of My Khe beach – the wartime playground American troops knew as China Beach. An emerging metropolis of luxury mega-resorts, it's a beach that is elusively out of sight from the road, but it points almost all the way to my day's goal of Hoi An. As the school day ends, I find myself in curious bunch rides. Boys sprint to ride beside me, dropping away only when they can no longer maintain the pace on their clunky single-speed bikes.

Hoi An is one of Vietnam's most charming towns, and the prime place to spend a rest day (or week!), if you intend to build one into the trip. Its name translates as 'peaceful meeting place', and it feels well named when its lantern-lit, UNESCO World Heritage–listed old town closes to vehicles at night. Its streets, which are lined with French-colonial-era buildings, are almost literally sewn in silk, with the town famed for its tailors. If the romance of old Vietnam is alive in any one place, it's here.

DAY 3

HOI AN TO QUANG NGAI (140KM/87 MILES)

Fishing boats crowd Hoi An's photogenic docks along the Thu Bon River as I pedal out of town the next morning, heading downstream towards the coast but not to the coast. A short way out of town, I join a stream of people boarding a ferry to cross to the river's south bank, squeezing onto a boat the size of a cricket pitch, with half-a-dozen motorbikes and 20-plus people. It's the most crowded I'll feel all day, with the coastal roads beyond, south of the river, carrying little traffic.

Once again, the ocean is tantalisingly close, but just out of sight, and the dunes are covered in casuarinas and human graves. At the roadside, fishermen patiently mend nets, while

others caulk their distinctive basket boats. There are brief and entertaining traffic jams caused by cows or ducks crossing the road, and quick manoeuvres to swerve around chickens and children who are so keen to high-five a passing cyclist that they almost run under my front wheel.

Around 100 kilometres (62 miles) south of Hoi An, I finally touch the coast, wrapping around the fishing village of Sa Ky, where colourful fishing boats are so plentiful they seem almost stacked atop each other in the harbour.

The ride's most sombre moment comes just beyond Sa Ky, and 15 kilometres (9 miles) before Quang Ngai, at the Son My Memorial, scene of the infamous My Lai massacre during the Vietnam War. Here in 1968, US troops killed between 347 and 504 villagers, and today you can tour the remains of the village and a museum of gut-wrenching photographs. It is history stripped raw, a sombre final stop before a late finish in the workaday city of Quang Ngai.

DAYS 4–8

QUANG NGAI TO MANG DEN (130KM/80 MILES); MANG DEN TO KON TUM (55KM/34 MILES); KON TOM TO PLEIKU (50KM/31 MILES); PLEIKU TO EA DRANG (100KM/62 MILES); EA DRANG TO BUON MA THUOT (75KM/46 MILES)

At Quang Ngai, I change the bearing of my ride, turning off the coast and into the green embrace of the mountains. The faces of the people are suddenly different (the Vietnamese replaced by ethnic highland groups), the trees are different (eucalypts yielding to rainforest), the sky is different, with the blue over the plains replaced by clouds that threaten the summits, and most noticeably to a cyclist, the gradient is different.

Beside the road, the earth cascades down from the highlands in layered rice fields, which are being prepared for planting as I pass. Buffaloes lurch through the water, with egrets hitching rides on their backs.

For the next few days I roll across this highland delight, pursuing nothing but the sense of journey towards Dalat. There are steady climbs, and descents so rapid that at times I'm passing motorbikes as I hurtle downhill. The road seems to roll through folds in the highlands, which are drier and hotter than the rainforests behind, but still I'm surrounded by plantations of coffee, bananas, rubber trees, papaya, pepper and corn. It's a shopping list as much as a landscape. Even away from the fields, the front yards of the homes are a mat of coffee beans laid out to dry, and the roadside is lined with drying rice and curious faces. I'm far from the typical tourist paths now, and some children squeal in delight as I pass while others run away in tears, surprised by the sight of a stranger.

Altitude isn't all that's different about the roads across the highlands. They are also universes away from the traffic crush of the plains, at least until Buon Ma Thuot, a city made wealthy by the spoils of the coffee plantations (*see* p. 178) that so thoroughly surround it.

DAYS 9–11

BUON MA THUOT TO LAK LAKE (55KM/34 MILES); LAK LAKE TO DAM RONG (45KM/28 MILES); DAM RONG TO DALAT (115KM/71 MILES)

It's Sunday as I pedal out from Buon Ma Thuot, with just three days to ride now to Dalat, but the road towards Dalat doesn't adhere to calendars. Traffic builds into a frenzy the nearer I get to the former French colonial-era hill station, but even over the sound of trucks, buses and horns, there's still the welcome sound of greetings from people I pass.

At the same time, the rice fields begin to flourish again, looking as green as new life against the surrounding hillsides smothered in dark forest and even darker clouds. I spend a night on the shores of Lak Lake, the largest natural lake in the central highlands, where elephants laden with tourists splash through its shallow waters.

I stay in the Mnong village of Jun, sleeping on the floor of a traditional longhouse on stilts, and then roll on south, where the road continues to serve dual purposes – carrying transport and the drying of coffee beans. Highland valleys provide long, flat sections broken by the intrusion of hills. Riding through stands of bamboo on a windy day is like listening to the rustle of pages of a book. As I climb through hills, I find myself peering down into forest canopies so thick it's difficult to imagine there's earth below.

Dalat is the highland destination that outshines all others. At around 1450 metres (4760 feet) above sea level, it was used by the colonial French as a cooling retreat from Ho Chi Minh City (then called Saigon), and it remains one of Vietnam's most popular tourist destinations, noted for its French colonial-era architecture, a strange Eiffel Tower-shaped communications tower, and even a nascent wine industry. Unless you've arrived sweating and weary in lycra, it's where Vietnam seems to come to fall in love and honeymoon. It's also the country's fruit bowl, surrounded by the likes of strawberry and vegetable farms instead of the ubiquitous rice paddies.

DAY 12

DALAT TO NHA TRANG (135KM/84 MILES)

For me, Dalat is also a springboard back to the coast, the point at which I depart the highlands and begin my final day to the coastal resort town of Nha Trang 1500 metres (4920 feet) below. It's a long day that can be broken into two, but it's a downhill day, swooping back to the plains and finally the beaches of Nha Trang. It's a day of such freewheeling beauty that there are tour operators in Dalat that offer this ride by itself as a daytrip.

I leave Dalat through a sea of glasshouses, beneath hillsides covered in artichokes, cabbages and daisies. It's a cool mountain morning that will end with a hot beach evening. For the first 40 kilometres (25 miles) the ride is undulating – short, sharp climbs followed by short, sharp descents – on what feels like the quietest, smoothest road in the country. After days of rain around Dalat and the highlands, there are bends in the road that are awash in mud and soon my legs are covered. When I stop in one village, the local mechanic wanders over and hoses down my bike and my body.

Around 50 kilometres (31 miles) from Dalat, the road tops out at about 1700 metres (5580 feet) above sea level, and soon I'm roaring downhill, across Khanh Le Pass and down slopes dotted with coffee plantations. The descent is glorious – free-flowing and fast, with barely the need to brake. Waterfalls filled with days of rain gush down the slopes, spraying over the road and showering me in water. It's as good a downhill ride as I can remember.

At the foot of the mountains I slow, and normal cycling pace suddenly feels strangely pedestrian as I follow the Cai River towards the coast. I've cycled more than 1000 kilometres (620 miles) along and behind Vietnam's coast, and yet the coastline itself has barely featured. Tonight this will change because I will be sitting on the sands at Nha Trang, awash in satisfaction. Even now, as the traffic builds, there are endless greetings from along the road, and children pedal beside me with wide, happy grins of welcome. There may be no friendlier place in the world to cycle.

Riding Resources

Some local tour companies, such as Indochina Holidays Travel (indochinabiketours.com) and Vietnam Bike Tours (vietnambiketours.com) run cycling trips through central Vietnam, usually with shuttle transfers along the way to reduce the time and effort.

Opposite Buffalo farming in the highlands

ASIA

Manali to Leh

INDIA

Cross the world's highest mountain range, with some of the wildest, fiercest and most spectacular scenery lining any road on the planet.

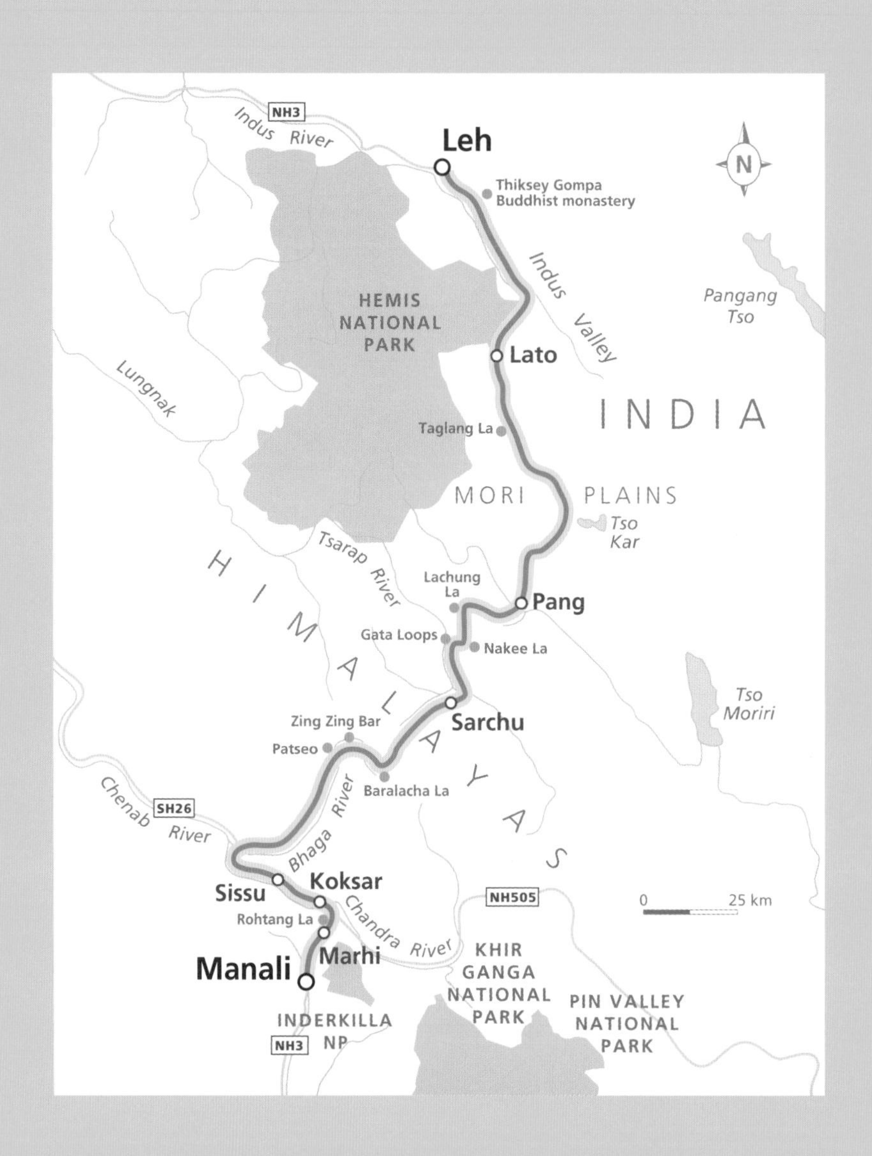
NH3
Indus River
Leh
Thiksey Gompa
Buddhist monastery
N
Indus Valley
Pangang Tso
HEMIS NATIONAL PARK
Lato
Lungnak
INDIA
Taglang La
MORI PLAINS
Tso Kar
Tsarap River
HIMALAYAS
Lachung La
Pang
Gata Loops
Nakee La
Tso Moriri
Sarchu
Zing Zing Bar
Patseo
Baralacha La
Chenab River
SH26
Bhaga River
Sissu
Koksar
Rohtang La
Chandra River
NH505
0
25 km
Marhi
Manali
KHIR GANGA NATIONAL PARK
PIN VALLEY NATIONAL PARK
INDERKILLA NP
NH3

Manali to Leh

WHY IT'S SPECIAL

Atop Taglang La, 5360 metres (17,585 feet) above sea level, I could easily be convinced that the only air present is that inside my tyres. My bike sits discarded at the road edge and, sucking at breaths, I lean back against a yellow road marker declaring that I'm: 'Passing through second highest pass of the world. Unbelievable is not it!'. At this altitude, there's only around half the oxygen compared to sea level. To pedal is to feel exhausted - to even think about pedalling is to feel exhausted. And yet I'm elated. I just don't have the energy to show it.

To reach this point of airless exhilaration, I've crossed four of the highest road passes in the Himalayas, and the satisfaction of cycling across the tallest mountain range in the world is immense. Conditions are rough and tough but the high mountain scenery is incredible, as is the feeling of arriving into the high desert of Ladakh at ride's end.

BEST TIME TO RIDE

The effect of the region's brutal winters - sub-zero temperatures, snow and ice - typically closes (and mangles) the highway for most of the year, so the window to cycle it is short (around July to Sept). This coincides with the monsoon on the southern side of the Himalayas, around Manali, but at any other time of year, the highway will almost certainly be closed. Monsoon conditions dissipate once you cross Rohtang La, the first of the passes.

RIDE IT

You'll cross four high Himalayan passes on this 507-kilometre (315-mile) cycling journey from Manali to Leh in India's far north. The ride follows a road that was constructed in 1987 to provide an alterative approach to Leh at a time of troubles in nearby Kashmir. The road opened to foreign travellers in 1989, and quickly became a favourite among hardy cyclists.

It's unquestionably one of the most dramatic roads in the world, typically open for just a few months of the year, and my favourite ride in this book. It's also the toughest, and most cyclists will likely only want to consider it as part of a guided ride. I cycled it over eight days with a group from Exodus Travels, but after hearing my stories, friends organised their own independent trip and had little difficulty with any of the logistics.

Only experienced cycle tourers will want to do this ride independently, for it's the kind of journey where things will likely not go all to plan - the knowledge and adaptability to get around any of those unexpected difficulties is as vital as spare tyre tubes. That said, the biggest task on an independent ride is likely going to be getting your bike to Manali - you'll probably need to put it on the roof of a bus from Delhi. Make certain your bike is mechanically sound and that you have knowledge of bike repairs

Nuts & bolts

Distance: 507 kilometres (315 miles)
Days: 8
Ascent: 8000 metres (26,250 feet)
Difficulty: Hard
Bike: Though this road is ostensibly fully sealed, ride a mountain bike with 2.0- or 2.1-inch tyres, as the fierce winters often destroy sections of highway, leaving some pretty rough stretches.

Previous Himalayan highs near Sarchu

and carry enough spares for remote-area travel. Also carry enough money with you for the entire ride – there's nowhere to source cash along the highway. Once you're on the road, dhabas (roadside stalls and restaurants) are plentiful, as are sleeping options of varying levels of comfort.

Altitude is the ride's biggest challenge, with each of the passes being above 3900 metres (12,800 feet), but on a bike it's so much easier to follow the acclimatisation maxim of 'climb high, sleep low', than it is on foot. Within minutes of rolling off a pass, you can be hundreds of metres lower, with your lungs and brain refilling with oxygen.

Nor are the climbs to be taken lightly. Across the ride, the road ascends more than 8000 metres (26,250 feet), or almost the equivalent of cycling from sea level to the top of Mt Everest. It's a landscape that breeds its own dangers, with precipitous drops from the road edge, and a tangled road filled with hairpin bends that trucks and other vehicles have to navigate as they also navigate around you. The roadside drop-offs should present no problem during the climbs, but you'll need to take the descents with caution, since speed (and you can get some real speed on these descents) can bring them into play.

After settling on an independent or guided ride, the next decision comes in your direction of travel. Many cyclists prefer to start in Leh and ride south to Manali, citing the overall loss of altitude (Leh is almost 1500 metres, or 5000 feet, higher than Manali), but it also means you have to cross the highest pass first. I'm an advocate for beginning in Manali, so that the passes rise in ascending order, and you get to finish in the desert-like beauty of Leh rather than in the hectic heat of Manali.

It's both a spectacular ride and a spectacularly ambitious road.

LOCAL SNAPSHOT

In Ladakh, the landscape and culture feel very Tibetan, so you could be forgiven for thinking that you'd arrived in Lhasa as you cycle past Thiksey Gompa, around 20 kilometres (12.5 miles) from Leh. This Buddhist monastery spills down a hillside and bears more than a little resemblance to Lhasa's famous Potala Palace. One of the most striking features inside is a 15-metre-high (50-foot) golden Buddha, constructed to commemorate a visit by the Dalai Lama in 1970. If you don't mind an early trip back out from Leh (it's about an hour's cycle), it's worth coming for the dawn puja (worship), which monks evocatively announce with the blowing of horns across the Indus Valley.

Opposite High times in the Himalayas *Left* Climbing towards Marhi from Manali

DAY 1

MANALI TO MARHI (37KM/23 MILES)

I'm riding the road in July, soon after it's clear of snow. The lands around Manali are dripping with the annual monsoon and a humid mist rakes through the forest like fingers as we pedal out of town.

For the bulk of the first two days, we will be climbing, with the road crawling steadily through a knot of hairpins for 50 kilometres (31 miles) to the first pass: 3978-metre (13,050-foot) Rohtang La, almost 2000 metres (6560 feet) above Manali. There are early reminders that this is a sub-continent highway – trucks crumpled at the base of cliffs below the road; a soundtrack of horns – but the volume of traffic isn't heavy and, as ever in Asia, I find myself in a peacefully fatalistic place on a bike. Trucks rumble past, coloured as brightly as parrots, but unlike in Europe, North America or Australia, drivers here take road obstacles as the norm (the only traffic jam this first morning is one created by cows being herded down the highway) and drive blithely around me. It's a strangely chaotic environment in which to feel completely safe.

As we ascend, the land seems to fold in on itself, with the wide valley contracting into deep, narrow gorges. Through switchback after switchback, the road climbs, passing through the tree line and into an alpine valley where we enter Marhi, a roadside smattering of buildings that is our first night's camp. Like every night along this ride, camp will be just a clearing of land - nothing formal, though in Marhi the stop has at least the faint semblance of a settlement, with a few stalls in which to buy snacks ready for the next day. In some ways it's a highway roadhouse stop little different from any other around the world, with people going about their transitory business, paying little attention to these newcomers on bikes. It feels as far from the in-your-face India of lore as the Himalayas feel from Goa. From here, there are vertiginous views back down over the road, which runs like spaghetti through the landscape but it is also clearly brilliant in its design – always climbing but never steeply, allowing for the limitations of the trucks, and now bikes, that journey along it.

The view above is even more fascinating. Rohtang La is still 1000 metres (3300 feet) up there somewhere, but with the monsoon still in force the road is covered in a poultice of mud. Long into the night, the road is lit like a Christmas tree by the headlights of hundreds of vehicles stuck in a muddy traffic jam.

DAYS 2–4

MARHI TO SISSU (51KM/32 MILES); SISSU TO PATSEO (78KM/48 MILES); PATSEO TO SARCHU (57KM/35 MILES)

As the climb continues the next morning, we are almost immediately weaving through the traffic jam, squeezing through narrow gaps between vehicles and pedalling at the road's edge, poised above precipitous drops. Our wheels sink deep into the mud but still we progress better than the cars and trucks, many of which are bogged. After three hours, we rise onto the wide pass whose name macabrely translates as 'Piles of Corpses'. Fittingly, vultures cruise the skies overhead but we are defiantly alive and well, even if we're as muddy as elephants at bath time.

Rohtang La is one of the most stark of this ride's moments, marking the point at which the green lands around Manali turn to the brown and barren high slopes of the Himalayas. It's a true watershed, of both rivers and rain, with the monsoon rains falling on the southern side but not making it across here.

The descent from Rohtang La rolls out for almost 20 kilometres (12.5 miles), hurrying down to the Chandra River, where

we lunch in a roadside dhaba (food stall) in Koksar village, looking over a bridge that lies crumpled in the river. Like the mud on the other side of the pass, and sections of damaged road still ahead, it's a sign of this highway's constant battle with nature in one of the harshest environments imaginable. As we ride on, little distinguishes the river from the dry, rocky slopes for they are the same dull colour, broken only by the crops of beans and potatoes that cover any rare flat patch of earth.

We camp this night by the road in Sissu, 15 kilometres (9.3 miles) past Koksar, and for the next two days, the Chandra River will be our guiding line towards the highway's second pass, 4900-metre (16,075-foot) Baralacha La. The land is almost contradictory in description, becoming more barren and yet more beautiful with almost every hour that passes. There are mountains coloured like mosaics, and others with surfaces brushed so smooth they resemble 6000-metre-high (19,685-foot) sand dunes. At the end of the third day we camp at Patseo, primed and poised at the base of the climb to Baralacha La.

The road to this pass ascends around 1200 metres (3940 feet) but with the kindness to be as gradual as is humanly possible in this terrain. The highway kinks and folds its way to Zing Zing Bar, a motley collection of makeshift teahouses that has no bar and little zing. It's a welcome break though, because approaching 5000 metres (16,400 feet) above sea level, the task of cycling and either eating or drinking on the bike is now beyond me. To take a sip of water or have a snack, I must now stop. There simply isn't oxygen enough here for both tasks at once.

It takes more than three hours to climb the 32 kilometres (20 miles) to the pass, and just minutes to descend into the Sarchu valley, where we'll camp this night on unusually grassy plains at the edge of a gorge filled with hoodoos. It's like finding a rogue piece of Bryce Canyon dropped into the Himalayas.

DAY 5

SARCHU TO PANG (81KM/50 MILES)

The day's ride out of Sarchu is arguably the most challenging of the trip, with two passes to cross to reach Pang, and for the first time the road rises above 5000 metres (16,400 feet). It's a day that you want to set out feeling fit, strong and well fed.

Some 25 kilometres (15.5 miles) from Sarchu, the ride arrives at the base of the well-named Gata Loops, and it's here that the highway gets truly limber, climbing out of the valley through 21 hairpin bends that corkscrew towards the third of the high Himalayan passes: 4770-metre (15,650-foot) Nakee La. To see the Gata Loops on a map is to see something resembling a seismogram but the hairpins at least negate the steepness of the climb. It's when you reach the top of the 21st bend and the highway straightens that, against expectation, things become a lot steeper.

The climb ends atop Nakee La, but only momentarily, with the highway dipping 200 metres (650 feet) into a barren alpine bowl and then climbing out again. I've barely got back what little breath I have anyway before the 400-metre (1300-foot) ascent to 5060-metre (16,600-foot) Lachung La has begun.

Such effort deserves reward, and it's plentiful beyond the pass as we descend past peaks shaped as if borrowed from the pages of fantasy novels. The road burrows through ever-narrowing gaps, until soon we're inside a deep gorge that seems to hang between mountains. Between the cliffs of the gorge, there's room only for the riverbed and the road squeezed tightly together.

By the time we reach Pang, beside a junction of gin-clear streams, we've been cycling for more than nine hours, covered more than 80 kilometres (50 miles), climbed two passes on a road that refuses to be smooth, and never dipped below 4200 metres (13,780 feet). Almost every rider is in bed by nightfall amid mutterings about the toughest cycling day of their lives.

DAY 6

PANG TO TSO KAR LAKE (51KM/32 MILES)

By morning, it's as though the gods have heard the grumbles, for this third-last day on the highway is the polar opposite of the one before it – a virtual and blessed rest day in the space between high mountains. After a short climb from Pang, it's close to an entirely flat ride across the Mori Plains, a stretch of land ringed by mountains that seems to have been ironed into the Himalayas. Salt lakes beam like novas and the road weaves between mountains without venturing onto mountains. By lunchtime we're turning off the highway and bumping across the plain to Tso Kar lake, the largest of the salt lakes in the area.

The afternoon is a momentary holiday, a chance to recover and rebuild strength ahead of the final and highest pass climb – Taglang La, which is the dividing wall between us

Above Yak skulls at Tso Kar Lake *Opposite top* Traffic jam below Rohtang La *Bottom* Cyclist at the base of the Gata Loops

and the desert lands of the Indus Valley. Here Buddhism will suddenly become the defining feature of the views, with monasteries balanced atop rocky ridges and chortens studding the valleys. It's a piece of Tibet that's wandered across the border, which is little more than 100 kilometres (62 miles) away.

Like advance notice of what's ahead, we camp this night between Buddhist chortens on the shores of the lake, where a spring has created an oasis of grass.

DAYS 7–8

TSO KAR TO LATO (73KM/45 MILES); LATO TO LEH (79KM/49 MILES)

I've slept the night on the grass, lying out watching the stars, and I wake to the sight of a yak herd grazing around me and a storm brewing over Taglang La. Even without the angry clouds, this 5360-metre (17,585-foot) pass has the fiercest reputation of all those along the highway, because unlike the passes now behind us, the road here largely eschews switchbacks, climbing as if determined (or weary) to be at the top as quickly as possible.

After a week of pedalling and altitude acclimatisation, however, the ride to the highway's highest point is less ferocious than its reputation. Road workers chip at the cliffs, cutting away rock to rebuild the road – as has become a common sight – after the destruction of the winter.

The climb stretches out for about three hours, until we round a cliff and emerge among a scraggly forest of prayer flags. We've crested the pass. The storm has cleared and light snow is falling. The prayer flags' entreaties hurry to the heavens on the strong winds. As I catch my breath against the yellow road marker, I figure out that I've reached a height above the highest point in Europe and approaching those of Africa and North America, and yet I'm on a road, riding a bike.

The scenery ahead is only rock – it's like riding into an enormous quarry site – but within a day, after a night camped by a stream in Lato, I'll be pedalling across the foot of the stunning Thiksey Gompa (*see* p. 186), a Buddhist monastery 20 kilometres (12.5 miles) from Leh, and into the swelling traffic of Leh, more than 2000 metres (6560 feet) below where I now sit. For now, however, atop one of the world's highest road passes, I'm hungrily eyeing not the snacks in my pack, but the air in my bike tyres. Might it be possible to borrow some for my lungs?

Riding resources

Himalaya by Bike, written by Laura Stone, is an excellent guidebook covering this ride, as well as other forays through the Indian mountains.

Only a few companies operate cycling tours from Manali to Leh, including Exodus Travels (exodus.co.uk), which has been running bike trips here for years.

Opposite Prayer flags at Leh Palace

Another turn of the pedals

Keep rolling with this selection of other bike rides from around the world.

North America

San Juan Islands, USA

Circuit a trio of gorgeous islands among a wealth of marine wildlife.

Best time to ride
The islands provide good riding from around April to October; aim to ride through the week to avoid the weekend visitor crowds.

Nuts & bolts
Distance: 205 kilometres (127 miles)
Days: 3-5
Difficulty: Medium
Start: Orcas Landing
End: Lopez Village
Info: visitsanjuans.com

Dotting the ocean between Washington State and Vancouver Island, the sunny San Juans are composed of more than 170 islands, but it's the three largest islands - San Juan, Lopez and Orcas - that make this archipelago one of the USA's most popular and compelling cycling destinations. Each island can be lapped in a single day or, better still, stretched across a couple of days of island time.

The evocatively named Orcas - there are indeed orcas in these waters - is the largest, hilliest and most challenging of the islands, providing a 90 kilometre (56 mile) return ride from the ferry dock at Orcas Landing out to Doe Bay, wrapping around East Sound, a fjord-like bay that almost cuts the island in half. If you have a strong pair of climbing legs, you might be tempted by the ascent to the summit of 731-metre-high (2409-foot) Mt Constitution, the islands' highest point, with a vast view over the archipelago and Vancouver Island. A stay at the turnaround point of Doe Bay is recommended, with the Doe Bay Resort and Retreat containing three rejuvenating outdoor hot tubs.

San Juan Island and Lopez Island provide shorter, easier loops of around 65 kilometres (40 miles) and 50 kilometres (31 miles), respectively. The San Juan Island loop sets out from the ferry port at Friday Harbor and crosses to the west coast and Lime Kiln State Park, aka Whale Watch Park, where the cliffs provide some of the world's finest land-based whale watching - resident orcas, minke whales, gray whales - from around May to September.

Lopez is the flattest and smallest of the trio, making it also the most popular among cyclists. From the ferry terminal in Lopez Village, roads head south through the skinny island, providing plenty of coastal views and easy pedalling. Make for Shark Reef Sanctuary in the south-west corner, where you can park up and follow a short walking trail through grand old-growth forest to the coast and sightings of seals and otters.

Previous Riverside on Rallarvegen, Norway *Top* Lime Kiln Lighthouse, San Juan Island *Bottom* The Great Divide Mountain Bike Route near Canmore, Canada

Great Divide Mountain Bike Route (GDMBR), USA & Canada

Tough and terrific – you'll find no more committing or rewarding ride, but it's purely for the hardened and determined bikepacker.

Best time to ride

If cycling south, as most riders do, you should aim to begin in July or August.

Nuts & bolts

Distance: 4963 kilometres (3084 miles)
Days: 45-80
Difficulty: Hard
Start: Jasper
End: Antelope Wells
Info: adventurecycling.org

Everything about the GDMBR is daunting, but what an epic achievement to cycle the length of the United States, with the Canadian Rockies thrown in as a party trick. Linking Jasper (Canada) and faraway Antelope Wells on the Mexican border, the ride traces the line of the Continental Divide through Alberta, Montana, Idaho, Wyoming, Colorado and New Mexico, and is a test of endurance and self-sufficient cycling rather than of your technical skills. Billed as the 'world's longest off-pavement cycling route', it predominantly follows unsealed roads and tracks as it crosses the Continental Divide 30 times. In doing so, it racks up climbs totalling more than 60,000 metres (200,000 feet), akin to scaling Mt Everest from sea level almost seven times! You should be exhausted just reading that.

It's not a ride to take lightly so do your research and plan carefully. With long remote stretches and few towns en route, you'll need to camp and self-cater most of the way, and much of the ride is through bear and mountain lion terrain. Long waterless stretches through the Great Basin and into the deserts of New Mexico require the ability to carry plenty of water on your bike. But the rewards are plentiful, with the route passing through Banff, skirting Yellowstone and Grand Teton national parks and following the stunning Wind River Range into the high desert of the Great Basin. Into Colorado, the GDMBR crosses its high point – the long haul over 3630-metre (11,910-foot) Indiana Pass – before rolling out across sparse New Mexico and into the largest desert in North America – the Chihuahuan Desert – before arriving at the lonely border post in Antelope Wells.

Route Verte, Canada

A web of rides among beautiful cities, national parks, blueberries and whales!

Best time to ride

Hit the warmest times around Québec, which are from about May to September. The weeklong Go Bike Montréal Festival is held in early June.

Nuts & bolts

Distance: Up to 5300 kilometres (3300 miles)
Days: Up to 100
Difficulty: Varies according to ride
Start & End: Varies along network
Info: routeverte.com

Once named by National Geographic as the world's best bike trail, Route Verte (Green Road) is a network of cycling routes through the French-speaking Québec province. It's a mix of roads – usually quiet ones – paths and bike trails, and while very few cyclists will pedal the entire network, it forms the framework for a series of fine shorter tours – you can come to ride one, or string a few together.

The spine of the well-signed network is the St Lawrence River, with the trail running along both banks between the major cities of Montréal and Québec City (the south bank is the more appealing option if riding between the two cities), and continuing north from Québec City to the wild Gaspé Peninsula, which is smothered in four national parks. Make a full loop of the peninsula on Route Verte 1 from Québec City and you have a ride of more than 1500 kilometres (930 miles).

Across the river from Route Verte 1, the network follows the 300-kilometre-long (186-mile) Véloroute des Baleines (Whale Trail). Stretching between Tadoussac and Baie-Trinité, this section mostly sticks to a wide road shoulder on Route 138, but as the name suggests, there's the likelihood of sighting whales – up to 13 species migrate into the St Lawrence River and the offshoot Saguenay Fjord between May and October each year.

Another enticing section is the 256-kilometre-long (159-mile) Véloroute des Bleuets, or Blueberry Route, which loops around large Lac-Saint-Jean, filling your eyes with lake views and your stomach with the wild summer blueberries.

One of the great pleasures of Route Verte is the Bienvenue Cyclistes! accommodation program. Participating hotels and B&Bs provide locked bike storage and often have bike tools, while member campgrounds guarantee sites for cyclists, regardless of bookings, and shelters so you can eat out of the weather.

South America

Carretera Austral (Ruta 7), Chile

A Patagonian spectacular of abstract mountains, glaciers and impossibly blue lakes.

Best time to ride
The southern end of the Carretera Austral is at the chilly latitude of 48°S, making summer (Dec to Feb) the most comfortable season.

Nuts & bolts
Distance: 1220 kilometres (760 miles)
Days: 20-25
Difficulty: Hard
Start: Puerto Montt
End: Villa O'Higgins

Stretching from Puerto Montt to Villa O'Higgins, near the southern tip of South America, the Carretera Austral (Ruta 7) has fast become a cycling classic. It's a stunning and remote journey that feels almost as though it's taking you off the edge of the map.

It's a ride effectively in two parts: Puerto Montt to Coyhaique (660 kilometres/410 miles), which is mostly along sealed roads, with three ferry crossings; and Coyhaique to Villa O'Higgins (560 kilometres/350 miles), where the road deteriorates into dirt, dust and washboard corrugations. More than half the road is now sealed, with more sections of asphalt being added each year. Expect wild weather at the best of times – Patagonia is a byword for high winds, with the prevailing winds favouring a north-to-south ride (Puerto Montt to Villa O'Higgins). The isolated nature of the ride means you should be confident about DIY bike repairs, with Coyhaique containing the only bike stores en route, and you need to be prepared to camp most of the way.

The views are sublime throughout, but there are a few standout sights. Near its northern end, the ride passes through Queulat National Park, where the Ventisquero Colgante hanging glacier sits poised atop cliffs. South of Coyhaique, the road runs along the shores of Lago General Carrera, where you can take a boat trip or paddle a kayak into the swirling patterns of the Marble Caves that puncture its edges.

Though the road ends in Villa O'Higgins, the journey for most cyclists doesn't finish here. Ferries and a brutally rough track – expect to do a lot of pushing and swearing – deliver you to the southern end of Lago del Desierto, from where it's about a 40-kilometre (25-mile) ride to the Argentine town of El Chalten. Here, you'll likely want to swap your wheels for hiking boots to explore the trails around the spectacular mountains of Monte Fitz Roy and Cerro Torre.

Gauchos and cyclists on the Carretera Austral

Europe

Baltic Sea Cycle Route, Denmark

A rewarding meander through the scattered islands of Denmark.

Best time to ride
Danish summers are comfortably warm, without excess heat, making May through to September the prime time to be on a bike.

Nuts & bolts
Distance: 820 kilometres (510 miles)
Days: 10-15
Difficulty: Easy
Start & End: Padborg
Info: balticseacycleroute.com

If you could create a country designed for leisurely cycle touring, it would look a lot like Denmark, a nation composed of more than 400 islands that reaches a high point of just 170 metres (557 feet) above sea level. It has around 7000 kilometres (4350 miles) of dedicated cycle paths, and a network of national cycle routes extending across more than 11,000 kilometres (6835 miles). The longest and most appealing ride in the national network is the Baltic Sea Cycle Route (National Route 8), which wraps across southern Denmark in a figure-eight loop.

The route is predominantly on quiet back roads and cycle paths, and is well signposted throughout. The islands and the Jutland Peninsula are connected by four ferries and eight bridges, including the 18-kilometre-long (11-mile) Great Belt Bridge (Storebælt) – one of Europe's longest bridges – which must be crossed by train.

The town of Padborg, resting against the German border, makes a good starting point. From here the route island hops east to Zealand, Denmark's largest island, before doubling back. Along most of its journey, it sticks close to the coast taking you through pretty harbourside towns. Highlights are plentiful, from some of Denmark's finest castles to its longest dike and the former capital city of Nyborg and, at the ride's eastern tip, the high chalk cliffs of Møns Klint.

If time is short, you could simply choose to ride the western (350 kilometres/217 miles) or eastern (470 kilometres/292 miles) loop, each of which could be cycled inside a week.

Gotland Trail, Sweden

Circuit an island seemingly custom-made for cycling, passing otherwordly sea stacks and entering a piece of movie legend.

Best time to ride
Summer provides the best weather but aim to come early (June to about mid-July) before the sun-seeking crowds arrive.

Nuts & bolts
Distance: 500 kilometres (310 miles)
Days: 7-10
Difficulty: Easy-medium
Start & End: Visby
Info: destinationgotland.se/en

Throughout Sweden, the popular holiday island of Gotland is almost a byword for cycling. As soon as you roll off the ferry into the capital of Visby, you'll find bikes in abundance. The Gotland Trail, or Gotlandsleden, makes a full lap of the Baltic Sea's largest island, sticking predominantly to roads along the coast and rarely rising more than 50 metres (165 feet) above sea level. Expect plenty of wind, though since you'll be pedalling a loop there's no real advantage to cycling in any particular direction – as you'll encounter headwinds (and tailwinds) at some point either way around.

Before you start cycling, build in at least a day to explore Visby, a medieval town so beautifully preserved that it's now a UNESCO World Heritage–listed site. If you set out riding north, you'll quickly pass Lummelunda Cave – one of Sweden's longest caves and a popular tourist attraction – before crossing (by ferry) to the adjoining island of Fårö. Movie director Ingmar Bergman lived on Fårö for more than 40 years, and today the island is home to a Bergman museum. There's also a striking collection of beaches and the slender sea stacks (known in these parts as rauks) that define the coastlines of Fårö and Gotland – the most striking rauks are at Langhammars, near Fårö's northern tip. Expect more rauks around Folhammar as you pedal down Gotland's east coast, before reaching the wild southern tip at Hoburg. As if by cycling design, one of Gotland's finest beaches, Tofta, can provide a spot to drop and flop just 20 kilometres (12.5 miles) before you arrive back into Visby.

Gotland is about a three-hour ferry ride from Nynäshamn and Oskarshamn, both south of Stockholm.

Rallarvegen, Norway

Climb through the Norwegian mountains, taking in the country's most famous cycling trail as you cross between the capital city and the coast.

Best time to ride
This ride is one for the Scandinavian summer, ideally sometime between July and September.

Nuts & bolts
Distance: 614 kilometres (380 miles)
Days: 8-12
Difficulty: Medium-hard
Start: Oslo
End: Bergen

Norway's most famous bike ride is an 82-kilometre (51-mile) stretch of gravel road built beside the Oslo–Bergen railway line. Known as Rallarvegen, or the Navvies' Road, it was designed for transporting materials and workers along the railway during its construction early last century. It's a spectacular one- or two-day ride, squeezing between mountains and along the shores of lakes between Haugastøl and the fjord town of Flåm. It's said to draw around 25,000 cyclists a year, but it also doubles as the show-stopping section of the country's National Cycle Route 4 (also known as Rallarvegen).

This long-distance route connects Norway's capital, Oslo, with the country's second-largest city, Bergen. From Oslo, the ride swings north to skirt the shores of Lake Krøderen before joining Rallarvegen at Haugastøl. Around 30 kilometres (19 miles) ahead, it reaches Finse, which, at 1222 metres (4010 feet) above sea level, is Norway's highest railway station as well as the highest point of the ride.

By the village of Myrdal, the cycle route turns off the main Rallarvegen, heading towards Voss, Scandinavia's wild adventure capital – yes, those may be BASE jumpers you see leaping off the cliffs. If you have time, you might want to finish the shorter version of Rallarvegen by making the 18-kilometre (11-mile) detour into Flåm, but you then have to return, which means an 800-metre (2620-foot) detour back through 21 hairpin bends.

From Voss, the ride offers a classically Norwegian finish, wriggling along the shores of fjords (with one more detour over the mountains from the town of Evanger) into gorgeous Bergen.

Apart from the main Rallarvegen section between Haugastøl and Flåm, which is vehicle-free, the ride mostly follows roads, many of which are lightly trafficked, though some sections can be busy with cars.

Hebridean Way, Scotland

Island hop through an archipelago at Europe's very edge.

Best time to ride
The summer months of June, July and August see not only the warmest conditions but also have the lightest winds.

Nuts & bolts
Distance: 297 kilometres (185 miles)
Days: 6
Difficulty: Easy-medium
Start: Vatersay
End: Butt of Lewis
Info: A Hebridean Way leaflet can be downloaded from the Outer Hebrides tourism website (visitouterhebrides.co.uk).

By their very nature, islands are enticing places to cycle since they are often easily circuited or, in the case of archipelagos such as the Outer Hebrides, strung together to create a series of stepping stones across the ocean. Created in 2016, the on-road Hebridean Way (or National Cycle Network route 780) traverses 10 islands that effectively form part of the western edge of Europe.

The ride connects the southern Hebridean island of Vatersay with the Butt of Lewis lighthouse at the archipelago's northern tip, and is best cycled from south to north in order to place the prevailing winds (which can be fierce out here in the Atlantic Ocean) at your back. The islands are connected by a puzzle of causeways and two ferry rides, and each day involves island hops until you reach the largest island of Lewis and Harris in the far north.

Ferries from Oban on the Scottish mainland arrive on the island of Barra, immediately to the north of Vatersay, so you'll need to make a short ride south to find the start proper on Vatersay, or you can simply set off from the ferry port at Castlebay, cutting out around 10 kilometres (6 miles).

The archipelago's highest point is just 799 metres (2620 feet) above sea level, and the Hebridean Way largely stays below 200 metres (650 feet), though there are a few sharp climbs.

Gaelic is the predominant language on these remote islands, and Lewis (the northern area of Lewis and Harris) in particular is rich with prehistoric sites, including the striking Callanish standing stones, which pre-date Stonehenge. The beaches around Lewis are also among the most beautiful in Europe, albeit tempered by the chill of the water.

Top left Cycling near the outer wall of Visby, Sweden *Top right* The Outer Hebridean island of North Uist *Bottom left* A woolly detour to Flåm on the Rallarvegen Trail *Bottom right* Château de Chambord, Loire Valley in France

Loire Valley, France

Royal chateaux and picturesque villages on a ride beside France's most famously beautiful river.

Best time to ride
In order to squeeze in between the crowds and the snows, May, June and September are ideal. Loire chateaux close through winter.

Nuts & bolts
Distance: 900 kilometres (560 miles)
Days: 14-18
Difficulty: Medium
Start: Cuffy
End: Saint-Brevin-les-Pins
Info: loirebybike.co.uk

The name alone - the Loire Valley - is an evocative siren call, bringing to mind regal chateaux, vineyards and sublimely French landscapes. Little wonder that the Loire à Vélo is the most popular touring route in France. The marked ride, which forms the western end of the cross-continent Eurovelo 6 route, follows France's longest river from the town of Cuffy to where it pours into the Atlantic Ocean at Saint-Brevin-les-Pins.

Logistics are simple - point the bike west and follow the river and cycling signs to the ocean - and the rewards are manifold. The route follows a mix of quiet roads and bike paths, and the region is particularly well set up for cyclists. There are lots of villages and hundreds of businesses - accommodation providers and tourist attractions - registered as 'Accueil Vélo', a national program of cycling-friendly operators.

The ride passes through all of the classic and historic Loire Valley cities, such as Orléans, Tours, Angers and Nantes, but it's the resplendent chateaux that will undoubtedly become the focus of your stops. A 280-kilometre (174-mile) stretch of the valley between Sully-sur-Loire and Chalonnes is UNESCO World Heritage–listed, and this section alone contains more than 40 chateaux. You'll pass the big and famous ones, such as Chambord and Amboise, and you can detour away to chateaux such as postcard-perfect Azay-le-Rideau on the Indre River. Be sure to make the detour to Chenonceau, about a one-hour ride from the Loire. The Renaissance chateau spans the Cher River, and though it's hardly a secret, it's well worth a stop.

From mid-June to mid-September, the Train Loire à Vélo, a dedicated train for Loire à Vélo cyclists, runs through the valley between Orléans and Nantes. More than 50 bikes can fit and are transported free, with an assistant to help you load and unload.

Danube Cycle Path, Germany & Austria

Bunny-hop between countries as you pedal beside Europe's second-longest river.

Best time to ride
This ride is on bike paths away from traffic, so peak tourist seasons are no impediment. Aim for the best weather window - May to September.

Nuts & bolts
Distance: 320 kilometres (200 miles)
Days: 5-6
Difficulty: Easy
Start: Passau
End: Vienna
Info: Esterbauer (esterbauer.com) publishes the excellent *Danube Bike Trail 2* guidebook, with full maps and details of the route from Passau to Vienna.

Europe's most famous long-distance cycling trail follows the course of its second-longest river, the Danube, on dedicated bike paths. You can choose any section, with the Eurovelo 6 bike route following almost its entire 2850-kilometre (1770-mile) length, but most popular is the flat 320 kilometres (200 miles) between Passau and Vienna. Here, trails are along both banks of the river - stick to one or make like the river and meander. Passau rests against the German–Austrian border, and if you set out along the north bank you spend the first 25 kilometres (16 miles) in Germany, but if you set out along the south bank you are almost immediately into Austria.

Around 40 kilometres (25 miles) from Passau, the river and path U-turn through the striking Schlögener Loop before passing through the city of Linz. It's worth detouring to Enns, said to be the oldest town in Austria. Passing beneath the crazily Baroque Melk Abbey, the ride enters its most beautiful stretch through the UNESCO World Heritage–listed Wachau region, where vineyards are interspersed with castles and churches.

The Danube Cycle Path is mostly flat, and accommodation and eating options are plentiful. There are regular passenger ferries across and along the river (especially in the Wachau region), allowing you to switch banks or cut out sections of riding.

To add an even more international flavour, consider pedalling on from Vienna, where the path leaps between capital cities - Vienna to Bratislava to Budapest - while crossing from west to east in the old European political divide. It's around 300 kilometres (186 miles) from Vienna to Budapest.

Berlin Wall Trail, Germany

Cycle a ring around Berlin, tracing the line of the Cold War-era Berlin Wall.

Best time to ride
Come for the finest of Berlin's weather - through to October.

Nuts & bolts
Distance: 155 kilometres (96 miles)
Days: 2-3
Difficulty: Easy
Start & End: Brandenburg Gate
Info: berlin.de/mauer/en/wall-trail

Who knew that the fall of the Berlin Wall in 1989 would directly lead to the creation of a fine cycling trail through and around the German capital city? The Berlin Wall Trail, or Mauerweg, is a smooth, shared-use (cycling and walking) path beside the double cobblestones that mark the one-time line of the Berlin Wall. It follows patrol roads used by soldiers manning the wall that divided Berlin into east and west from 1961 to 1989.

Though it covers a distance almost equivalent to cycling from Berlin to Dresden, the trail barely leaves Berlin, making a wide loop of the city as it traces the course of the wall that came to represent the divide between East and West in Europe. Fitting to the theme, the trail provides an historical journey through the tragic life and times of the Berlin Wall. Signs along the trail tell the story of the wall and the people it impacted. Memorials to those who died along the wall are also dotted along the route.

There's more than just history to discover along this trail. In the city centre, the ride is akin to a greatest-hits cycling tour, passing by the likes of the Brandenburg Gate, the Reichstag, Potsdamer Platz and Checkpoint Charlie. Out west, it rolls along the shores of beautiful lakes such as Griebnitzsee and Groß Glienicker See, and to the north it disappears into woodlands such as the Spandau Forest. The palaces and gardens of Potsdam are also less than 5 kilometres (3 miles) off the trail.

One of the beauties of this trail is the ability to ride it without the need to cart all of your gear, since it's easily accessed at many points by Berlin's trains and S-Bahn, allowing you to stay in the city and branch out each morning to the trail.

Top Checkpoint Charlie *Bottom* The Austrian Danube town of Spitz an der Donau

Africa & Middle East

Jordan Bike Trail, Jordan

Cross a holy land through deserts, deep valleys and ancient civilisations.

Best time to ride
April and May is best, when the rains have stopped and the wildflowers are blooming. September and October can also be good.

Nuts & bolts
Distance: 730 kilometres (453 miles)
Days: 12
Difficulty: Medium-hard
Start: Umm Qais
End: Aqaba
Info: jordanbiketrail.com

If the Middle East doesn't spring immediately to mind as a cycling destination, meet the Jordan Bike Trail. Stretching the length of the country from north to south, this new creation of a local adventure-tour company (but open to all cyclists) is an adventurous, non-technical mountain-bike route – 60 per cent on sealed roads, 40 per cent unsealed – with the good sense to take in many of the country's pin-up tourist attractions.

It's designed to be cycled from north to south, beginning in the olive groves of Umm Qais on the Syrian border and finishing (like Lawrence of Arabia) in Aqaba on the shores of the Red Sea. It passes through a range of altitudes, rising as high as 1700 metres (5575 feet) above sea level and as low as 220 metres (720 feet) below sea level in the Jordan Valley. If you cycle it over 12 days, the average daily ascent is a significant 1600 metres (5250 feet), so come well seasoned in hill climbs.

The route runs almost due south the entire way, with Jordan's natural and cultural treasures threaded along its course. It passes through the city of Madaba, with its famed mosaics, and then dips into Wadi Mujib, the so-called Grand Canyon of Jordan (try not to think about the 1000-metre, or 3280-foot, climb back out) before entering the wildlife-rich Dana Biosphere Reserve, Jordan's largest nature reserve. From the trail's highest point, there's a glorious descent into the fabled 'rose city' of Petra, where you really should stop for a couple of days. You'll then set out across the magnificent desertscape of Wadi Rum to Aqaba.

Bikepacking set-up is recommended, and the official website has accommodation recommendations, as well as a difficulty rating and elevation profiles for each of the 12 stages.

Garden Route, South Africa

One of the world's great drives is even better on a bike.

Best time to ride
The Garden Route can be cycled year-round. The autumn months of March and April bring the most stable weather conditions. Avoid the Christmas holiday high season.

Nuts & bolts
Distance: 1000 kilometres (620 miles)
Days: 10-12
Difficulty: Medium
Start: Port Elizabeth
End: Cape Town

The Garden Route is South Africa's premier scenic drive, and though the route proper stretches for only around 200 kilometres (124 miles) between Mossel Bay and Storms River, the most satisfying way to cycle it is to pedal between Port Elizabeth and Cape Town (or vice versa), covering much of the southern nib of Africa.

Towns along the route are spaced so that you really need the fitness to be able to cycle more than 100 kilometres (62 miles) a day, and much of the riding is on busy highways, but the reward is one of the most beautiful stretches of coastline in Africa.

If you leave from Port Elizabeth, the most enticing route follows the coast to Mossel Bay, before swinging into the hinterland to cross through the desert-like Klein Karoo area. Returning to the coast and the southern tip of Africa at Cape Agulhas, it's largely a coastal run into Cape Town.

The route passes through a chain of South Africa's finest visitor attractions, with so many active distractions along the way that you could almost turn the ride into a multisport event. A day's ride out of Port Elizabeth is Jeffreys Bay, regarded as one of the world's best surf spots, before the Garden Route squeezes between Tsitsikamma National Park and Garden Route National Park. Near here, you can take the plunge with a bungee jump from 216-metre-high (710-foot) Bloukrans Bridge, Africa's highest bridge. In the Klein Karoo, Oudtshoorn is ostrich-farm central, while past Cape Agulhas are the marine marvels of Gansbaai and Hermanus. The former's stock-in-trade is cage diving with great white sharks, while Hermanus, just 40 kilometres (25 miles) away, is regarded as one of the finest whale-watching locations on earth – the whale season runs from June to December.

Top Cycling on the Jordan Bike Trail *Bottom* Pincushion Proteas in Cape Town's Kirstenboch Botanical Gardens

Australia & New Zealand

Munda Biddi Trail, Australia

Ride beneath towering trees and beside a wild coastline on Australia's premier off-road cycling trail.

Best time to ride
Spring (Sept to Nov) and autumn (Mar to May) are prime time for the Munda Biddi. Avoid summer (Dec to Feb), which can be brutally hot.

Nuts & bolts
Distance: 1000 kilometres (620 miles)
Days: 20-25
Difficulty: Medium-hard
Start: Mundaring
End: Albany
Info: mundabiddi.org.au

Completed in 2013, the Munda Biddi Trail is a purpose-built off-road cycling route that curls through Western Australia's south-west corner, beginning near Perth and finishing in the south-coast town of Albany. Constructed to parallel the course of the hikers' Bibbulmun Track, it's a ride suited only to mountain bikes, preferably with a bikepacking set-up (pretty much the only time this ride goes on sealed roads is to cross them). It's less a test of your technical skills than an enticing off-road tour.

The trail starts in Mundaring, 35 kilometres (22 miles) east of Perth, and passes through some of Australia's most impressive forests – in those around Pemberton and Walpole you'll fast come to appreciate the tall timbers of karri, tingle and jarrah trees as you pedal along far beneath their canopies.

The ride has remote stretches, with towns up to 150 kilometres (93 miles) apart, making camping the only option along much of the route. Dedicated cyclist campsites have been dotted along the trail, usually no more than 50 kilometres (31 miles) apart. Each campsite features tent sites, shelters that sleep up to 25 people, rainwater tanks and bike-storage areas.

The Munda Biddi has a number of towns and access points along its length, making it possible to cycle smaller portions of the trail. If you're eyeing off a shorter ride, the most appealing sections are through the eastern half between Pemberton and Albany, where the tall forests scrape at the sky and the south coast comes into view.

Opposite The majestic Annapurna Circuit *Top* Cycling the Otago Central Rail Trail near Lauder *Bottom* The tall timber of tingle forest near Walpole on the Munda Biddi Trail

Otago Central Rail Trail, New Zealand

Scenic gorges, pubs and golden history on a gentle rail trail.

Best time to ride
Autumn (Mar to May) is golden on this trail, though it can be cycled throughout most of the year.

Nuts & bolts
Distance: 152 kilometres (95 miles)
Days: 3-4
Difficulty: Easy
Start: Clyde
End: Middlemarch
Info: otagocentralrailtrail.co.nz

New Zealand's craze for cycling trails can be directly linked to the impact and success of the Otago Central Rail Trail. This converted railway makes a horseshoe-shaped journey between the South Island towns of Clyde and Middlemarch, through what was one of the world's richest gold-bearing areas in the 19th century. When the trail opened in 2000 as New Zealand's first dedicated long-distance cycleway, the area had been all but forgotten by tourism, but it now draws more than 15,000 cyclists a year.

Like rail trails the world over, the gradient and terrain along the wide, unsealed path are gentle. Even the frighteningly named Tiger Hill, the only climb of any note, has more growl than bite, with an average gradient of a mere 2 per cent. Add to this the presence of around a dozen pubs along the trail's length - about a pub every 12 kilometres (7.5 miles) - and plentiful accommodation options, and the trail becomes about as civilised as any bike ride in the world.

Trail highlights include a pair of spectacular gorges - Poolburn Gorge and Taieri Gorge - where the ride clings to the cliffs, burrows through dark railway tunnels (having a light on your bike is a good idea) and crosses a host of railway bridges - there are around 70 bridges in total along the trail, some of which are as striking as the scenery.

The trail can be cycled in either direction and whichever way you ride, the first half is gently uphill and the second half gently downhill. If time isn't an issue, worthwhile detours include the Vulcan Hotel, a classic gold rush-era pub in St Bathans, around 20 kilometres (12.5 miles) off the trail; and trying your hand at the icy sport of curling in Naseby, 15 kilometres (9 miles) off the trail near Ranfurly.

Asia

Annapurna Circuit, Nepal

Ride a lap around one of the grandest mountain regions in the Himalayas.

Best time to ride
The Annapurna region has two good weather windows: October to November and March to May.

Nuts & bolts
Distance: 230 kilometres (143 miles)
Days: 7-9
Difficulty: Hard
Start: Besisahar
End: Beni
Info: Scour bookstores in Thamel (Kathmandu) or Pokhara for a copy of the detailed 'The Eagle's Loop: Biking Around Annapurna' map.

There was a time when the Annapurna Circuit was the go-to trail for trekkers in Nepal – at the turn of the 21st century it was said that two-thirds of all the country's trekkers came to the Annapurna region, the majority of them to walk the Circuit. Then roads began pushing up the valleys through which the trail ran, and the trekking crowds began to evaporate. In their place are coming more and more mountain-bikers.

The ride, which is best suited to a bikepacking set-up, makes a lap of the vast Annapurna massif, home to two of the world's 20 highest mountains (Annapurna I and Annapurna II). Beginning in Besisahar, a 100-kilometre (62-mile) drive east of Nepal's second-largest city, Pokhara, the ride ascends for the first 110 kilometres (68 miles) to the ramshackle village of Thorung Phedi, crossing vertiginous suspension bridges as it goes. There will be plenty of times you'll be pushing or carrying your bike to here, but that's good practise for the crux day out of Thorung Phedi, when you'll almost certainly be pushing your bike pretty much all the way up the 1000-metre (3280-foot) climb to the trail's highest point atop the oxygen-starved 5416-metre (17,770-foot) Thorung La mountain pass.

Things speed up beyond the pass as the route descends through Muktinath and Jomsom – gateway to the famed Mustang desert region – and into the Kali Gandaki Gorge. Pinched between Annapurna I and Dhaulagiri, this gorge is the deepest on the planet.

The ride ends in the village of Beni, but you'll likely want to build in an extra day and finish with the 85-kilometre-long (53-mile) road ride back to Pokhara.

The Circuit is strung with teahouses offering basic trekking-style beds and meals. Be sure to add in one or two rest days to help acclimatise on the approach to Thorung La.

Index

Note: **Bold** *entries refer to major cycle routes.*

D

E

F

G

H

I

J

K

L

M

N

O

P

Q

R

S

T

About the author

Andrew Bain discovered cycling the easy way, on a 14-month, 20,000-kilometre bicycle journey around Australia. He's since pedalled across large parts of Europe, Asia, North America and New Zealand, and continues to trundle across the roads and trails of Australia. He once spent five months towing his children across Europe in trailers. He's the author of *Headwinds*, the story of his ride around Australia, and his travel writing has won multiple awards. He continues to dream of cycling, well, everywhere.

Acknowledgements

Thanks to the many and varied who have accompanied or assisted me in my various cycling journeys over the years. To Jason and Meg Hopper for sowing the seed, and to Kiri, Cooper and Janette for the European and Australian journeys. To Alice McDougall for being the very best of cycling company across Wales, Sandra for some very rainy laughs on Old Ghost Road, and Ramon for accepting you were no longer riding with a pro team when you had me in tow along the Camino de Santiago. Happy trails to you all. Big thanks also to the likes of Michele Eckersley, Sue Finn, Louisa Day and Virginia Haddon for being ever-supportive of my cycling wishes. For the generosity of their time and knowledge, a tipped hat to Dan Buettner, Kate Leeming, Josie Dew and Charlie Walker. And most of all, thank you to my other wheels on this project – Mark Watson, Jen Murphy and Ethan Gelber – and the team that steered once my hands were off the handlebars: Melissa Kayser, Megan Cuthbert and Alice Barker.

Photography credits

All images are © Andrew Bain, except the following:

Note: (a) (b) (c) (d) refers to placement on page, top to bottom, left to right.

Front cover: Stocksy; p. ii, 36, 38 (a)(d), 41 (b), 42, 44 Mark Watson / Highluxphoto; xvii Unsplash / Ryan Stone; 2 (a), 5, 18, 126 Alamy; 2 (b) Unsplash/Dimitar Donovski; Banff, Canada; 2 (c), 8, 23, 32, 38 (b) (c), 41 (a), 45, 86, 199 (a), 201 iStock Photos; 2 (d) Unsplash/ Abben Salacu; 4 Unsplash/ Justin Hu; 9 Unsplash/Louis Paulin; 20 (a)(b)(d) Kristine Keeney; 20 (b) Patrice Goodwin; 24 Lisa Watts; 26-27 Dan Buettner; 28 Unsplash/ Dylan Sauerwein; 33 Unsplash / Glen Rushton; 34 (a) Unsplash / Donald Teel; 6-7, 34 (b), 41 (c), 65, 192, 194, 196, 199 (b) (c) (d), 203, 204, 205 Shutterstock; 35 Unsplash / Dulcey Lima; 56-57 Josie Dew; 112- 113 Charlie Walker; 120 Visit Victoria; 132-133 Kate Leeming.

Published in 2020 by Hardie Grant Travel, a division of Hardie Grant Publishing

Hardie Grant Travel (Melbourne)
Building 1, 658 Church Street
Richmond, Victoria 3121

Hardie Grant Travel (Sydney)
Level 7, 45 Jones Street
Ultimo, NSW 2007

www.hardiegrant.com/au/travel

All rights reserved. No part of this publication may be reproduced, stored in a retrieval system or transmitted in any form by any means, electronic, mechanical, photocopying, recording or otherwise, without the prior written permission of the publishers and copyright holders.

The moral rights of the author have been asserted.

Copyright text © Andrew Bain 2021
Copyright concept, maps and design © Hardie Grant Publishing 2021

© Map Resources (World map)

A catalogue record for this book is available from the National Library of Australia

Hardie Grant acknowledges the Traditional Owners of the country on which we work, the Wurundjeri people of the Kulin nation and the Gadigal people of the Eora nation, and recognises their continuing connection to the land, waters and culture. We pay our respects to their Elders past, present and emerging.

Ultimate Cycling Trips World
ISBN 9781741176964

10 9 8 7 6 5 4 3 2 1

Publisher
Melissa Kayser

Project editor
Megan Cuthbert

Editor
Alice Barker

Editorial assistance
Jessica Smith

Proofreader
Rosanna Dutson

Cartographers
Brenda Thornley and Emily Maffei

Design
Andy Warren

Typesetting
Megan Ellis

Index
Max McMaster

Colour reproduction by Megan Ellis and Splitting Image Colour Studio

Printed and bound in China by LEO Paper Products LTD.

The paper this book is printed on is certified against the Forest Stewardship Council® Standards and other sources. FSC® promotes environmentally responsible, socially beneficial and economically viable management of the world's forests.

Publisher's Disclaimers: The publisher cannot accept responsibility for any errors or omissions. The representation on the maps of any road or track is not necessarily evidence of public right of way. The publisher cannot be held responsible for any injury, loss or damage incurred during travel. It is vital to research any proposed trip thoroughly and seek the advice of relevant state and travel organisations before you leave.

Publisher's Note: Every effort has been made to ensure that the information in this book is accurate at the time of going to press. The publisher welcomes information and suggestions for correction or improvement.